THE ADVENTURES OF FLO AND ALICE

A. L. MOTTLEY

DEDICATION
For everyone I love.

This is not a chapter by chapter story of Flo and Alice's lives. it is a series of observations/conversations that chronicle their friendship.

CONTENTS

tribulations

ACKNOWLEDGMENTS

Thank you to every person who ever said "I enjoy your stories"

INTRODUCTION

1: Meet Flo and Alice

FLO

In the year of our Lord, nineteen thirty-ish. A young Sheffield lass by the name of Florence - Flo for short, arrived in the leafy - *Well there were trees in the cemetery* - suburb of Moston, Manchester, to work in service for a local doctor.

Moston was mainly a community of smart terraced houses, donkey stoned steps and immaculate back entries. The main thoroughfare, Moston Lane had an immense variety of shops. Shoes could be cobbled, Knitting wool obtained, and Iced fingers bought. Without any need for 'going in to Town'

It was a world away from her rural upbringing, but the Sheffield lass soon settled in to her job, and became a familiar face around and about.

Moston would be where she met her future husband Bob. A widower, thirty years older than her, who lived next door with his teenage daughter. In the years to come, the Sheffield lass would give him a second daughter. her beloved 'only child' Joyce.

The courtship of Bob and Flo began slowly. And if truth be told, unintentionally. In those days a single dad was a rarity and her initial feelings toward him, were of sympathy. He was after all, a grown man in his forties, whilst she was barely eighteen. I guess you could say proximity played a big part in their blossoming romance. Hardly a day passed when she didn't see him walking past the surgery or on the 'Lane' heading home from work. Head up, hat on. Probably mindful of the fact he was the subject of gossip by the local women gathered on street corners, shop queues, or bus-stops.

"Aw look at him. He's a widower you know...Fought in the trenches...Not a scratch on him...Comes home and his missus dies of consumption. She was only 20 odd..Int life a buggar"

"Ooh the poor sod...I bet his house is a hovel"

"Speak for your bloody own house!...I've never been in but his window sills and step are spotless. He's raising his child an' all"

"On his OWN?"

"I think his sister pops in now and again. But in the main..Yeah"

"What the bleedin' ell does he feed her? My Jack would die of starvation if I popped my clogs...Name me a man who can cook and I'll show you a 'fairy'"

"You're not wrong Ada"

***

Flo, by now firmly ensconced in the community, listened to

these conversations quietly. She was yet to find her own inner gossip and hadn't met her best mate and big gob extraordinaire, Alice - *known behind her back, as 'The malice'* - yet. But more of her later

She was an excellent cook and food was bountiful in her employers house. One day, after months of head nodding and "Looks like rain" comments, between her and Bob. She plucked up the courage to 'knock on' with some leftover Shepherds pie. Which one can only presume, was gratefully received, as the following days and months saw the regular occurrence of meals being passed over the back wall.

Years later, when reminiscing, Flo would re-iterate that her initial feelings towards him were sympathetic but soon she noticed the little things. His lovely head of hair, the twinkle in his eye... Bob was a 'looker' and quite obviously the feeling was mutual because shortly after she'd given him a cottage pie, with a side of beetroot, a romance of Romeo and Juliet epicness began...The only differences being, just one of them was young. The families got on...sort of. And neither died for ages.

Thus began a marriage that was to last through the middle and latter years of the twentieth century. Through war and austerity to the 'never had it so good' years and beyond.

They were to be blessed with a much loved child Joyce. Who was to carry on the family tradition started by the dyed in the wool Lancashire lad, when he wed his Yorkshire lass, of marrying a foreigner. A proper foreigner an' all! Oh it caused all manner of kerfuffles when she brought a 'coloured lad' home but time and grandchildren are great healers.

Flo and Bob stood up to Hitler - Single handedly according to

2

the tales they told the grandkids! and lived in a world devoid of washing machines, vacuum cleaners and Television. To only be parted by Bob's death a good thirty five years later...Which is a bleedin' miracle when you bring Alice into the mix.

ALICE

There's no actual proof that Alice was ever born. Some say she arrived on earth as a middle aged whinging old battle axe. Some say she came from Hell. But they would say that wouldn't they? Because ninety-nine percent of people around Moston way, had fallen out with her at some point!

Her mam was an ambitious woman. Eager to live the middle class life. Dad had his own window cleaning round and a good life insurance policy.She grew up at the top end of Moston lane. Where the 'posh' houses were. In a semi detached house, with bay windows. And although she was to spend all her adult life in a terraced, albeit one with an inside loo!, she still maintained a 'semi' state of mind. Which made the lion statues in her back yard, look a bit daft.

She was born with a 'gift' for causing offence . A gift that came so naturally to her, she permanently had a 'what did I say?' look on her face. Coupled with her penchant for a tight curly perm-from her late teens onwards. It made for a frightening sight.

Alice was an enigma. An 'idiot' who didn't suffer fools gladly. A two-faced cow, who'd lay down her life for her best friend... First to your door in times of trouble. First to the bus stop to share your business with random strangers.

Married for 'minutes' to a man she couldn't stand but blessed with his early death and a works pension for life.

No kids - Thank god, for the kids...Oh she wouldn't have harmed them but imagine a world full of little Alice's. *Shudder!*

***

2: THE FIRST TIME THEY MET

THE FIRST MEETING BETWEEN FLO AND ALICE WAS TO BE A 'COMEDY OF ERRORS' INSIDE THE DOCTOR'S SURGERY WHERE FLO WORKED. AND WAS TO SET THE TONE FOR THEIR LIFELONG FRIENDSHIP...

ALICE BARGES INTO THE DOCTOR'S SURGERY AND COMES FACE TO FACE WITH HER FUTURE BEST FRIEND

"Bloomin' eck. You gave me a right fright. Can I help you?"

"Well you're obviously not a doctor. A: You're a girl and B: You're wearing a pinny. I'm here to see the doctor"

"It's seven o'clock in the morning! He's still having his breakfast. And how did you get in?"

"Through the back door - Murial leaves it open for me. Not that it's any of your business -How did YOU get in?"

"I live here!"

"Since WHEN? Where's Murial?...MURIAL!"

"Shurrup! You'll wake the dead"

"Oh my god! Is Murial dead?... She was only twenty ... Oh my god!"

"When you DO get in to see the doctor, tell him you're going deaf! I NEVER said she was dead"

"Well where is she then?"

5

"If she's who I think she is, she left to get married, I think, a couple of weeks ago. That's why I'm here. I'm the new housekeeper"

"LEFT?... MARRIED? ... TO WHO? ... She weren't even courting!... My Eddie - That's my 'financee' used to walk her home after she'd been anywhere with us - Me mam only lets me go out with him if I take a friend ... Alice, she said - That's me name by the way - What's yours?"

"Florence Kime -And I need to get on with me chores"

"Alice Shufflebottom. Pleased to meet you. You carry on luv ... Florence? Like the nurse? Well you're in the right place, even if you're just a maid"

"I'm NOT a maid. I'm a live in housekeeper"

"Yeah, if you say so - Anyway, me mam's from Cheadle Hulme, so she's used to standards ... Alice, she said 'Only a certain type of girl walks out with a man on her own' So anywhere I go with Eddie, Murial comes too. Bloomin eck, she kept her cards close to her chest, dint she. I only saw her a couple of weeks ago. She never said a word. Mind you, she had her head down the toilet, at the time. Couldn't stop being sick. That's why I didn't come round for a bit...You can pick up all sorts here"

"Sounds like she's in the 'family way' to me. I worked for another doctor before I came here. That's how they all go on when they're 'you know what'"

"MURIAL?... Did you ever see her?...I'm not saying I'm a beauty, although people have compared me to Mary Pickford - It's the curls - But if you had to compare Murial, I think the nearest you could get is Rin-tin-tin ... I knock about with her, more out of sympathy than anything else. Heart of gold though ... My Eddie took ill once in Bogart Hole Clough. And she was passing. She stayed with him for ages til he felt well enough to walk home. Even sat in the bushes with him cos it was warmer"

"REALLY?"

"I'm not sure I like your tone...She's probably sent me a letter. It's not like her to just get off... Wait till I tell my Eddie. He'll be proper gobsmacked"

"He might have an inkling already"

"Come again?"

"Nowt! ... Anyway I've got to get on"

"Well like I said, don't mind me. I've only come for summat for me mam's corns. Me mam and the doctor attend the same soirees. So he gives her special service. Do you know what a soiree is?"

"It sounds painful whatever it is"

"It's a social gathering ... We live in in the posh houses at the top of the lane...Soirees coming out of our ears ... What do you do for entertainment"

"I go to the pictures a lot"

"How quaint ... Anyway I'm gonna nip home and see if the letter from Murial has come. Tell the doctor Clara Shufflebottom's daughter came for the medicine but she'll be back after luncheon ...That's dinner to you ... Nice meeting you, I might see you around ... Toodle-oo"

7

Not if I see you first. You snobby cow!

A FEW DAYS LATER

"Hiya again. Flo int it?"

"Hiya Alice? Nice to see you at a normal time … Did Murial get in touch?"

"Not seen head nor hide of her …It's a funny to-do"

"Int it just! … How's your fella? Not took ill in the park again, I hope"

"NO He's been as right as rain. We're getting wed next year. Once he gets his proper qualifications"

"Oh! … What does he do?"

"Summat in an office. He works for a builder's merchant … In the office"

"Yeah, you said!"

"I'm half middle class"

"Does it hurt?"

"You're a tad cheeky you, aren't you?"

"Yeah cos you're a tad daft! What the eck is half middle class?"

"Me Mam married beneath her and she doesn't want me doing the same"

"What does your Dad say about that"

"Nowt he's dead!"

"Aw ...The War?"

"Kind of...He got drunk celebrating armistice day and choked on his vomit. I don't really remember him, I was only a baby. But me Mam was fuming ...'Don't do what I did, Alice' she said ...'Marry someone with a proper job, not just a twinkle in his eye, because twinkles don't pay bills' ... I keep a tight ship with my Eddie. None of that going to the pub nonsense ...He's going places. This time next year, When he's fully qualified and we've wed, we'll be putting down a deposit on a semi detached ...What about you? Are you walking out with anyone?"

"I've got me eye on someone"

"Round here?"

"No ... Spain! Of course they're round here. I wouldn't have me eye on 'em otherwise"

"Who? I know most folk round here, and there's only a couple of Schools. So I bet I went to school with 'em"

"I bet you didn't"

"Is it a foreigner?"

"Can I just say something luv. So you don't put your foot in it anymore than you need to ... My Mum and Dad came here from Russia"

"DID THEY? You'd never know. You look proper English ... So is it a foreigner?"

"NO! It's a ... Mature chap"

"Well I wouldn't say no to Rudolph Valentino - 'cept he's dead. But one of them old 'uns round here?"

"Aren't you dead cheeky? Age is but a number... I don't care what he's got. He seems really nice"

"Who is it?"

"I don't think I know you well enough to say"

"I won't breathe a word! ... Cross my heart and hope to die. But if you say he's married, I'll faint cos I think you're talking about the Doctor"

"Do you take me for some sort of brazen hussy? Am I bloomin' eck talking about the doctor... I'm talking about him next door"

"Next door?"

"Yeah"

"Mr Holden?"

"Yeah"

"The widower, next door to you?"

"It takes you a while to take stuff in, dunt it?"

"I'm just making sure ... Bob Holden?... He's ninety if he's a day!"

"Don't be daft. He's only forty seven"

"ONLY FORTY SEVEN? That's practically dead!"

"Is it eck!"

"So how did all this come about?"

"To be honest I felt a bit sorry for him at first. And one day I made too much Shepherd's pie"

"You've completely lost me!"

"You could try not butting in til I've finished me sentence"

"Ooh! Well pardon me...Go on? I'm all ears"

"Like I was saying, I made too much Shepherd's pie, and doctor thingy said "why don't you pop next door and see if Mr Holden can make use of it" So I did"

"What did he say when he saw you stood on his step?"

"I wasn't stood on his step. I could see his pipe smoke wafting over the back wall so I stood on the bin and passed it over"

"How romantic!"

"If you've got better things to do, don't let me stop you " *You sarcky cow!*

"Aw sorry ... Go on, I promise to keep quiet"

"He asked me what my name was yesterday. When I told him, he said 'Florence' is a beautiful name"

"Have you set a date for the wedding then?"

"I know you're being sarcky, but between you and me, if he asked I say yes ... He has asked me something though"

"What? -No, don't tell me. Is it summat rude? I'll faint ... I bet them widowers have 'desires' and all sorts"

"Did you ever watch 'The Perils of Pauline' at the Pictures?"

"I loved it. It's one of me favourites"

"I can tell! He's not some Cad trying to take my honour. he's a fella that lives next door and who just happens to be a bit older than me ... And he's asked me if I want to go to the Pictures... And I've said yes"

"Well you're not going on your own!"

"I know! ...I 'm going with him"

"FLORENCE LUV? I don't know how you do things in Sheffield, but you can't go walking out with a fella on your own, round here...Your name'll be mud! ... Especially with him being... y'know?... A man of the world ... A man whose previously had his desires filled ... Gawd knows the trouble I have with my Eddie. He's forever trying to touch me knee when no-one's looking. But I'm raised proper... Not til there's a ring on me finger... Now Bob, well he's had a taste hasn't he. What if he can't control himself?"

"We're only going to watch George Formby!"

"Well I'm coming with you"

"Y'what?"

"I'm coming with you. It'll be more respectable if you've got a chaperone"

"Nowt to do with you being a nosy cow then?"

"You'll thank me during the intermission ... what day are we going?"

"Er, tomorrow"

"Tell him to meet us on the corner of kenyon lane at seven... I'll knock on for you at about six thirty ...What are you wearing?"

"Clothes!"

"Tut! Well at least take that pinny off... I've got to dash. Me Mam's waiting on her carbolic and if I miss the shop me life won't be worth living... I'll see you tomorrow ... Aw I'm glad I met you. I think me and you are gonna get on fine ...Ta - ra "

***

Thus began a lifelong friendship. Through wars -most likely caused by Alice and her 'mouth'. Through heartbreaks ... Flo's attempts to have children, finally rewarded with the birth of her only child Joyce.

A friendship that encompassed Alice's short lived marriage to Eddie and her tears of joy upon finding out he was dead and SHE got the pension instead of his trollops... And Flo's lifelong marriage, spanning over thirty years, to her beloved Bob.

A friendship that lasted despite the fact they often got on each other's nerves.

A friendship that endured Alice's ever so slight bigotry towards ANYONE.

A friendship built on Common sense and daftness ... A lethal combination.

 A friendship built up over brews, shopping trips and the odd excursion to Blackpool.

 A friendship known by women on every street, in every town and city.

 A friendship so ordinary that one would wonder what was worth writing about.

 But turn the page dear reader and you shall find out. For this is the story of genuine love, dressed in down to earth normality.

THESE ARE THE ADVENTURES OF FLO AND ALICE.

3:HOW FLO AND ALICE GOT MARRIED

NOT TO EACH OTHER! A BRIEF HISTORY OF BOB AND EDDIE'S COURTSHIPS

THE PROPOSALS

FLO AND BOB

"Aren't you ready yet? The film starts in a bit, and we've still got to walk up Kenyon lane. Is Bob meeting us outside or are we knocking on for him?"

"I'm ready. And he said he'll meet us outside. he's had to pop out on an errand"

"Flo! You're not in Sheffield now. Can't you wear something smarter?"

"Alice! You're vergin' on dead cheeky. What's wrong with me? We're going to WATCH Clark Gable, not have our tea with him. Bob likes me in this dress"

"That's cos he's used to it. And we're not just watching a film. We're going somewhere after it"

"Do you know something I don't know"

"NO! ... Yeah"

"Go on then. Spill the beans"

"I can't. I'm sworn to secrecy"

"YOU? Someone's trusted YOU with a secret?"

"What do you mean by that?"

"Alice. I was only here five minutes and you'd filled me in on everyone's business"

"Oh! Well pardon me for making a stranger feel welcome. Anyway change that dress"

"Not til you tell me what's going on"

"I can't...I CAN'T...Cross your heart and hope to die"

"Just bloody tell me...Oh for gawds sake. I cross my heart and hope I don't kill you!"

"Flo. Say it properly or I'm not telling you"

"Alice. I PROMISE I won't breathe a word"

"Bob's gonna propose to you"

"Let me sit down ... How do you know?"

"He told me ... Remember the other morning when I popped round. You were donkey stoning your step, and he was stood on his, with his pipe, watching you"

"Was that the day you asked him what life was like in the olden days? And I threw me wet cloth at you, and it got you right in the gob?"

"No ... And I still haven't forgotten that *You'll get yours!* It was the day after the Coal man had been cos you was moaning about the messy footprints. And do you remember you had to pop inside for a minute cos the doctor couldn't find his 'listening to your heart' thingy and went mad cos you'd put it to soak in the sink"

"Well it looked filthy... I know what day you mean now. So what did Bob say?"

"I shouldn't really be saying"

"Are you daft? You've already told me the main part"

"I know. But he wanted it to be a surprise"

"You'd think he'd know better than to tell you then"

"I'm your BEST FRIEND! And the nearest thing you've got to family round here... Anyway don't tell me you weren't expecting it. You practically live together"

"I BEG YOUR BLOODY PARDON! Are you saying I'm a trollop? LIVE TOGETHER? I'm raised not dragged up. Are you insinuating we've had 'relations'?"

"NO! I meant because you live next door to each other...But have you? You can tell me. I won't judge"

"Have we 'eck...Not that I haven't been tempted...You know we've kissed, and when we do, me tummy gets butterflies...He's so...Manly" *sigh*

"I've let Eddie touch me knee - In clothes!...But that's as far as it goes til that ring's on me finger... Speaking of rings. I bet that's the errand, Bob's popped out on"

"How do you know all this?"

"Cos I've seen it"

"Seen what?"

"The ring you daft lummox"

"Could you possibly wipe that smirk off your face and tell me what's going on?"

"Right. When you went in to sort out the doctor's thingymajig. Bob asked me if I could pop round to his when you went to the shops. That's why I didn't want to come with you"

"Oh! So you were prepared to sneak behind me back and go in MY fella's house when I wasn't there?"

"Shurrup Flo. I already had an inkling what he was on about cos I'd bumped into him coming out of the Jewelers in Town, the other day. And he'd said not to breathe a word to you cos he was getting a you a special gift. You don't need to be genius to work it out"

"So have you seen an actual ring then? What's it like? Is there a diamond in it?"

"Yes I've seen it. That's probably why he's meeting us outside the Pictures. He's had to take it back"

"Why? Was it horrible?"

"Aw no it's a lovely ring. And he's spent a good bob or two on it. But I said to him "I know Flo's got stumpy fingers, but that'll swamp her. It's more like a bracelet than a ring"

"STUMPY FINGERS?... Remind me again. Are you an actual FRIEND?"

"Well you have, a bit. Anyway it's all sorted now. I lent him mine and told him to get yours done two sizes up"

"THANKS!"

"Well go on then. Put your blue two piece on"

"I only wear that for church and special stuff. He's gonna know I know"

"Men his age don't notice stuff like that. Get it on. I've brought me special perfume round. I love Elizabeth Arden. You can have a squirt when you've changed...Aw look at ya. You look lovely Flo"

"Let's go then...I don't know why you had to tell me. I'm a nervous wreck now"

"There's no pleasing some people. Anyway you haven't told me if you're gonna say 'yes' "

"Of course I'm gonna say yes, you daft sod"

"Well don't give it away, til he mentions something. He'll fall out with me. I promised not to say a word"

"I won't say anything"

"Stop that humming then"

"What's wrong with a bit of a song. I'm always singing"

"Well hum summat other than 'A bicycle built for two' Talk

about giving it away"

***

ALICE AND EDDIE

"Aw Flo. I've missed you. And I've got loads to tell ya?"

"I've only been away for a weekend. it still feels a bit weird being in here rather than next door but I wouldn't change a thing"

"Well you did have a few weeks to settle in before going off for your hols. How was it?"

"Couldn't be helped. The new girl couldn't start immediately at the doctors, and there was no way I'd let them down. They've been good to me. And if I hadn't worked there, I wouldn't have met my Bob...Aw it was lovely, Alice. You can't beat a bit of Blackpool. The fish is heavenly"

"What about the rest of it? Did you ... y'know?"

"Course we did. We did that on the wedding night. But It was our belated honeymoon. So we did it some more ... You single girls don't know what you're missing"

"Did you just wink at me?"

"Yeah? I'm a woman now. I CAN wink ... Pop in the scullery and put the kettle on. I've got loads to tell you, and I've got a stick of rock for you. If I can find it"

"Well I've got me own news, Flo"

"Ooh. pass the sugar bowl, and spill the beans"

"Me and Eddie have set a date for the wedding, and I want you to be my Matron of honour"

"I'd be honoured ... Honoured to be a maid of honour ... I should be on the stage"

"It's Matron when you're already married. And you're as funny as a verruca"

"Aw don't be so nowty...Anyway tell me all about it. How did he propose? Was it as romantic as my Bob's?"

"What's romantic about being nudged during the intermission, and asked "Do you want to get wed"?"

"You're just jealous cos he waited til you'd gone to the toilet. To me it was the most romantic thing in the world ...So how did he do it?"

"That doesn't matter. what matters is we've got a date for Jackson's row and you need a new outfit cos I've got a colour scheme"

"Why aren't you getting wed in church? I had to marry Bob at the register office cos he's been married before, and we're both different denominations, but you and Eddie can have a church wedding"

"We've put a deposit down on a house in Ivy street. So we can't afford both. I couldn't bear the thought of having to live with his mam...She's a slut! And after all that's gone on whilst you were away. We need a place of our own. It's a good job I've had him saving up for the past four years"

"Well I did think her grating needed a good clean, when we visited. But its not that bad, is it?"

"Me and her had a bit of a row. She won't be coming to the wedding"

"What do you mean by a bit of a row?"

"The cheeky cow implied I wasn't right for her Eddie...I told her straight. Your Eddie, I said, would be emptying bins, like his dad if it weren't for me. You'd be happy for him to have nowt, I said. He passed his eleven plus and he's going places cos of me... Guess what the cheeky mare replied?"

"The mind boggles... Go on? what did she say?"

"She said. I'll tell you where he's going. He's going up the wall because of you...Oh is he? I said. Well he couldn't go up yours cos the mildew would make him slip off. And why don't you stop treating him like a bloody kid. He's got qualifications. He's a man and he'll get married to who he wants to"

"What did Eddie have to say about all this?"

"Nowt. I told him to sit down and shurrup. he's been sleeping in me mam's parlour for the last few days...Anyway the wedding is in two weeks, and you'll need something in puce"

"What's puce when it's a home?"

"Gawd Flo. It's a colour"

"What type of colour?"

"A colour, colour!...It's like a purplish reddy brown"

"Maroon? I hate Maroon"

"Puce and maroon are totally different. There's a nice outfit in kendals, that'd suit you"

"KENDALS? I've just got wed meself. I can't afford Kendals"

"Well what could you afford?"

"No more than five bob"

"I'll put the rest to it. I want you in puce"

"What colour are you wearing"

"White! you cheeky cow"

"Even after you and him went behind the Adelphi?"

"TO TALK!"

"You must be one of them people whose hair gets muzzed up when they talk"

"Ha, bloody ha...Anyway, it's just gonna be a small affair. Sandwiches back at me Mam's afterwards, cos we get the house keys two days later and we've got to get furniture...You don't know how lucky you were, marrying a man with his own three piece suite"

"Yeah. I would have refused his proposal if he hadn't had a dining suite an' all...You've still not told me how he proposed"

"Well between you and me. It wasn't really a proposal. We both sat there in me mam's parlour, after the row with his mam. He said "I'm buggered now" and I said "we can't afford to lose that deposit, we'd better get wed as quick as"

"Like summat out of a Rudolph Valentino film"

"Shurrup!...I must admit it wasn't what I'd thought my wedding proposal would be, but we've got the rest of our lives to be romantic...Well once the mortgage is paid off"

"Are you sure you're doing the right thing Alice? Bob say's he's a bit of a rum 'un and he's seen him with the odd 'lady' or two"

"Tell Bob to mind his own business. I can't stand old people poking their noses in others people's affairs"

"Oy! That's my husband you're trying to slander...I won't have it, Alice. He's been good to you"

"Oh I don't mean it like that. But me and Eddie have been together since we were twelve. We HAVE to get married"

"No you don't...Unless you're...You're not in the family way are you?"

"Am I bloody 'ell. He's never touched me, and he'd be 'dead' if he tried...Me and Eddie are just meant to be together. Even if he does get on me nerves"

"Well you'd know...So when are we going shopping and when do I get to see your dress?"

"The dress is already in me wardrobe. me and me mam made it about five years ago"

"You're like them boy scouts. Always prepared...Can I see it?"

"I want you to. Cos I've put a teeny bit of weight on and I need you to help me take it out at the waist. I'm no good at sewing and me mam's up to her eyes with the cake"

"Good to know I have my uses...Right shift yourself. My husband will be home from work soon and i need to make his tea...Eh? you'll be saying all this soon"

"I know...I can't wait"

"This time next year Alice, we might be mothers...What's up with your face?"

"Nowt...I'd hadn't really thought about kids"

"It's all I think of. I'm gonna be dead disappointed if I get my little visitor this month"

"Do you mind. I've not had me tea...Babies?...Ooh I'm not sure about that. I want a chaise lounge under me bedroom window"

"Well get one that'll double as a cot"

"You don't even know what one is"

"I know. But I also don't care. Now sod off before me husband thinks he married you as well"

4: A WEDDING TO REMEMBER AND A WEDDING TO FORGET

FLO AND BOB

"Oh Flo … Flo … Flo!"

"WHAT?"

"You look beautiful...Like a Princess...Gawd don't you scrub up well? I wouldn't have gone for that style with your hips but you've proved me wrong"

"What's wrong with me hips?"

"Nowt! They're just on the largish size and I thought all the detail would make you look like a gable end -But you DON'T"

"Thanks for THAT Alice... I'm getting dead nervous now. We're not gonna miss the bus are we? Have you seen Bob? Has he set off yet? I don't want to get there before him and have to hang about like a lemon"

"Bloody 'ell girl. Take a breath...Bob's already set off, and you're not gonna miss any bus...Just have a look out of the window and tell me what you see"

"It's sunny, thank God... Other than that I can't see owt - Oh hang on! They've put a new advert up... Ew, I hate Bovril"

"Look again...Just outside the front door"

"I can only see the doctor's car"

"And WHY can you see the doctor's car?"

"Because YOU just told me to look out of the soddin' window"

"That's your 'Bus'"

"Come again?"

"We all arranged it behind your back. We're going to the registry office in the doctor's car. Him and his missus were delighted to do it...They actually like you...Though God knows why -DON'T CRY! it'll ruin your make-up"

"I'm not crying...Yes I am. You're a cheeky sod sometimes. But you're a bloody good friend"

"Right! Shut it with the daftness. We're not Americans. Are you ready Miss Kime?"

"As ready as I'll ever be Miss Shufflebottom"

"Just think, you'll be Mrs Holden in an hour or two. And once my Eddie gets his skates on, I'll be Mrs Clough"

"Sounds weird dunt it?"

"Destiny luv, destiny. Now come on. They're waiting for us...I must say, I'm a bit worried about Bob"

"WHY? is there summat you're not telling me?"

"No...it's just...At his age, the shock of seeing you all dolled up might...Y'know?"

"You can't go a day, can ya?"

"I'm only kidding...Come on chuck. Your audience awaits"

It was a lovely wedding and all went smoothly. Everyone went back to Bob and Flo's house for the 'wedding spread' Where rumour has it, Alice overdid the Sherry and caroused everyone with several choruses of 'Inka Dinka Doo' before being carried home in a semi comatose state.

ALICE AND EDDIE

"Alice?...Come on sleepy head. It's your wedding day and we have to make you look beautiful...Which is gonna take some time"

"Shurrup Flo...I've not slept a wink anyway. Your bed is lumpy"

"Well talk about ungrateful"

"Aw I'm not really. I'm just nervous. I'd always expected to be going to my wedding from my own house...Eddie's mam is a cow for throwing him out"

"It was lovely of your mam to take him in. And its bad luck for the groom to see the bride the night before the wedding. But I couldn't have had him here instead of you. Not with my Bob being away at his sisters. It wouldn't have been seemly...You know what people are like round here - But what am I telling you for? You're their leader"

"Tut! Have you brewed up?"

"Is the Pope a Catholic? Do you want a fried egg?"

"No I bloody don't!...How you sat down to a full breakfast on YOUR wedding day is beyond me. I couldn't eat a thing"

"I couldn't have faced all that without summat in me stomach. I told you to choose an afternoon slot. You'd have had more time for the nerves to settle"

"What time is it now?"

"Eight thirty?"

"EIGHT THIRTY? We've gotta be there for ELEVEN!"

"Calm down Alice. Everything's in hand...Whilst you were busy NOT sleeping on me lumpy bed, I was running round doing all sorts. All you need to do is get ready"

"I can't cope Flo...Am I doing the right thing?"

"Course you are . *I just wish you hadn't chosen such an 'orrible sod* If anyone can make an honest man of Eddie, you can. *It'll never happen. He a swine!* Having said that, if you want to change your mind. I'll stand by you"

"Why would I want to change me mind?"

"I'm not saying you want to change your mind. I was just answering your question"

"No you wasn't. You was insinuating summat...You don't like Eddie do you?"

"He's alright"

"Just 'alright'"

"Well what do you want me to say, Alice? I don't really know him that well. *Bob does though. Should I tell her about the barmaid in the 'Ben'? -No! It's only gossip. I'm sure she'd know. And I'd only get shot for being the messenger.*

"He's shy that's all"

Keep your gob shut Flo. "Anyway less of this daft talk. Let's get you ready"

***

"Alice. You look a vision of loveliness. Just like that film star. What's her name?"

"Do you mean Norma Shearer? I've been told I'm the spitting image of her"

"No not her....That's it! Shirley Temple"

"The kid? I look like a kid?"

"Yeah. It's not an insult luv. It's the dress"

"What's wrong with it?"

"Nowt! Stop looking on the bad side of everything I say...The dress is lovely. But when I let it out for you, it seemed more of a simple design. It's all them bows on it. I don't recall it having bows when I last saw it...It's them that remind me of Shirley. Was it your idea to put so many bows on it?" *Cos if I'd known,I'd have slapped ya.*

"It was me Mam's idea. When she had a good look at it, it looked a bit plain. And with Eddie wearing a bow-tie"

"Eddies wearing a bow-tie?"

"Yeah. He's hired a dead posh suit and it comes with a bow-tie. It's a shame your Bob couldn't be his best man. He'd have got one too"

Well that explains a lot "Bob thought he should have someone nearer his own age as best man. Plus he's been planning this trip to his sister's for ages. *God forgive me. So many lies!* So who is best man?"

"Some lad he works with. He's not really one for mates is my Eddie"

"Well not the masculine kind"

"What was that Flo?"

"Nowt...Well just let me titivate meself a bit, and we're ready to go...Gawd, me mouths all dry. I've got no spit for me mascara"

"I can't help. Mine's as dry as a bone...And now me legs are shaking...I'm scared Flo"

"You'll be as right as rain. Come on chin up. Everyone on the street is outside for a nosy at the car...And you. Let's get a move on. Look in that mirror, and say bye-bye to Miss Shufflebottom. It'll be Mrs Clough that comes here next...You really look lovely. Give us a hug"

"Yeah but mind me perm...Thanks Flo. You're a brilliant mate. I'm glad Murial left the doctors. So I could meet you"

"So am I luv. So am I"

***

The wedding went well. The after do was a classy affair in Alice's mam's front parlour - with bay windows. Which every guest, and I mean EVERY, was invited to admire.

Flo got tipsy and repaid Alice by singing more than a few choruses of Oh my darling Clementine before being escorted home by half the guests. Because the butties had ran out and she had an Hot-Pot with some beetroot going spare.

***

Alice and Eddie left that night for two nights in Scarborough. Too posh for Blackpool and upon their return, settled into married life in their new house on Ivy street. Their wedded bliss last for weeks. Then Eddie ran away.

***

Flo and Bob's marriage lasted til death did them part. When Bob passed away some thirty odd years later.

***

Flo found great comfort in her daughter and grandchildren.

***

Alice and Eddies's marriage lasted barely five minutes. Some weeks after the wedding he left her for another woman and shortly after, he died -Not at Alice's hands! from natural causes. Although Alice believed the wrath of God had something to do with it.

Alice never remarried, and remained childless. She was left with the house and a tidy little pension for life.

***

Although Chalk and Cheese, in many respects. Flo and Alice managed to maintain a life long friendship. Firmly based on the premise that, even if your friend is an idiot, with daft ideas that in no way concur with yours. You should still respect your friends right to be that idiot.

The following observations prove this premise...

These conversations/events are not in chronological order. But they all take place during the time span of the 1930's to the 1970's

5: A CHILD OR TWO

A COUPLE OF YEARS BEFORE WORLD WAR TWO. FLO GAVE BIRTH TO HER ONLY CHILD.

ALICE, BY THIS TIME, WAS DESERTED, WIDOWED, AND ON HER SECOND POODLE.

ALICE MEETS JOYCE

"Cooey? Is it alright to come in Flo?"

"You're halfway up me hall before you ask! What do you want?"

"What do you mean? What do I want? I don't want anything. I've come to check on you. The baby was due three days ago"

"What baby?"

"Oh I see you're not running short on the sarcasm...How are you feeling?"

"Fat!"

"You look it too. Did you take the castor oil and orange juice?"

"Can't you tell by the fetching shade of green me face is?"

"Have you run up and down the stairs"

"Several times"

"Well it's obvious you're meant to wait...You might as well put the kettle on then"

"ALICE! I feel like there's a football between me legs. And I look like the side of an house. YOU put the kettle on. I'm knackered"

"Get up and walk around. It'll do you the world of good...Half a sugar less in mine. Looking at you has made scared of getting fat - OW! Did you just pinch me?"

"Sorry. I thought I was having a nightmare...But you are really here"

"If you want me to go just tell me. Flo?... There's a puddle on the floor...Have you gone THAT lazy? Gawd I'd have got the potty for ya"

"Bloody 'ell me waters have gone. This is it Alice. Nip next door and get the doctor"

"What should I tell him?"

"Tell him, it's half day closing on a Wednesday! WHAT THE BLEEDIN' ELL DO YOU THINK I WANT YOU TO TELL HIM? TELL HIM THE BABY'S COMING"

"No need to shout"

Several hours later

"Aw Flo...It's lovely"

"It's not an 'it' It's a little girl. I've got a little girl, Alice...I've got a daughter...I'm a mum"

"Do you think your Bob'll be disappointed? Cos he's already got a girl. I bet he wanted a boy"

"Do you think you could shut your gob! Bob will be over the moon. She's absolutely perfect. Int she?"

"Yeah, course she is. *I still prefer dogs* So what are you gonna call her?"

"Don't know yet. Bob said if it was a girl, he wanted to call her after his mam. Julia"

"That's a nice name"

"I can't stand it. I told him a fib and said I went to school with a girl called Julia who got rickets. So every time I thought of our baby having that name. I saw it with bandy legs"

"To be honest, she does look a bit bandy"

"That's cos of the nappy, you daft sod...Anyway I compromised and said we'd choose a name that started with J"

"What about Loretta?"

"Did you hear a word I just said?"

"Oh yeah...What about Jean. Like Jean Harlow"

"I'm not naming her after someone who plays brazen hussies"

"JOAN...Like Joan Crawford"

"Oh no! I can't stand her mouth. It's got a life of its own. And it doesn't have to be a film star she's named after"

"What was you gonna call a boy?"

"Clark or Rudolph"

Dunt have to be a film star she says! "How about Jacqueline?"

"I don't think you pronounce the 'Q' but no. Too long. And it might turn her 'funny' if she gets called Jack for short. I want a name that can't be shortened"

"Jane?"

"Too short"

"Janet?"

"She's called Janet, in the paper shop. She's got a wart"

The kid'll be starting school before you think of a name "Here's a good 'un...Joy! Can't be shortened, and she has brought you a lot of joy"

"Do you know what Alice? I think you've got it...I'm gonna call her Joyce"

"I didn't say Joyce"

"I know you didn't. But Joy's a tad too short and I love the name Joyce...Now I'm looking at her. She LOOKS like a Joyce" *Also I don't have to lie when Bob says he hopes you've had nowt to do with the naming.*

"So is it Joyce then?"

"Well Bar 'r' Bob putting his foot down, cos he hates it. Which I don't think will be the case. I'm saying yes"

"I'm thinking of getting another poodle, to keep Pluto company. I might get a girl one and call it Joy"

"You'd better bloody not. I'm not taking my child anywhere wheres there's a dog with almost the same name!"

SOME YEARS LATER ALICE HAS A BRUSH WITH PARENTHOOD.

LOVE CHILD

BANG, BANG!

"Alright! Hold your horses. I'm coming... Who's that? - Alice! What's up luv? It's the middle of the night. You'd better come in but keep quiet. Our Bob's asleep in the parlour with his leg. Have you been crying? What is it? It's got to be something to drag you round here at - bloody 'ell look at the time. It's five to twelve...At NIGHT! And you've still got your rollers in. Has someone died? Is it the dog? *If it's the dog, I'm gonna bloody kill you* Aw Alice, what is it?"

"If you let me get a word in edgewise I'll tell you *sob* Oh Flo...It's Eddie. He's got a kid!"

"Eddie?... Eddie who died years ago Eddie? Eddie your husband? ...Your very late husband? Have you been going to them daft fortune tellers again? Did you have a nightmare?"

"Oh for gawds sake Flo. How many questions do you want me to answer at once? YES my Eddie. NO, I've not been to see a psychic. I've had a bloody knock on my door. That's what I've had. And guess who was there?"

"If you say Eddie, I'm getting the van with square wheels.Cos it int funny Alice. Our Bob gets up at five?"

"Why?"

"Why what?"

"Why does your Bob get up at five? He's been retired for ages"

"Cos he DOES! Anyway what's that got to do with anything? Why are you sitting in my back room at this time of night waffling on about your dead husband having a kid? I'd get down to Crumpsall hospital luv. You might be having a stroke"

"It's a wonder I'm not stood here dead, after what I went through tonight . Any chance of a brew? I'll tell you exactly what happened. I'd just finished doing me doings before going to bed..The last thing I do before I go up is put the dog's breakfast in a bowl on the window sill - I can't face food first thing in the morning . So if I prepare it the night before I just have to shove it in front of her"

"Get to the bloody point Alice. Here's your tea"

"I am getting to it!...Nice cup of tea is that...Oh yeah, so I've just put out half a tin of Pedigree chum, and I hears a knock on the door. I thought it might have been that trollop from over the road. Wanting to borrow a clean cup or something so I stormed to the door, ready to give her a piece of my mind...And there he was large as life...Looking at me, with Eddie's face"

"Who was?"

"Have you not been listening?"

"Well I now know what your dog has for breakfast, but beyond that, Alice, you've completely lost me!"

"A fella knocked on me door. Saying he was Eddies son. and he was the exact spit of him"

"OHHHHHHHH!"

"Exactly! I tell you what? If my Eddie wasn't already dead. He would be!"

"So who's the mother then?"

"Some Tart without a heart...The poor lad thought it was me at first...Raised in an orphanage he was and just found out about his dad, the other week. Took me a while to set him straight. No lad, I said to him. You're not mine cos your cheating, poor excuse for a dad, went missing years ago. His last words to me were 'You know I don't eat porridge' and that was it til the funeral parlour in Nottingham got in touch"

"Well I'll say this Alice. You think you've heard it all, but...That poor lad must be in bits.The joy of thinking he's found his parents then the pain of finding out his dad is dead"

"I know...And if I'd known at the time, I'd have took him in meself. I wouldn't put a dog in an orphanage...The poor mite. But I'm not surprised, my Eddie always had an eye for 'good time' girls. The ones I caught him with, didn't look very maternal to me"

"And yet he married you! Nowt so funny as folk"

"What do you mean by that?"

"Nowt Alice - And keep your voice down. You'll wake our Bob

up. So where's the lad now. Are you letting him stay for a bit? Are you gonna help him come to terms with all this?"

"Are you mental? I don't know him from Adam. I sent him off before the last bus went. He could have been a murderer or anything"

"But you just said you would have raised him if you'd known"

"There's a big difference between an eight pound baby and the big lummox that towered over me on me doorstep"

"Are you SURE he's your Eddie's?...I mean, from what I can remember of him. He was a 'slight' man. Shorter than our Bob as I recall...Not far off being able to join the Munchkins"

"Of course I'm bloody sure! Luckily for me, Eddie didn't live long enough for me to despise him in his old age. My only memories of him, are as a young man...About this lads age. And I'm telling ya, they could be Twins! - 'cept for the nose"

"So does he have no idea who his mam is? Eh! maybe we know her, if she's local"

"Whoever she is, she's got a big soddin' nose cos the one on that lads face come in me house five minutes before he did...I'd better be getting off. We'll do some digging about tomorrow. I'm getting to the bottom of this, if it's the last thing I do"

"Alright luv. Don't forget to tiptoe past the parlour. He's a dead light sleeper is my Bob...It'll all seem better after you've had a good nights sleep - Well what's left of it...Bye, I'll watch til you get to the end of the street"... ...BOB! WAKE UP. YOU'VE GOTTA TO HEAR THIS"

OVER THE COURSE OF THE COMING WEEKS MONTHS AND YEARS. THE ISSUE OF 'DID EDDIE HAVE ISSUE?' REARED ITS HEAD AT THE TEA-TABLE MANY TIMES

WHO'S THE MUMMY?

"Flo, I told you having a phone would come in handy. He called me on it. He's coming round later with the bits of paperwork he's got"

"Who is?"

"Are you senile?! I've not stopped talking about it for days"

"Yeah, but you don't expect me to listen to everything do ya? I'd be living in a hovel if I stopped to listen to every word you said"

"Great friend you are!... Eddie jr - Well he's called Billy, but to me he's Eddie jr. I want you to be there when he comes, but just act casual, like you don't know nowt"

"Well I don't know nowt, do I?"

"Yeah you do. I told you the other night and every day since. See what happens when you don't listen...I've got my suspicions though"

"What's new"

"I mean about who his mam is. There's something about his face that's dead familiar"

"Wouldn't that be cos he's the spit of Eddie?"

"I hate it when you do that, Flo"

"Do what?"

"Answer everything sarcky"

"ALICE CLOUGH! Pot, kettle, black, is all I'm saying"

Tut! "There are other people I could be telling...Anyway stop being moody and listen to this. Do you remember that night they had a pie and pea supper at the 'Ben'?"

"How far back are you going?"

"A good few years"

"Oh THAT night! -No I don't" *You daft sod.*

"Yeah you do! I ended up on your doorstep in floods cos Eddie had gone missing, and you said, very sarckily if I recall. *Before you call Sherlock Holme, why don't you pop in the Ben. They're having a lock in* And I said *Come with me* And you said, *But I've got my rollers in* And I said-

"ALICE! I remember. Get on with it!"

"Well if you remember, where did we find him?"

"Erm...In the 'Ben'?"

"EXACTLY! And who was he with?"

"The barmaid?" *Like I've got the faintest idea.*

"Remember her nose?"

"Like it was yesterday" *Do I buggery!*

"Well you don't get many of them to the pound do you. She had to bend backward when she pulled a pint, so her nose didn't get covered in froth...What was her name?"

"It's on the tip of me nose- I mean tongue- What? Why's your face like that?"

"You're taking the mick aren't you?"

"NO! *yes* Weren't it something beginning with S?"

"Slut, probably...That's it! her name was Sadie. We used to call her Sadie Siegfried cos her nose was longer than the 'line'"

"You might have done. I just called her Sadie"

"Oh yeah. I forgot you were practically perfect in every way, and you don't call people . But do you remember her?"

"Int she the one who didn't turn up for her shift one night, and no-one's seen head nor hide of her since? And you thought she'd had been killed by Haigh, the Acid bath murderer...Even though he never came anywhere near Moston"

"Well it was dead funny, her just disappearing like that, at the same time as all them acid bath disappearances. But we know why now... I'll bet me own Grandma's cameo brooch that she's Eddie jr's mother. I could see the guilt all over her face, when my Eddie said he'd just been helping her change a barrel"

"Oh yeah. I remember now. Your Eddie looked like he'd had a bath in beetroot juice. Redder than me embers, he was. And the state of that skirt she was wearing? I say 'skirt' my Bob's got braces that cover more...So do you think it's her?"

"You ever seen anyone else with a nose that big?"

"Well her mam still lives up here and she isn't short in the nose department"

"Whereabouts does she live?"

"Why do you want to know Alice? It's not her fault is it? and she's getting on a bit. I'm not having you show me up, going round there with your shrieky voice, stirring up old news"

"I don't shriek! and I wouldn't dream of starting with an elder. I was raised proper you know...Eh, does Sadie's mam get a pension?"

"I would imagine so. She's eighty if she's a day...WHY?"

"No reason, Flo... ... ... So which Post office does she go to?"

"Hang on, Alice, whilst I just get my who goes to what post office, book out - How should I bleedin' know that!"

"You said you know where she lives. It stands to reason she's gonna get her pension from the nearest one...Mind you, do you remember Wilma Whatsherface? We seen her coming out of that post office in Marple when we were on the sharra going to the Peak district...Her face when you knocked on the window, and she saw half her street waving at her"

"Oh yeah. Sending a telegram my backside! Who does she know, that can read?"

"That's where vanity gets you, Flo. She was pushing thirty when I was sweet sixteen. Next thing I hear she's having her fortieth, two days after I turned Fifty!...It must be three buses at least, to Marple. Imagine doing that every Tuesday just cos you've knocked a decade off"

"It's not the only thing she was knocking off. I'm naming no names...Jack Slater"

"Ew. He's got enough room in that beer belly, for every hot dinner I've ever had. But WAIT! Didn't he go to school with your Joyce?"

"Three years above, And why do you think she lied about her age!"

"That's nowt so strange as folk. Anyway we was talking about Sadie 'Siegfrieds' mam. He could be her Grandchild you know? Could Eddie jr. We could be depriving her of a helping hand in her old age...He could definitely give her a budge up from her chair, with that nose. Aw go on. Tell us where she lives?...I'll find out meself anyway, eventually"

"I tell you what. Bring him round to mine and I'll have a good look at him. Then I'll have a look at her, the next time I'm up her end. If I feel it in me water. I'll let you know where she lives"

I give it two days, before you give in and tell me. "Alright then Flo. I'll bring him round at seven"

"You bloody well won't! I'll be watching Coronation street. Come at half six. Just don't get comfy"

THE SAGA CONTINUES. AND GETS AS THICK AS ALICE'S GRAVY

"Cooey Flo. It's only me ...Well it's not technically -I've brought someone with me to meet you...This is Billy. Int he the spit of Eddie?...'Cept for the nose"

"Hiya chuck. Ooh you do favour your dad. Sit yourself down. You look like you're gonna charge me for something, stood up all formal like that...Alice, why don't you come in the scullery and help me brew up"

"Ya'What?"

"Help. Me. To. Make. A. Brew! *How thick are you? I want a word!*

"Oh! Yeah. Billy, you watch the telly for a minute. I'm just going in the back, to help Flo make a brew...She's got a bit of arthritis in her wrist...And we're just gonna pull the door to. Her kettle's got one of them whistle's that go right through ya. Like chalk on a blackboard...The Magic Roundabout's on. Do you like the Magic Roundabout?"

"Not really"

"Well it's only on for five minutes! *You ungrateful sod* and the news is on next. *Mr 'I'm too good for Zebedee* I won't be a minute"

***

"He's getting like a millstone round me neck, Flo"

"Now you know how I feel -And eh! you cheeky cow...Arthritis?!"

"Well I had to say something. To stop him getting suspicious"

"He got suspicious when I had to spell out what was supposed to be a subtle hint!"

"How was I meant to know you were hinting? I thought you were showing off"

"SHOWING OFF? What bit of 'Come in the scullery, is 'showing off'?"

"Well it's only a step down from where we were stood. I thought you were trying to make out your house was bigger than it was...Like you had to walk a mile to brew up"

"You are really, really, not normal, Alice, and I don't know how long I can put up with your daftness - No way is he Sadie's. He looks nothing like her...Yeah she's got a massive hooter but you've seen it yourself. Her nose is as big as his, but in a different way"

"What d'ya mean, Flo?"

"What do you mean? 'What do I mean. It's as plain as the...It's bleedin' obvious. Hers is long. His, is more splodged on his face.

Like a cauliflower ear. But not an ear - A nose! And while we're on the subject of 'looks' I have to say, Alice. He's a plain lad. There's no one to carry on for you and Eddie and I don't think it'll carry on for Eddie with his mystery son...Very plain...Bordering on downright ugly"

"Oy you! You're not wrong though - And thank you very soddin' much! I hadn't even thought of descendants or anything like that, til you put it in me head. Always wishing me dead you are"

"Stop bloody exaggerating! When did I ever mention death?"

"When did you NOT"

"You really are a nutter!...So, we've established he's not Sadie's, and Coronation street is coming on soon. So get rid and we'll have a think about who else it could be tomorrow. We can narrow the field down a bit, by leaving out anyone attractive... I don't know why, but he puts me in mind of her who used to sell them cheap nets on Conran street"

"The one with a gammy leg?...And two bits of extra cleavage cos her bra was too tight? She was always flirting with my Eddie. The cheap tart! I think I know what you mean. I reckon she used her bust to distract from her ugly face...Like they say 'You don't look at the mantle-piece when you're poking the fire' - My God! If it's her?...The shame of it...i could bloody kill him for showing me up like this. It's a good job he's already dead...And how am I supposed to get rid of junior? He's not even had his cup of tea yet. Neither have I. Would you want people thinking I was mates with a tight sod"

"Other way round luv! Coronation street is coming on soon...I'll get rid. Watch and learn Alice... I bet you thought we'd got lost in there, Billy luv. Me bloomin tea caddy only went and got wedged behind the mangle. I'd make you a cup of Ovaltine but I'm short on milk and there's no shops open at this time. Anyway we don't want you falling asleep on the bus home do we? So Alice is gonna walk you to the bus stop, aren't you Alice?"

"Am I?" *What just happened?*

"Yes you bloody well are. And tomorrow. When Coronation street ISN'T ON, we'll try and sort out who his mam is, won't we? *Will you hurry up and shift yourselves*"

"I think we're being chucked out Billy. She's changed since she got that telly - Alright Flo, put your face straight. We're going!"

"Bye Alice - *I'll be having words with you tomorrow. You cocky cow* - Bye Billy luv, and don't you fret. We'll find out who your mam is. Anyway, look on the bright side. At least it isn't Alice"

"You cheeky sod! Come on Billy. You can have a quick cuppa at mine. The bus doesn't come til quarter to...And I've got teabags, so at least you can drink it down to the bottom without a mouthful of CHEAP leaves"

"DON'T BANG ME -" *She banged me bloody door. If any of my plaster heads have come off the wall, she's dead!*

UNTIL THE DAY FINALLY COMES. AND 'MUMMY' IS REVEALED

"Bloomin' eck Alice. Did you wet the bed? It's not even nine o'clock yet. What's up? Have you no milk for your morning cuppa?"

"I had my breakfast at six...Couldn't sleep"

"So you thought you'd come round here and disturb mine. Well you're here now. You might as well put the kettle on whilst I make myself look decent. Our Bob's just gone out...He's having a day at the 'dogs' with some old mates from work"

"Yeah I know *You've told me ten times this week, already* Anyway hurry up I've got something to tell you. Flo? You've got your pinny on over your dressing gown!"

"It's weekend...So what've you got to tell me?"

"Make a brew first" *You're gonna need it*

"I thought it was important"

"It is, Florence my luv. And when i tell you, you're gonna say you need a brew. So you might as well be prepared...Were you never in the Girl guides?"

"I can tell you were, by all the knots in your hearth rug"

"You're a Philistine, Florence Holden. That rug is shag pile and it cost an arm and a leg. It's meant to have knots. Proper shag always has knots. Not that you'd know. I've got more pile on my lino then you have on that thing in front of YOUR fire"

"You want to mop it more often then, Alice. Here's your brew. Now explain the big smirk you've had on your face, ever since you walked in"

Why am I not mixing with the type of people who read Cheshire Life "It is NOT a smirk. I'm being enigmatic...Like the Mona Lisa"

"I prefer The Haywain meself. At least you can see a proper view. I thinks that the Mona Lisa is dead plain. I don't know why they call it priceless cos it dunt look worth two bob to me...And I don't know what 'enigmatic' means, but if it's something that can be cured by Senna pods you're definitely it! Now spill the beans. What've you done? You haven't popped the little lad next door's ball have you?"

"I will next time the little sod kicks it over. All the flowers in me trough, are bent"

"Straighten them out then, and stop pretending they're real. You're not fooling anyone with that display of Chrysanthemums in November. Now stop waffling and tell me what it is you have to tell me"

"I know who it is"

"Who what is?"

"Billy's mam. I know who she is...Go on then! Pick up your bottom lip and ask me?"

"Who is it?!"

"I'll give you three guesses"

"Alice!"

"I'll give you a clue then. And you guess. Right - that's not the clue. The clue is..."

"Alice! For Pete's sake. Just tell me who it is!"

"Hang on. I'm still thinking of a clue...Here's the clue - She used to work with you"

"Where at? - Ferranti's? - The Ben? - The Doctors. That place I only lasted a day cos they were idiots? Bloomin' eck Alice. I've had loads of job's, if you're gonna play guessing games at least narrow the soddin' field"

"The Doctors"

"What year? I've been there for over twenty"

"After you married your Bob, but definitely before you had your Joyce, cos you was slim then and I had my suspicions about you and my Eddie, cos he went through a phase of wanting to go to the doctors a lot?"

"Am I hearing what I'm hearing?! What the eck?"

"I know Flo. All them people we thought of and it was someone right on our doorstep"

"NOT THAT ALICE! YOU!, even thinking I'd mess about with your Eddie. For one, I'm a married woman, and for TWO, we're mates!"

"Yeah I know...Aw don't take it the wrong way. I didn't really know you then. I had you down for 'brassy' when in fact you're just loud. I had some horrible mates before I met you. Me best friend from school ran off with John Arkwright when me and him were courting. It affects you, makes you not trust people til you get to know them. I'd trust you with me pension book now. And you're the only person who knows where I keep me best brooch"

"You had a lucky escape with John Arkwright. I was stood behind his missus the other day in the Wool shop. The amount of balls she had to buy for one jumper! I could have knitted our bob a suit, with a matching waistcoat...If I could knit . Anyway, stop changing the subject and tell me, who it is, and how you found out?"

"Doreen Bradley"

"Dunt ring a bell ?"

"DOR-REEN BRAD-LEY!...Short-arse red head. Looked like a librarian"

"Was she the one with the bandy legs? Couldn't stop a pig in the entry? If me memory serves me right, she finished work on the Friday and I ended up doing a stint on reception the following Monday cos she didn't show up. The things you learn about people when you do reception! Gertie Morris who never sat down anywhere when she visited people wasn't a snob. She had hemorrhoids...Big ones! Doreen Bradley!? He left you for Doreen Bradley? Bloomin eck, Alice. You're no oil painting, but Doreen BRADLEY? Was he starting to get cataracts? I can see where the 'nose' comes from now. hers weighed more than the rest of her combined. They built ten planes during the war, from the scrap metal off her spectacles...Who'd have thought...Doreen Bradley. Well they do say watch out for the quiet ones. Her mam said she'd found 'God' over the weekend and joined a convent. We thought nowt of it...She was a plain girl. It seemed to make sense. It's a good job old Maisie Bradley is dead. She's die anyway if she knew people knew...Why's your face like that?"

"I'm just thinking, with friends like you!...What do you mean,

I'm no oil painting?"

"Oh shurrup Alice. You know what I mean. You were a decent girl. You dressed decent and you spoke decent...ish. I'd have had Eddie down for getting off with some tart, not Cyrano de Bergerac in a frock. The conniving little madam. You were having problems with your 'bits' around that time weren't you? I bet she went rooting through your notes so she could give Eddie a bit of what he was missing"

"WHEN HAVE I EVER DISCUSSED MY BITS WITH YOU?"

"You never shut up about 'em. So how did you find out all this?"

"The orphanage Billy grew up in, had the decorators in and they found a room behind a false wall, full of old files. They remembered him from the other month when he was making enquiries and sent him his real birth certificate. Doreen bloody Bradley. When he told me it was - Doreen bloody Bradley, I felt dead shown up. And can we just get summat straight Flo? My Eddie DID NOT leave me for that trollop. She must have left cos he didn't want to know. He was still with me when she got off..Don't you remember? You came round to mine the day she didn't turn up for work, and made me cross my heart and hope to die, before you told me that Gloria Anderson's husband had problems with his waterworks. And as we were laughing, Eddie came in...And to this day I've never breathed a word"

"Didn't breathe a word? The next time you saw them, WHAT did you blurt out? *Is your Walter ok Gloria? He looks like he's dying for a wee*' I didn't know where to put me face"

"You still laughed though...Anyway back to Billy. A lot of water's gone under the bridge since it all happened "

"Literally, in Walter's case"

"Ha, ha, bloody ha, Flo. What I wanted to ask you was, do you know any relatives who might know where his mam is? I want to help the lad move on with his life. And it's cost me a fortune in extra milk and sugar since he started popping round, every soddin' five minutes...And not just that - He looks so much like Eddie it's making me ill. I have to keep fighting the urge to smack him in the face with a pan"

"Well like I said before, her mam is dead. Her dad died during the great war. Not doing war stuff, he got drunk on gin and fell in the canal. She had a little brother though. Last I heard, he was living in Miles Platting, in one of them high rises"

"This country's going to the dogs Flo. You grow up with a drunkard for a dad, a trollop for a sister and you end up in a posh apartment with everything inside. Me and you have struggled through two wars and you've still got to walk through wind and rain just to have a pee"

"Stop showing off cos you've got an inside toilet. I use the potty in bad weather...An' it's not his fault is it? He was only a nipper when Doreen got off...Tommy, his name is. I'm sure I saw him on Grey Mare Lane Market the other week"

"Is that where you got them new Toby jugs from? You told me your Joyce had got them for you. I've been wanting to go there for ages...as well you know!"

"She did! We weren't planning on going we was just passing, on the way up here, and decided to pop in"

"How do you just pass Grey mare lane market, on your way from Collyhurst to Moston?" *You LIAR!*

"Oh give it a rest Alice. So what are you gonna do now? about Billy"

"Well it's gonna break his heart to find out his mam is an ugly cow but the lad deserves to know the truth...He's a bit 'slow' an' all - must get it from her side. So I can see me having to ring every bell in them flats trying to find his uncle Tommy. Aw now the truth is out and he can get on with things, I think I'm actually going to miss the lad"

"Really?"

"No, but I'm gonna keep in touch and I'll tell him, when he finds his mam, if she's still alive. He must bring her round to mine"

"REALLY?"

"Yeah...I'm gonna kill the trollop! Carrying on with my husband"

6: SPECIAL DAYS

THROUGHOUT THE YEARS. FLO AND ALICE CAME TOGETHER TO CELEBRATE MANY OCCASIONS...BUT MAINLY TO MOAN ABOUT STUFF.

PANCAKE DAY

"Alice. Have you seen the size of this queue?"

"Well I'm stood here with you and me names not Helen Keller"

Tut "Why do people wait til the last bloody minute to get their eggs for Pancake Tuesday? We'll be here all bloody day. Oh God! Look who's next but three from the counter - Don't let her see you looking, you daft sod"

"Flo? I was only leaning forward a bit to see who it is...Who is it?"

"Shout a bit louder. There's a few people in Salford who didn't hear you. It's that Ivy Wilson. We'll be here til Easter. You know what she's like with her gob. *I'll pay you for my goods. But first, you have to endure one of my many tales of illness and woe. Whilst I hold up the queue"*

"Do I know her?"

"She lives on your street!"

"You mean Ivy, from Ivy Street Ivy?"

SIGH "YES"

"I can't stand her. It's a shame there's no Trollop street round here. That's the street she should live on"

"I know what you mean Alice. If I had varicose veins like her, I'd be making sure me hems were a bit lower. And just between you and me. Ted, the chiropodist told me he has to use industrial strength Corn ointment on her feet. Dunt stop her propping up the bar in the Bluebell every night. She's brazen. Shush, here she comes...Hello Ivy. I was just saying to Alice, there's Ivy from your street. Dunt she look well?"

"Hiya Flo. Don't let looks fool you. It's a miracle I'm still alive with my medical problems"

"Well you're bearing it well. Just don't give up tablets for Lent"

"Ooh don't make me laugh Flo. It could trigger off my Rheumatoid 'Artisticness' - Hiya Alice. Don't see much of you nowadays"

"You wanna try coming to mine. She's always there - Put your face straight Alice. I'm kidding *I'm NOT* Them eggs you've got look lovely Ivy"

"I got brown ones with it being a special occasion. You pay a bit extra than you do for the white ones. But at the end of the day it's for Jesus. Are you getting your Pancake stuff?"

"Good God no. Me and Alice got ours in days ago. Didn't we Alice?"

"A week ago last Wednesday" *Stop making me tell fibs. Without giving me notice!*

"Well I'll love you and leave you Ladies. Me pancakes won't toss themselves"

"Have a good 'un, luv. See you soon"

Ivy leaves the shop.

"I thought she's never go Flo"

"I know. Dunt her voice 'grate'?"

Flo and Alice reach the counter

"Hello Flo. What can I do you for?"

"Six eggs, half a pound of plain flour and a Lemon please?"

"Brown or white eggs?"

"Whatever's cheapest. Should I treat us to a packet of biscuits Alice? I could murder a custard cream, and I've only got Rich Tea at home"

"I fancy a Ginger Nut meself"

"So buy yourself a packet. I'M getting custard creams. And I'm not made of money"

"I'll make do with a custard. Why did you want me to lie to Ivy. About us getting in our pancake stuff the other day?"

"I just felt like disagreeing with her"

"Oh"

CHRISTMAS SHOPPING, ON A PENSION

"Hiya Alice. You're lucky you caught me. I've just this minute come back from Christmas shopping with our Joyce. That eighty eight's dead handy for us both. She got off on Oldham road and I carried on.

You'd have laughed on the way there. We'd arranged to meet on the twenty past, going to town and she was a bit late dropping the kids off at school cos one of 'em lost her mittens. I could see her coming, but there was no else at the bus stop. So I pressed the bell, like I was getting off and pretended I had a bad leg. I was sitting upstairs anyway cos I wanted a fag. So by the time I got down the stairs, she was there. I just turned round and said *Oops, wrong stop* The 'dirty' look he gave me when we did get off could have curdled milk whilst it was still in the Cow.

Anyway, do you want to see what I got for the grandkids? They're coming here Boxing day, and I want them to have something to open"

Not really "Go on then. How come you didn't tell me you was going to Town?"

"Because I didn't think I had to! And we was only going to Woolworths for the last bits for the kids, and you're not one for kids are ya?"

Not yours I'm not "Well go on then show me what you spent your pittance of a pension on. I hope them kids are grateful when you're living on bread and dripping for the next month"

"First of all, it's MY business what I spend me money on, and it's NOT out of me pension. It's called 'Saving up' and never pretending to be out when the Club man comes. Fifty quids worth of Provident cheques go a long way"

"You know what Flo? Your Bob would be turning in his grave, at the thought of getting you 'tick' for anything"

"Well he's cremated, so there's nowt to turn. Do ya want to see what I got or not?"

"Go on then. And a brew wouldn't go amiss either"

"I'll do one in a minute. Right, they've all got one of these Selection boxes, shaped like a stocking. Aren't they lovely? These books are for our Lesley and the others have got a Doll each, apart from our Wayne of course. I don't fancy Liberace the second for a grandson. I got him this fire engine.

All I need now is me Sprouts and some Blancmange for the Trifle and not only is Bob me dear departed husband. He's me 'uncle' too.

I'm putting the kettle on. What do you want? Tea or Tea? *ha ha ha* I should have been on the stage"

"Yeah you're bleedin hilarious Flo - Oy! Put an extra sugar in mine. For the 'shock' I've just seen how much you paid for them selection boxes. They've charged you two bob extra for the wrapping. Still, like they say 'No fool like an old fool'"

"Have you ever been round the back of the Adelphi with Charles Dickens? Makes me wonder where he got the idea for Scrooge"

"I can go to better places to be insulted, you know!"

"Alice luv. I can't think of many places round here where you AREN'T insulted. They can't stand you at the 'Over sixties's club. There's only me who sticks up for you, and what do I get in return? whinge, whinge, bloody whinge"

"I'm going. I've got me own tea at home. And proper china cups. Unlike some"

"You know where the door is"

"Yeah I do. Don't worry I'll remember to wipe me feet on the way out ... Am I still invited for Christmas day?"

"I invited ya didn't I?"

"I'll see you then, then"

"Yeah"

YOU SHOULD ALWAYS KEEP YOUR GOB SHUT. ON THE ELEVENTH HOUR OF THE ELEVENTH DAY.

"Bloody 'ell Alice, you're cutting it fine. It's quarter to eleven"

"I overslept. Forgot to wind me alarm clock up and it never went off. If this is what they call modern technology they can soddin' keep it. It was loads better when the knocker upperer used to come round"

"Well you're here now. Make yourself useful and pass me that Pledge and a duster. I'm not standing in silence with dust on me sideboard"

"My knees are killing me. Would it be alright if I sat down?"

"ALICE! There are men out there who don't even have knees. They lost their knees protecting the likes of us. But if YOU can't stand for TWO minutes, ONCE A YEAR, so be it. Just remind me not to stand near you when it's thunder and lightning"

"I'll stand! *You're a hard cow!* Have we got time for a brew?"

"We would have had, if you'd got here in time. You'll have to wait now. Turn the radio on, Our Bob's already tuned it in for me, so don't mess with the knobs"

"It's a bit hissy. Should I -

"DON'T MESS WITH THE KNOBS!. Right, It's gonna start in a minute...Where's your Poppy?"

"It's on me coat"

"Get your bloody coat back on then! - Hurry up!"

"Am I alright to lean on the back of this chair?"

"SHUSH!"

BONG, BONG, BONG,- **KNOCK, KNOCK** - BONG, BONG, BONG, BONG -**KNOCK, KNOCK, KNOCK** -BONG, BONG, BONG.

The two minutes silence goes unbroken

"I don't bloody believe it! What idiot was knocking me door during the bongs?"

"I heard it too Flo, but I didn't like to say anything" *Mainly cos I didn't want me head ripping off.*

"No one's supposed to say anything. It's supposed to be two bloody minutes silence. When I find out who it was, I'll have their guts for bleedin' garters. I'll put the kettle on ...What sort of 'animal knocks your door during THIS TIME OF YEAR"

"Well it definitely wasn't your Roger. Your knocker's too high up" *And your dog's too daft anyway.*

"I didn't literally mean an animal Alice. I meant who in their right mind would knock a person's door at the eleventh minute of the eleventh hour?"

"Probably a German or it could be a Japanese. Mind you I can't say I've ever seen someone Japanese round here. Unless you count them who live in Chinatown"

"I never heard owt so daft. Who's gonna knock on my door from Chinatown!"

"Should I knock on next door's and see if it was them? Or if they saw anything"

"It wouldn't have been Mrs Wilson. She lost two of her lads in the last war. Plus she can't walk. She's ninety if she's a day. And anyway, her wheelchair squeaks. I'd have heard it trundling up her lobby. These walls a paper thin. But I'll get to the bottom of this, if it's the last thing I do ... BLOODY HEATHENS. Do you want a biscuit?"

"I wouldn't say no. What kind have you got?"

"The beggars can't be choosers kind. You can have a rich tea or a rich tea"

"Well put an extra sugar in me tea. They're verging on being a cracker are rich teas. I like a sweet biscuit, me. A custard cream would go down well now"

"I'll nip to the shop if you want and get an assortment. Let me get me coat on and then stick that sweeping brush up me backside. Might as well sweep the street on the way round!"

"You're being sarcky, aren't you? I'll manage with a rich tea!"

"I can do you a Salmon paste butty, if you're hungry?"

"Aw why didn't you say so before? What am I supposed to do now?"

"Either have it, or don't. It's not bloody compulsory to have a butty!"

"I meant I've just ate two biscuits, and now you're offering me a butty. That's having a sweet before a savoury. What's that gonna do to me insides? It's supposed to be savoury THEN sweet"

"You're not normal you! ... Here, keep hold of those rich teas. Have a butty then a couple more biscuits. That'll put you right"

"Makes sense"

"You, saying I make sense? Hang on, whilst I just pick up me jaw!. Do me a favour Alice? You stop thinking you're Albert Einstein's Teacher and I'll stop saying I can bite my elbows.

We're both lying ... What ARE you bloody doing?"

"Hey Flo. You're right...You CAN'T bite your own elbows"

*Tut! **KNOCK! KNOCK!*** "Who's that at the door? I hope it's who I hope it is"

Flo answers the front door. A short conversation ensues

BANG!

"I thought the house was gonna fall down around me, Flo. The way you just slammed that door. It's a good job you'd shut the middle door, or I had been deafened. Who was it?" *Why did you shut the middle door? I couldn't hear a thing.*

"I. AM. FUMING! Top that brew up for me... It was only Mandy Crompton asking me did I want an Avon book?"

"Was it her knocking before? She's still in her teens, her, in't she? They're the worse for it. I hope you gave her a good telling off"

"*Go and ask your mam how important today is,* I said to her. *After all YOUR mam's got more than her fair share of soldiers to grieve over ... And the odd sailor or two.* And then I slammed the door in her face"

"You didn't?"

"I did"

Both pause for thought, and personal remembrances

"She didn't half get about, did Ada Crompton. And I don't mean to the shops!"

"She was 90% of the war effort, Alice. She entertained more Yanks than Glenn Miller"

"I like Moonlight Serenade, me"

"Ada's favourite must have been 'In the mood"

"Ooh! Florence! ... These rich tea taste a bit sweeter. now that I've had that butty ...You could have still taken the Avon book off her Mandy. We could have had a look through it before your Bob came home"

"Definitely, not normal!" ...

THE BITCHIN' HOUR

"Waste of a good turnip is that. Look at all the waste where you're carving it"

"Did you buy it, Alice? NO. So shut it! I'm doing for the grandkids. And next week I'm getting them fireworks and treacle toffee. Who doesn't like it can lump it"

"It's your money you're wasting. Hey? Is your Bob upstairs?"

"My Bob hasn't been upstairs for twenty odd years, as you well know. Not with his leg. That's why we have the bed in the parlour"

"Well I heard a noise ...There it is again. Did you not hear it?"

"Like a scraping scratching noise?"

"Yeah!"

"No, I didn't hear a thing. But it's funny y'know. People have mentioned it before ... Bob says it's the ghost of Martha Hodgkins, who was murdered under this very roof in nineteen hundred and two"

"You never told me that before?"

"You never asked"

"Well I'm asking now! Who was Martha Hodgkins? And what happened to her?"

"Don't blame me if you have nightmares"

"ME? Have nightmares? I usually cause 'em luv. Go on then, spill the beans. Or the blood *he he he* I'm dying to know"

"That's an unfortunate turn of phrase Alice. Especially in light of the murderous tale I'm about to tell you"

"Ooh it's like one of them true crime stories. I love me true crime. Go on then?"

"Well it wasn't long after these houses were built, that Martha and her husband moved in here"

"I thought your Bob's first wife's family had it from new?"

"They did! for all intents and purposes, cos within five days of Martha and her husband moving in, she was dead! And my Bob's in laws bought it a couple of months later ... When all the blood had been cleaned up"

"Oh my God! So what happened?"

"You see that cupboard under the stairs Alice?"

"The one you keep your Ewbank in?"

"No the one next to it *sigh* YES the one I keep my bloody Ewbank in. How many soddin cupboards under the stairs are there? I hate telling you something, you interrupt all the bloody time"

"I'm just getting the facts right. There is another door there"

"But that's the door to the stairs! I said CUPBOARD - Oh never bloody mind!"

"Aw I promise I won't interrupt again...Go on? You was saying about the cupboard"

Sigh "Well, Martha's husband was a man of routine. A bit like my Bob. Every night come rain or shine, he was home for seven o'clock on the dot ... Anyway with it being 'All Hallows eve' She must have decided to give him a bit of a fright, by hiding in that very same cupboard ... What time is it now?"

"Ten to seven"

"Ten to seven? Bloomin' eck, that's a bit of a coincidence, cos it was at that very moment, Martha decided to settle herself down in the cupboard and wait - Before you say anything. I know it was at that time, because at the inquest, her neighbour, who was the last to see her alive, testified that at a quarter to seven, she'd knocked on to borrow a cup of sugar. And funnily enough she thought Martha's husband was already there, cos as Martha had gone to close the front door, her next door could have sworn she'd seen the shadow of a man come across the living room wall ... Right there, where you're sat now"

"Ooh let me move...So go on?"

"Anyway, the neighbour went back in her own house. Later on at the inquest she stated that she'd heard thuds coming from next door, and heavy footsteps coming down the stairs, but she hadn't knocked on to complain cos it would have been cheeky after getting a lend of some sugar. The thuddin' apparently started at seven and went on til after nine. By which time she was regretting ever having had, a sweet tooth"

"Bloody 'ell Flo! And what happened after that? Was it her husband that killed her?"

"Oh no. It wasn't him. Turns out he'd received a telegram at work saying his brother in Chorlton had been badly hurt in a tram accident. He just rushed off from work without being able to get word to Martha. It turned out to be a cruel hoax. But it meant that he didn't get home til gone ten, and he was fumin' .... Then he found her ... Dead! Not a mark on her that he could see...Just dead, with a frozen look of fear on her face. That's when HE heard the footsteps ...What time is it?"

"Nearly seven...Flo, I'm not sure I can ever come in your house again? Did the husband die too? Did they find out who did it?"

"The husband didn't die but he was never the same again. And the Police had no more luck than they did finding 'Jack the Ripper' - Some say it was HIM. That he'd moved up north and the urges had started again. But like I said, it was a crime that was never solved ... But here's the next 'mystery'. They say that every year on this date you can hear the sound of footsteps coming down me stairs...But I'm usually out, so I couldn't say if it was true or not"

"Flo? I CAN hear footsteps!"

71

"Bloomin' eck Alice, so can I"

"What should we do? WHAT SHOULD WE DO?!"

"keep calm woman! Grab an ornament. We'll face it together"

The stair door creaks slowly open. Alice faints ... A small child appears at the foot of the stairs

"Nana? You told me to tell you when it was seven o clock. So you could make me some Horlicks ...Why's Aunty Alice lying on the floor?"

"She's just having a rest luv. Get back in bed and I'll bring it up to you" *When I've stopped laughing ... I wish I had a camera.*

BLACKPOOL HERE WE COME

"Flo? I can see the Tower"

"We're lucky we're not still staring at the Simpson Memorial. Cos of YOU, Alice. What sort of idiot is going on a Sharra to Blackpool, and gets halfway up the road before they remember they've forgotten the butties. I could feel my Angina 'starting' when we had to run from Ivy street to the 'Ben' We nearly missed it. *Cos of YOU* How, on bloody earth, do you forget the bloody butties, when you're going to Blackpool of all places?"

"YOU put me off. Doing that daft dance, up the lobby. I could see your knickers. Mind you, they do come down to your knees. You made me want a wee, and I won't let it be said that I'm the kind of woman who takes food to the toilet. So I put the bag down while I 'went'...And then I forgot it. Cos of YOU! So you needn't be casting stones. Not with the state of YOUR windows!"

"You're barefaced you are! Anyway pass us the flask. I could murder a brew"

"Save some for when we're on the beach"

"Stop fretting. There's a good six or seven cups in this flask. Are you having one?"

"Go on then...Dunt tea taste funny from a flask?... Nice, but 'funny'"

"I know what you mean Alice. It's the water. It's not the same as at home"

"You got it out of YOUR tap"

"Yeah! Well it doesn't travel well does it. Neither does she, three rows behind us, by the look of her -Don't make it obvious, by turning round, but when you can, have a gander ... It's her from the market. Dora whojamaflip...The one who sells wool"

"How am I supposed to look if I can't turn round? And what did you look at her with? Them eyes in the back of your head?"

"I clocked her when we was getting on. She'd obviously took a shortcut through some privets ... Backwards"

"Why didn't you tell me then?"

"I wasn't talking to you, for making us nearly miss the Sharra altogether"

"You weren't talking to me? Well you could have told me! I

thought you was quiet with excitement. Aw I want to look now"

"We'll be getting off in a few minutes. You can look then...WHAT ARE you doing?"

"I'M JUST STANDING UP AND TURNING ROUND TO STRAIGHTEN OUT MY SKIRT...Oh, hiya Dora. You're looking well ... Bloody 'ell Flo. I see what you mean. She mustn't own an Iron OR a mirror"

"I thought I said wait til the sharra stops. You didn't half make it bloody obvious you were having a nosy!"

"No I didn't! Everyone thought I was straightening out me skirt"

"I KNOW! I bet they bloody heard you saying what you was doing, back in Moston"

"I don't know who died and made you the boss of me, Flo. Ooh! we're stopping now. Let's stay on til she gets off. I want to see her from the back ...Look at the state of it. Sells wool yet can't manage to get a Cardi that fits. What ARE them lumps ? She looks like she needs another bra for her back fat"

"That's why you'll never catch me in a full length girdle. The fat's gotta go somewhere, when you're squeezing in your middle bits. Do you think she knows she's got bits of her waist hanging off her armpits?"

"Are you gonna tell her?"

"What? and hurt her feelings? That's your area of expertise Alice"

"Have you brought a camera?"

"No. It's the Butler's day off and I don't know which of my hundred cupboards it's in! - When have I ever had a camera?"

"You've got an hoover!"

"Does it take photo's? *You IDIOT!* And it's second hand. It was our Joyce's. I've said you can borrow it whenever you want. It's you that chooses to be a martyr with your Ewbank"

"It'd break me back, carrying it round to mine. She's got a camera an' all has your Joyce. I just thought she might have given you that as well"

"Well you thought wrong, Alice. Anyway why were you asking about a camera?"

"I wanted a photo taken, but with Doreen's back, in the background. She needs help, the poor luv. It's a bit hard telling someone they've got things protruding out of 'em. We could discreetly pin it up in the Pub and hopefully she'd get the full picture. So to speak"

"If that's your idea of 'discreet' Remind me, not to take you with me to the Clinic"

"WHY? What's wrong with ya?"

"Shurrup and get off this Sharra, before it's time to go back - OY! The butties!?" *GOD GIVE ME STRENGTH*

THE KIDS ARE ON HOLIDAY AND ALICE ISN'T BEST PLEASED

"Don't go near my bottle of milk, you'll curdle it. What's up with your face Alice? Have you found something new, to get on your nerves?"

"We can't all be a ray of sunshine like YOU. It's a wonder you haven't been murdered, all them strangers you smile at. I bet more half of them, thought you was simple. Anyway I'll tell you what's wrong with me. Having to nearly have to stand up, on the bus from town. That's what's wrong!...The bloody kids are on their six weeks holidays"

"i could have told you that"

"I wish you bloody had done Flo! I'd have avoided Tib street like the plague. Anyone would have thought Clark Gable was running the Joke shop, the amount of kids stood outside it"

"Clark Gable?! You're a bit behind the times Alice"

"Well whoever or whatever it is they like nowadays. I was mad about Clark Gable. Remember when we watched 'It happened one night' at The Adelphi? Three times"

"Yeah...You trying to tell the usherette we were triplets, taking it in turns!"

"I did not! - Oh yeah, I did. Weren't we daft buggars when we were young?"

"Speak for yourself. Anyway, what did you mean by 'Nearly' had to stand up?"

"I went to town to get a copy of my Eddie's death certificate. The original one is getting tatty. When I'm feeling down I like to look at it. Cheers me up no end"

"You're not normal!"

"It's alright for you, with your 'Perfect' marriage. Even if people do think he adopted you. But some of us had to put up with lying philanderers"

"I did try to warn you. Should have been an 'Old man's darling' like me, then. Instead of the 'Young man's slave' you turned out to be"

"Slave? I'll have you know that once I clocked on to what he was doing, I stopped lifting a finger for him. He was close to starvation and didn't have a single clean sock when he left me!"

Tut "You still haven't told me why you almost had to stand, on the bus?"

"Because you keep changing the subject Flo. I ended up getting the sixty three bus, cos I needed to get off at the bottom of the lane. A load of kids got on in front of me - The cheeky beggars. In my day, we wouldn't have dreamed of getting on the bus before grown ups... They all had Duffle Bags or rolled up towels so they must have been going to the Baths. Anyway two of 'em decided to sit on the front seats. The cheek of it! - *Oy! move it* I said to them. *The BACK of the bus is for kids. Or have YOU got bad knees?* - They soon shifted"

"What's wrong with a child sitting at the front? Me eldest granddaughter loves to sit on the front seats"

"That's your business if you want to raise selfish gits. I've lived through two wars. Why should I struggle, with my knees.

They're only kids. The back of the bus is where they belong. Out of sight"

"Have you ever lived in Alabama?"

"Is it anywhere near Newton Heath?"

God give me strength "No, that's Ardwick, you thick sod. Make yourself useful and put the kettle on"

ALICE 'WINS' A CRUISE

THE BEFORE

"FLO! Guess what?"

"The Pope's a Catholic?"

"No you daft sod - Well, yes he is, but it's not that. Go on, have a guess?"

"We'll be here all bloody day . Why don't you just tell me?"

"Aw can't you have a guess?- Ooh that face would curdle milk! Sit down then and I'll tell you"

"Gawd, Alice. What is it? you're not pregnant are you? Hurry up then. I've got a pile of mangling to do"

"I've only gone and won a cruise. Two weeks abroad. It was a competition in the paper and I had a spare stamp, so I thought...Anyway, I won, and it's for two. So get packing"

"Aw thanks for thinking of me but I can't go. Not with my Bob's leg. Plus I don't have a Passport"

"I wasn't inviting your Bob's leg! And it doesn't say anything about needing a passport. We'll be at sea anyway, it's not like we'll be popping in and out of foreign places. Aw can't you come?"

"Sorry luv. I couldn't leave my Bob on his own for two weeks. He'd starve to death, and our Joyce has got her hands full with the kids, so she couldn't help"

"Well I'm going even if I have to take the dog. THE DOG! What am I gonna do about the dog?"

"I'll pop in everyday. I'll feed him and let him have a run in the entry - Even better, he can come and stay here. I've still got our Roger's old kennel...And I'll still pop in yours every day to open and close the curtains"

"Aw you're a good 'un. I'm gonna get off now. Got loads to do before we sail. Do ya know what? I might ask her next door if she wants to go with me"

"Jean? You can't stand her"

"I know. But she's got an extra set of matching luggage. Hasn't been able to part with it since her Ted died. Have you still got my spare key?"

"No I gave it to Burke and Hare! - Of course I've still got it. It's in the button tin drawer"

THE AFTERMATH

"Hiya. Welcome back, our Alice. I've missed you *I really have!* How was the cruise? You don't look very brown. I bet you're dying for a proper brew? Sit down, I'll put the kettle on. Have you brought me back a stick of rock? Did you sit at the Captains table in your pearls" *Your FAKE pearls*

"It was RUBBISH Flo. And if I never see that Jean Ogden for the rest of my life, it'll be too soon"

"You'd better hope she moves then. It's hard not seeing the person you share a back wall with. You don't want a shortish life do you? Mind you, you have had a good innings"

"Oh shurrup, and put the kettle on. She's a COW. But that aint the half of it"

"The brew's in front of you. Go on then? I'm not sitting here cos I'm waiting for piffy"

"Well Flo. Do you know how I told you it was abroad?"

"Yeah? Don't tell me they took you to Germany?"

"I WISH! Even if they ARE all Nazis. NO! It wasn't even abroad - It was the Norfolk Broads. That taxi you waved us off in, only took us as far as Chorlton street Coach Station. And the journey was horrendous. It took hours"

"The ones in Norfolk? I knew someone who went there...I know two now - three if I count Jean" *Chuckle*

"Are you mocking me?"

"No luv - Anyway the Norfolk broads are lovely, so I'm told, an' it WAS free"

"Not in soddin March they're not. It did nowt but rain. I'd have been even more fuming, if I'd paid"

"It did here too. You could have stayed home and had a paddle up the entries. Was the boat nice though, Alice?"

"Some may call it a boat. I'd say it was more like a floating sharra, 'cept the seats on a sharra are comfier than the so called beds...They were bunk beds Flo. BLOODY BUNK BEDS!"

"Bloomin' eck, who had the top one?"

"Well not ME! Your Bob only thinks he's suffering with his leg. He wants to try having my knees"

"Oy you! I've told you before. My Bob has a war wound. God only knows how you got dodgy knees...But dunt Jean only have one eye? And a recent hip replacement?"

"You don't need two eyes to climb a ladder. And I waited underneath in case she had a wobble"

"You're a Saint luv!"

"And you're a sarcky mare Florence. Eeyar I got you a tea-towel. You see that bit there? Just under the crease? That's the bit we went on. Never- a- soddin- gain"

WEDDING GUESTS

"I'm sorry Flo, but to me a wedding's not a wedding if it isn't in church. With a Vicar. Registrar? What's that? Only registrar I know is a school 'registrar'"

"You weren't saying that on your wedding day"

"That was different. We were between wars...And we had to buy our own houses. Nowadays they get a council house thrown at em, like confetti. They don't know they're born!"

"I was wondering when you'd start. I half expected having to gag you with me gloves when she entered the room"

"Well it WAS an hideous outfit. And at her age too, but I wouldn't dream of making someone feel bad on their wedding day. Anyway I'm saving myself for the reception. There's some equally hideous creations in the row behind us... Don't let her see you looking, but get a look at 'Mutton dressed like lamb' - immediately behind you, but four up - going towards the door...See what I mean?"

"Alice. I wish you'd learn to whisper properly. How can I look now that half of Deansgate has heard you? But blinkin' eck I see what you mean. Is that dress made of Crochet? She'd have been struck by lightening if this was St Lukes. I've used more balls of wool knitting a dress for 'Tippy Tumbles' Bloody disgusting...Not that I'm judging"

"Should we make a move? Before the butties start curling up If we get there before the others,we can have a good nosy at the parlour - Seeing as they're too tight to have the reception somewhere proper. And don't start about mine being at me mams!"

I'm not even listening to you. You moaning cow!

"You look lovely though Flo. Cornflower blue really suits you"

"You scrub up well yourself. You've always suited a dress. What colour is that ?"

"Puce"

"Looks maroonish to me...Like dried blood. In't that the colour you wanted me to wear, at YOUR wedding? I'm glad I told you to sod off"

"Well it's not! It cost a fair bit of me pension did this. Do I look daft enough to buy something the colour of dried blood?"

"No, but you look daft to believe in 'Puce' C'mon, let's walk to the bus stop and get there before the babycham runs out. I'm not stopping long though. Wrestling's on at four"

"I wonder how we 'get on' sometimes Flo. we're so different. I think Wrestling is dead common"

"Bet you'd watch it if Mick Macmanus wore puce knickers"

"Flo? Shurrup!"

Chuckle "D'ya know what's just come to me?"

"What?"

"By the look of them on the groom's side, there'll be some 'puce' stains on the parlour lino later on. Once the beer runs out. I might give Dickie Davies a miss and stay for the real thing - Aw look? The bus is coming - walk fast Alice but don't run. The buggars speed past if they think you're running for it"

"RUN? With my knees!"

SOON BE CHRISTMAS

"It'll soon be Christmas, Flo. Have you got owt planned?"

"Ya what?"

"Have you made any plans for Christmas?"

"Bloody ell woman, we've only just got Bonfire night out of the way. Give me chance to get me breath back, before I start thinking about Christmas. And what do you mean 'Plans'? I'll only have to look at the Butcher, first week in December, and me name'll be in the book for a nine pound Turkey"

"No I don't mean like that...I've been reading Cheshire Life -

"Has someone given the doctors some new magazines?"

"Do you want to see a copy of my paper bill? - Now, before I was so rudely interrupted, I was saying, The Cheshire life gives you some wonderful ideas for Christmas"

"Alice? Why would you need ideas for Christmas, at your age? Have you not had one every year, like the rest of us?"

"You can't help it can you? *Sarcky cow* There's more to Christmas than a Turkey"

"Don't I bloody know it! I've got half a dozen Grandkids to buy for. The only time of the year kids get presents on some other buggar's birthday"

"You can't call Jesus a buggar!"

"I just did!"

"Don't blame me when you're in hell and damnation. Anyway, when I come to yours for Boxing day, I'm not bringing mince pies this year. I'm bringing volumevonts"

"What's a volumevont when it's at home?"

"It's like a little cup made of pastry, filled with stuff"

"A PIE?"

You heathen! "No, Flo, NOT a pie. For one, It's not made with pie pastry. It's made with puff pastry"

"Like a Vanilla slice? I certainly won't complain if you bring vanilla slices" *Your mince pies are horrible.*

You're doing me head in. "Yeah. Like a vanilla, but with no vanilla. And a completely different shape"

"What's in it then?"

"Creamed mushroom"

"And?"

"Well you can have other stuff, but I'm a pensioner. I'm not shelling out on Stilton and Asparagus for no buggar!"

"Oh it's alright for you to say buggar?"

"I wasn't aiming it at Jesus!"

"So you're coming here on Boxing day, with a vegetable pie? *hmm* That'll go down well with our Bob"

"Mushrooms aren't spuds you know! Truffles - Not the chocolate ones - are mushrooms and they cost more than Gold. The Queen eats truffles"

"So we're having pies fit for a queen, are we? And where are you getting the mushrooms from? Beaverbrooks?"

"No. The Co-op...You know I'm on first name terms with the doctor's wife"

"Well you do spend more time with him than she does"

"You can have my knees if you want! You don't know the meaning of pain. Anyway, Diana - That's her name, was telling me, you can use undiluted Campbells cream of mushroom soup to fill volumevonts - Why's your face like that?"

"Undiluted tin soup? In a PIE? Posh people eat that? No wonder half of them are chinless wonders. Alice, if you don't want to bring mince pies, why don't you do a trifle. No one's gonna eat them voluwhatsits round here"

"Aw Flo. I wanted to do summat different for a change"

"Why don't you try smiling? That'd be a novelty. Or join in stuff. You never join in anything. When was the last time you did the Hokey-Cokey?"

Sniff "There's never been a first time. You don't half go

common at Christmas, you. I was raised proper. We don't do common!"

"I can tell you were at the front of the queue, when they was giving out cheek! You've always thought you were better than people. When we all went to town for VE day, you had a face like thunder. D'ya know how many times I had to tell people you weren't German"

"That's an outright fib!"

"No it isn't. You were glummer than Lord Haw-Haw and Tokyo Rose combined. We're all celebrating and you looked like your dog had died"

"Oh. So cos I don't go round grinning like an idiot, I must be a traitor? Anyway I'm not doing the hokey-cokey in your house. And do you know why? Cos you can't keep it to the hokey cokey. Once you've had more than one tonic wine. YOU have to turn it into the Can-Can and show off your knickers"

"I do that for the kids. It makes 'em laugh"

They're idiots too. "Well I'm not arguing with you Flo. I've got an appointment with the doctor"

"AGAIN?"

"Like I said. If you want my knees ... Am I still coming for me tea tomorrow?"

"Of course you are. I'll do you caviar and chips, and divide your brew between six sherry glasses. Don't want you feeling out of place ... DON'T BANG ME DOOR" *She banged me door. Next time I see her, she's dead!*

FIREWORKS!

"What's up with your face, Alice? You look like you've seen a ghost"

"I'm lucky I've still got a face. Some hooligan just came at me with a firework"

"Where?"

"Outside the paper shop on Moston lane. I'll tell you all about it, when I get me breath back"

"Never mind your breath. We're going round there, RIGHT NOW! Hang on whilst I get me coat on. The bloody buggars. They want to bring back National Service. It's getting worse every bonfire night. Thank god it's only one day a year!...why've you sat down?"

"I'm in shock!"

"Well when we come back, I'll put an extra sugar in your tea. Come on, before they go. By the time I've finished they'll wish they'd never been born"

"Aw leave it Flo. Just make us a brew. I'll be as right as rain after a nice cup of tea"

"Well you do look a bit peaky. I'll put the kettle on. They'll have probably scarpered by now, anyway. Would you recognise any of 'em if you saw 'em again?"

"It dunt matter now. I might have over reacted a bit. It just caught me off guard"

"Normally I'd agree with you -

"Agree with me about what?"

"Well you do tend to go on a bit, about the slightest thing. But you're a bloody pensioner. You can't go round shoving fireworks in a pensioners face. If I'd have shoved a firework in one of my elder's faces. I'd be dead by now. Was it a Banger? I hope it went off in the little sod's hand. I'm bloody fuming Alice. And if you didn't look so awful I'd be dragging you round there"

"What do you mean, I look awful? I'm wearing rouge!"

"The shock of what happened, must have wore it off. Maybe we should call the doctor?"

"Maybe you could just give me that brew you offered me half an hour ago"

"Bloody ell. I'm sorry. Why didn't you remind me?"

"I couldn't get a word in edge ways"

"Well I'm fumin' luv. We didn't win two world wars for a pensioner to be treated like this. Eeyar get this down. It's proper brewed is this. I've put an extra, extra sugar in it as well. That'll put the colour back in your cheeks"

It's like hot treacle "Do y'know what Flo? I think I'll just go home and have an early night" *And a decent brew*

"Let me get me coat on - Oh! I hadn't even taken it off. Bloody hooligans, getting me all in a kerfuffle ... Come on, I'll walk you round"

"You don't have to Flo. It's only two streets up. I'll go through the entries"

"It was only two streets, coming here and look what happened? A woman the other day got murdered on her own doorstep"

"WHERE?"

"It was an in an episode of 'Gideon of the yard' But they're all based on true stories"

"Ooh it doesn't bear thinking about. Where did your Bob go in the Great war?"

"Italy...Why?"

"Well. Look at that. All the way to a foreign country, with a bloody great big war going on. And he comes back without a scratch. Yet some people only get as far as their front door and a murderer murders them"

"We need to count our blessings luv...Come on I'll walk you to the top of your street" *And hurry up. I don't want to miss Armchair Theatre*

"Aw you don't have to"

"I want to!"

THE TWO FRIENDS MAKE THEIR WAY UP THE LANE. FLO SEES A FAMILIAR FACE COMING TOWARDS THEM

"There's our Joyce's friend, Betty. Is she waving at us?"

"Cooeey!... Auntie flo?"

"Hiya luv. Int the little un growing. How old is he now?"

"Just turned six ... I'm glad I caught you. Hiya Mrs Clough. Sorry about that before. He was just so excited. He didn't get your coat dirty did he?"

"Erm, no"

"Tell Aunty Flo what you did? Aw he's gone shy. He was so excited about having a Sparkler, he went running round in circles, like a dog chasing its tail, and nearly knocked Mrs Clough flying"

"Did. He. Indeed?... Alice?"

"WHAT?"

"Teenage hooligans?"

"It was YOU that made THAT assumption!"

CHRISTMAS, DONE AND DUSTED

"Oh dunt it look bare once you've taken the decorations down, Alice?"

"I don't know why you even bother at your age Flo"

"I do it for the kids!"

"I didn't put any up"

"Well you didn't need to did ya? What with being as barren as your ceiling at Christmas and spending every day of it round here"

"I wasn't here the day after Boxing day - and what do you mean 'Barren' ? It was him that had funny parts not me. If I'd met the right fella instead of that wrong 'un I'd have probably had a pair of lovely little angels"

"You were only in your late twenties when he died. I know it's getting on a bit for babies, but look at her next door but two. She was forty five when she had the twins"

"And look at 'em Flo? They're Mongolians"

"AND? They're lovely lads. Our Lesley's always knocking on for them. They're her best mates round here"

"Well that says it all. An eight year old girl and two forty year old men. Playing out together? Come on Flo. That's not normal... Mind you, neither is she"

"Oy! that's my grandchild you're talking about. She's more than normal. She's 'intellective-a-gent' or whatever they call it, and I've known them lads since they were born. They wouldn't harm a fly. So shut it!"

"You started it. Saying I was barren and it's not like you're Mary Poppins. You only had the one"

"You only need one. Look at all the lovely grandkids I got from our Joyce"

I bet she gets a fortune in family allowance "Anyway, are you putting the kettle on? or is it your new year resolution to not offer anyone a brew"

"I tell you what Alice. Whilst I'm stood on this chair, balanced on me table, trying to get the last of the tinsel from round the big light. Why don't you pass me the teapot and I'll pour you a brew!"

"Ooh! sarcky. I'll pour me own ... Are there any biccies?"

"No, I've not done me shopping, but you can have a Turkey butty. I need it finished by Easter"

7: STRANGE RELATIONS

*FRIENDS, NEIGHBOURS, RELATIVES.
EVERYONE GETS THE FLO AND ALICE
TREATMENT*

DING-DONG. AVON CALLING

*ALICE POPS ROUND FOR A BREW AND ISN'T BEST PLEASED THAT
FLO HAS 'OTHER' FRIENDS*

"Cooeey Flo? It's only me. Do you know your door is wide
open? - Oh! Hello Renee. What are you doing here?" *Yeah.
What is SHE doing here?*

"Course I know it's open. I've washed down the woodwork and
I'm just letting the hallway air out. Guess what Renee's doing
these days?"

Prostitution, by the look of her "Not got a clue! What ARE you
up to, these days, Renee? *And shift your fat backside. That's my
chair you're buckling* Budge up whilst I sit down then? You can

fill me in whilst Flo fills up that tea-pot"

"There's a cup and half left in there, Alice. Just pour yourself a cup"

"It looks stewed to me Flo. Can't you be bothered to make a fresh pot for your BEST friend *Did you hear that Renee? BEST FRIEND - ME!* I bet Renee's was fresh"

"Oh for god's sake, pass me the pot - Renee luv why don't you tell Alice about your new business thingy"

"I'm doing Avon. I'm an Avon Lady"

LADY? Don't make me choke "REALLLLLLY? Makes me glad I don't have a doorbell - Only kidding luv *I'm not!* Looking for a bit of 'pin money' are we? For all them holidays you go on? or has your Tony lost his job?" *Again!*

"A bit of both to be honest. His hours haven't been shortened but it's hard to get overtime. We've just bought a Caravan an' all. So we had a chat and I thought I'd have a go at Avon. The kids are practically grown and I've got a bit of time on my hands"

You wouldn't if you cleaned your house properly "Oh! Well good for you. Shouldn't you be out there ding-donging?" *Instead of being sat on my chair.*

"That's why I'm here. I dropped a book off with Flo the other day and I'm just picking up her order"

"How come I never got one?"

"Oh you can have one, I didn't get as far as your street when I was posting them through. I'd need your order today though"

"I can't be rushed. *Gawd. Some people will do owt to make a bit of money* Tell you what? Leave one with me for next time - What've you've ordered Flo?"

"A soap on a rope for our Bob. It's his birthday soon"

"Soap on a ROPE! How deep IS your tin bath?"

"Ha, ha bloody ha! Ignore her Renee. She was born sarcky- Are you off now luv? So a week next Wednesday it's coming? ... I'll see you then. Aren't you saying bye, Alice? Renee's going now"

I can see that. I'm not Helen Keller "Bye Renee. I'll let Flo know if I want something, seeing has you're always round here!"

RENEE LEAVES. FLO GIVES ALICE A DIRTY LOOK

"You're a proper cow, you Alice. I could see she looked uncomfortable. Don't think I didn't hear you having a dig"

"Well I can't stand her and she knows it"

"What IS wrong with you? If you wrote a book of people you can't stand, it'd have more pages than the Bible"

"Don't you remember the time she threw a bucket of water over me, Flo? You don't forget summat like that"

"She THREW a bucket of water over her step. Just as you were passing. She didn't mean it"

"She bloody did mean it! Me courts were ruined. I got them from KENDELS I'd only worn them once when me cousin Maggie got married to that waste of space Alan ... Alan, who

used to go out with Renee's big sister. She's had it in for me
since day one!"

"You'd take offence in an empty room you would. So why are
you ordering something off her if she's such an enemy"

"I was being POLITE! And who said I'm gonna order anything?"

"YOU DID!"

"No I didn't. I said I'd have a look. I'm not ordering nowt. I'm
not putting my money in that cow's purse, so she can go
swanning off on caravanette holidays. She wants to clean her
house properly instead of sitting in other people's all day long"
"You're just jealous cos she was here when you walked in, and
you think you missed something"

"Jealous of Renee Tompkins? Have you had a stroke, Flo?
What's to be jealous of? One- she's a slut and TWO -She's
welded to that Swing coat she always wears. I'm jealous of
Ginger Roger's legs, but nothing about Renee bothers me"

"So you say. But I bet if Ginger was sat here when you came in,
you'd moan she was bandy"

"Oh shut up! - Eh, do us a favour? Put this Topaz perfume on
your list for when she comes. It smells lovely and it's cheaper
than 'Evening in Paris' It's page fifty six, but I can't see the order
number without me glasses"

"I thought you said you wouldn't be ordering anything?"

"I'm not - You are. Are you making another brew? ... And
fumigate the pot. She was breathing all over it"

IF YOU HAVE A PROBLEM WITH MY CHILD. YOU HAVE A PROBLEM WITH ME!

ALICE AND JOYCE, DON'T GET ON.

"MAM? It's me Joyce. What've I told you about leaving the door open? Anyway I'm not stopping I got halfway to the bus stop and remembered I'd left me brolly - Oh hiya Alice, Is that seat warm enough for you? *You'd jump in me grave if you could* How come I didn't see you coming up the street. I only left two minutes ago"

"I come through the entries" *Not that it's any of your business.*

"Right I'm off. Mam, you don't need to see me to the door. I was born here, I know where it is"

"Well I want to! ... Joyce do you have to be so rude to Alice all the time?"

"No - Just when I see her. She's two faced, mam. I don't know why you even bother with her"

"I can handle both her faces. She's not as bad as she lets people think. You worry about your own business -Oy! give us a kiss ... I'll see you tomorrow"

Flo closes the front door and returns to the back room

"Your Joyce doesn't like me. I can tell"

"Don't feel special, Alice. She doesn't like anyone. She's what me own mam would call 'A little miss snooty drawers' She's always been a bit like that. She must get it from Bob's side, although I blame the war as well. With her being an only child, me and Bob wouldn't let her be evacuated, so to make up for it - She had her heart set on going to the country. I think she thought the Queen would take her in. That's what watching Shirley Temple films does to your mind. Our kids are being corrupted by Talking Pictures - Anyway, to make up for it, we used to let her spend a lot of time with her cousins in Cheadle Hulme. I soon put a stop to that, when she came home one Sunday and demanded - not asked mind you, DEMANDED that we start using the best china, even when we was on our own ... I got that set for me Wedding and I'm saving it for a special occasion. I don't even get it out at Christmas. Cept that one just after the war ended. So if I'm not getting it out for Jesus, I'm certainly not getting it out for a kid. Even if she is my one and only child"

"She made me laugh, Flo, when she come in shouting 'Mam it's me Joyce'... I was gonna shout back ' You're an only child, you daft sod. She knew who you was at mam' *chuckle* What? Why's your face like that?"

"Who are YOU calling a daft sod? That's my daughter, remember. She isn't daft, she's considerate. But you wouldn't know that. Not having had any kids of your own"

"Flo! You've only had the one. That doesn't make you Florence Nightengale"

"What's SHE got to do with it? Anyway, One is better than

NONE. So shurrup and make yourself useful. Stick the kettle on whilst I put this Blancmange in the Parlour, to set"

"Blancmange? On a weekday? Ooh get you! Int it usually an Eccles cake?"

"I'm having two of me grandchildren for the day. That's why our Joyce came round. She's got an appointment at the ante natal, and she's gonna take two of 'em with her and leave two of 'em with me. They don't like Eccles cake. They think the currents are dead flies. So I'm treating them to some Blancmange and a walk round the cemetery - Oh! that means I won't be able to go to the Cobblers with you. But it's only at the end of your street, and I'm sure you don't need me there to watch you inspect every bit of the shoe before you part with a penny?"

"Good money deserves good service. Only an idiot would pay for something they hadn't seen. An' what did you just say? TWO with her, and TWO to you? Whilst she goes to see the MIDWIFE? How many is she aiming for ? A baker's dozen? I know Catholics with less kids"

"She's Church of England as you very well know. You was at her christening"

"Oh yeah. I was, wasn't I? ... I remember that christening well. Well anyone would, if it was their best friend's baby's christening and they hadn't been asked to be Godmother. What was it you told me? - St Lukes had a rule that you had to have children yourself to be a Godparent" *hmmph!* Anyway. Don't worry about letting me down. You won't be the first.

How can you 'Godparent' if you've never been an actual parent? "That's what the cleaner at the Vicar's house's friend told me -Anyway, never mind that, Alice. You're making me feel 'tight' now. *DELIBERATELY!* Can't you go to the cobblers a bit earlier? She isn't bringing the kids til dinnertime"

"No I can't. He said they wouldn't be ready til after two"

"Aw. That's the time I'm taking them to the Cemetery. They love it in there. Our Lesley loves reading the headstones out loud. She's got a morbid side, if you ask me ... Oh well, there's worse things to be"

"She's only half christian though int she? Do they have proper graveyards in her dad's country? Or do they have them bonfire things instead? Where we have Ham butties, do they have Treacle toffee?"

"ONLY HALF CHRISTIAN? Where do you get rubbish like that from Alice? He's more bloody christian than you are. When did you last go to a church service that didn't involve a dead body and the merest hint of a buffet?!"

"I'm one of the most christian people I know. And christian people can admit when they get it a bit wrong"

"A BIT?"

"Yes Florence. A bit! ... Did I or did I not, say HALF christian? A half is a 'Bit"

"If I go to the butchers and say I fancy a bit of Steak. He doesn't shove half a cow on the scales, but I'm done mithering with you, Alice. If there's anything you don't like about my family, keep it to your bloody self, or me and you are gonna fall out. And that would be daft"

"I've got to go anyway.You know I didn't mean to offend. It's just the way I say things. I try to be more Common but the Upper middle class in me takes over, and it's always been in our nature to look down on people ... I'll see you the day after tomorrow. Or you can pop round to mine after the kids have gone home if you want?"

"Get an extra cup out around five-ish. I'll see you tomorrow"

JEALOUSY REARS ITS UGLY HEAD

And that head is on Alice's neck

"Alice? Name me a day you didn't take offence at something?- and don't say february the thirty ninth"

"I haven't said owt!"

"You don't have to. It's written all over your face"

"Look Flo. Let's get something straight ... I. Am. Not. One. Bit bothered that you didn't ask me round to play gin rummy with you and The Beverley Sisters"

"Ohh! Is that it?... Well firstly, you don't like playing cards"

"I could have watched!"

Tut! "Secondly, Anne and Brenda are my mates as well as you. They're lovely girls. You don't give anyone a chance. You've barely said two words to them in the five years they've lived over the road from me. And anyway, there's three Beverley sisters. If you're gonna make comparisons, get your sums right"

"Have you seen the size of Brenda? I had her down for the Twins. My sums are spot on luv"

"Don't be tight! She is a big girl though. Her thighs must chafe summat rotten. I've got one of them powder puff things you get with a tub of Talc. Our Joyce bought it me last Christmas - Pass us the tea-pot? - I can't stand the stuff"

"What? Tea?"

"You're not even listening properly. Don't be daft. I love Tea. It's talc I can't stand. . It makes me cough more than a Senior Service. Brenda's birthday's coming up. I'll re-wrap it and Bob's your Uncle. Her no chaffing, me no coughing"

"I hope I don't get second hand, used goods on MY birthday? I bought you Evening in Paris for yours"

"What did I get you for yours, last time?"

"A Blackpool Tea-Towel. Lovely views of the pier. I've got it nailed up on me kitchen wall"

"Well there you go Alice. You're not an idiot. You wouldn't have put it up if it had gravy stains on it...Brand new was that" *And it cost nowt, cos our Joyce brought it me back from her holidays.*

"How old is she gonna be then?"

"Who?"

"And you say I don't listen properly- Brenda?"

"Erm...Thirty-ish"

"And the rest! How come she's not married?"

"I DON'T KNOW Alice. I'm not her bleedin' manager"

"Oooh. Pardon me for breathin'... It's a funny to-do though. Two women of their age, and both unmarried"

"Perhaps they're Nuns in civvies"

"Would a Nun play Gin rummy?"

"What about that song 'Deck of Cards'? He's a Soldier and he's all Godly"

"Shurrup Flo"

"You shurrup Alice ... I tell you what. Next time we play cards YOU can be guest of honour"

"I don't like Cards. I have to keep chopping and changing me glasses so I can see them"

"Get some Bi-focals, like our Bob has"

"Ooh no! I'm not looking like an idiot in them ugly things"

But you don't mind sounding like one "OY! leave my Bob out of it. I think he looks lovely in his"

"I'm not saying he doesn't. They're just not my cup of tea. Speaking of which?"

"I wonder you don't drown in tea. Let me just freshen up the pot - Who's that knocking at the door? Just go and see who it is whilst I rinse out these cups"

Alice answers the front door

"Who was it?"

"Mother Theresa from across the road. Bringing back the plate from the pie you made her. How come you never told me you was giving away pies?"

"Oh for God's sake Alice! It was half a pie left over from me and Bob's tea the other night. I didn't want it to go to waste and you was out gallivanting somewhere. I'm presuming that you meant Brenda ... Anyway why didn't she come in?"

"I don't know!"

"You told her I was out dint ya?"

"NO. I just mentioned you were dead busy" *And then I shut the door in her face.*

"You need to expand your circle of friends Alice"

"What. Like her thighs have expanded?"

TUT! "What would you do if something happened to me? You'd be a right 'Billy no mates'"

"I'll cross that bridge when I come to it ... And nothing's gonna happen to you. So stop talking daft, Flo"

"You're right. It makes no sense us BOTH being daft"

"I'm not staying here to be insulted!"

"Get outside then. There's probably a queue forming as we speak"

THE POND

Alice gets to have a 'nosy' round someone else's house

"Aw Alice,I know we're meant to go shopping but I'm running late and I've just had Mrs Charlton from Scarbourgh street on me doorstep. Pleading with me to give her house the once over cos she's got visitors coming. I told her me usual day is Thursday but she was desperate, and she offered me an extra five bob , so I said yeah. I'll only be an hour at the most and we can jump on the bus from there"

"And what am I supposed to do whilst you're in there? Play two ball in the street?"

"No you daft sod. You can come in with me. She's gone

shopping for cream cakes and caviar or whatever it is them snooty types eat"

"I'm NOT cleaning"

"I don't clean. I house-keep! and I don't need an assistant I'm a bloody expert. You can just sit down and wait for me. Come on then? Let's make tracks? or we'll never get to town"

"It's you and your 'housekeeping' that's stopping us, Flo. Not me" *You're not kidding me. It's CLEANING!*

"Oh shut up moaning. You can have a nosy at her Pond whilst I'm doing me bits"

"She's got a Pond?"

"That's what she calls it. I call it a puddle. It's only the size of a sixpence. Who the bleedin' 'ell wants a pond in a terraced house back yard? She's got a Rockery 'an all. A bleedin' rockery in a back yard that's already made from brick. Which at the end of the day, is just rock, squared"

"Ooh, I think it sounds nice"

"You would! . It's a pity you've filled your backyard with them two lion statues. You've no room for a pond. And I'll tell you what. I'm sick of getting the Ewbank stuck every time I try to sweep round them bleedin' columns she's had put up either side of her front window. How bloody daft is that? They're not even bay windows, just the same sash ones you and me have got. AND she hasn't taken down them silly festoon nets she had put up for Christmas. I took our Joyce with me the other week, cos me sciatica was murdering me and I couldn't reach the top of the window frames. She loved 'em. I think it's looks like she's got Shirley Temple nailed up at the window"

"What colour are they?"

"What colour are what?"

"The nets"

"What's that got to do with anything? They're pink"

"Ooh Flo? I'm dying to see it. Sounds all 'Hollywood-ish'"

"It's not even smart enough for Hollinwood, luv. The poor buggars who live next door must get a migraine every time they pass her window. The street is ruined. And she'd better not try asking me to take them down. I don't do nets ... Polishing sweeping and mopping. That's what I do"

After a shortcut through the entries, they arrive at Mrs Charlton's

"Here we are then. You just make yourself comfy *As usual* whilst I get on. And don't touch the grapes. She counts 'em"

"Bloody ell Flo. I see what you mean. It's like something out of Them Olden days films, only smaller and more rubbishier. What are them column thingys made of? and what do they do?"

"They don't do nowt Alice. Just get in the bloody way. They're supposed to be concrete but give 'em a little push ... Go on! They don't bite. See what I mean? Have you ever seen concrete that wobbled? Plaster of Paris. That's what they're made of. More money than sense, some people"

"I'd be ashamed if I had to pay people to clean me house, and it was just a little terrace"

"Don't get me wrong. I'm not complaining, it's my living, but all me other jobs are in the big houses at the top of the lane. I can be in one of them and if I have to chat to the owner I'll send a letter cos it's quicker than walking to the other side of the house. But a two up two bleedin' down? She's in me pinny pocket half the time, when I'm 'doing' here"

"You'd think she'd move to somewhere posher with her money"

"Firstly Alice, it isn't her money. She just dropped lucky marrying her Arthur two months before his premium bonds came up. And secondly she's as common as muck under them twin sets she wears. She'd be like a fish out of water in a posh area. She prefers to be a big fish in a small pond does Bessie Charlton - And speaking of ponds. What do you think of that monstrosity?"

"She's lucky she's got a back gate on. If the corporation saw that, they'd fill it in thinking it was a pot hole ... Is it leaking? There's water coming out of the ornament on top"

"That's the fountain! I know. Hideous int it? Supposed to be a mermaid. Looks more like a fish wearing a balaclava to me. Anyway, I'm getting on with the dusting. I get nauseous if I stare at it for too long"

"It's making me want a wee, Flo"

"The toilets upstairs. You're in for a treat. It's advocaat or something ... Looks green to me"

"She's not normal is she? Can't wait to see it"

Alice goes to the loo

"Well what did you think of the bathroom?"

"Who the 'eck wants a bath the same colour as everyone's front door? Hurry up Flo, It's making me eyes hurt in here"

"I'm all done. And think yourself lucky. I have to come here once a fortnight. Let's get that bus whilst we've still got our eyesight"

JOYCE GETS A NEW FLAT

"I was knocking on earlier, Flo. But you weren't in"

"That's cos I was out"

"You don't normally go out on a Thursday morning?"

"You know what they say. A change is as good as a rest"

Hmm "Everything alright with you and Bob?"

"Well sometimes I wish he looked a bit more like Rudy Vallee - When he young. But other than that, we're fine"

"Are Joyce and the kids -

"ALICE! Why don't you just ask me where I've been? We'll be here all bloody day whilst you do your Miss Marple act!"

"I'm not bothered where you've been. Not my place to pry into other people's business - What are you looking at me like that for? I was just concerned that me best friend, who's normally ALWAYS in of a Thursday. Wasn't. So pardon me for caring!"

"Yeah, right! Our Joyce has been offered a Corporation flat and I went with her to see it"

"A 'Flat'? One of them things without an upstairs? Where is it?"

"Well you have to walk up two flights of the buggars to get to it. Which is gonna play havoc with my angina, so don't worry about her having no stairs to contend with. But once you get inside, it's lovely. Got a separate toilet and bathroom, three bedrooms and a massive kitchen. And it's in Collyhurst, so she's only a bus ride away. I'm over the moon, and so is she"

"COLLYHURST? Ew! it's dead rough round there"

"Well it doesn't stop you going through it on the number eighty, so you can visit your mate in Miles Platting, and anyway, you won't have to go there will you? *So don't be expecting an invite. Joyce and the kids can't stand you* And it didn't look rough to me. The neighbours were lovely. Our Joyce said they were being nosy sods but I told her not to be such a cow" "is she taking it then?"

"Too bloody right she is. I love her and the kids to death but it's getting cramped here"

"Is HE going with her?"

"Yes Alice he is. That's what husbands do. They move in places with their Wives. 'Cept yours of course who moved in with someone else's"

"Excuse ME! I'm a widow NOT a deserted wife!"

"You WAS a deserted wife. Now you're the widow of a man who deserted you. If truth be told. You don't even know if he's really dead"

"I've got a pension and an urn of ashes that say different, and stop being so cruel Flo"

"Yeah well you stop being so nasty about my son-in-law"

"Did I say ONE bad thing about him?"

"No, but that's cos I seen it coming and stopped you. I wasn't born yesterday Alice. He's coloured and you've got some kind of problem with that"

"I HAVE NOT! I love Nat King Cole and the Platters. And I always watch the Black and White Minstrel show"

God give me strength! "Anyway, like I saying, it's a lovely flat. The kitchen has got a stainless steel sink and an 'immersion'"

"What's that when it's at home?"

"A big boiler in the cupboard. So you can have hot water

whenever you like"

"Ooh Flo. They don't know they're born nowadays. Getting all that luxury for free"

"It's not free. She has to pay rent"

"Yeah, but me or you couldn't just say to the immersion people 'Chuck us one of them immersions in and bung it on me rent. All this Corporation business is making people lazy. They expect everything handed to 'em on a plate"

"If someone gave you the Crown jewels you'd moan about the extra work polishing them"

"I'm not moaning Flo. I'm just saying"

"Why don't you make yourself useful whilst you're stood standing and shove that kettle on. I'm nipping to the loo"

"You should have had one on your Joyce's inside lavvy and saved yourself the journey outside"

Jealous cow "I hope I'm not as bitter as you, when I reach your age Alice"

"You cheeky sod! you're barely minutes younger than me. You can brew that tea yourself now. Should I get the biscuit tin out?"

I'D RATHER BE AN OLD MAN'S DARLING...

Alice gets personal ... But what's new!

"Cooeey... Flo, are you in?"

"Of course I bloody am"

"Where are you?"

"I'm in the library! Where the eck do you think I am? It's not a stately home. I'm here in the back room"

"I thought you might have been in the parlour. I didn't want to walk past and have to go back again"

"It's a lobby, not Moston lane. You wouldn't have to walk that bloody far"

"Ooh! someone got out of bed on the wrong side. What's up Flo? Have you and Bob had a row"

"Me and Bob don't have rows. My Bob is the gentlest most kindest Man I have ever known. So shove that in your pipe and smoke it. Having said that, he does have some old fashioned views. Me knees have been giving me gip so I mentioned getting a Twin-tub on 'Tick' but he won't have it"

"What have your knees got to do with a twin-tub?"

"The mangle's wobbly and I have to push up against it - Anyway, never mind that Alice. Help me stick these green shield stamps in the books"

"Can you get a Twin tub with green shield stamps?"

"I don't think so, BUT you CAN get a windproof metal pipe lighter. And what sort of fella would refuse his beloved a Twin tub, when she's bought him a pressie for his upcoming birthday? I'm gonna have it engraved at the cobblers too"

"He'll still say no"

"I've not finished. With the money I've saved by using the stamps - But he won't know that. I'm gonna buy one of those nelly gellys"

"With your chilblains? And Bob IS getting on a bit. You don't want him having a stroke ... Or do you?"

"Have you got summat wrong with your eye Alice?"

"I'm winking you daft bat! A stroke? ... Do you get it?"

Tut "You go on like he's got one foot in the grave"

"Well he is thirty years older than you Flo"

"AND?"

"Nowt. I'm just saying ... Aw I remember his first wife. Lovely woman. Died of consumption just before you moved up here. Eh? Just think, if she hadn't died you might have still been a spinster. It's a true saying. Every cloud has a silver lining"

"You know what another true saying is? Some people thrive on other people's misery" *Especially you.*

"You did in a way. Married and straight into a furnished house. Husband with a guaranteed pension. And not too long to wait for it-"

"I'd shut my gob if I was you. I didn't marry my Bob for his assets. I married him cos I loved him, and he loved me. Here's another saying for you. I'd rather be an old man's darling than a young man's slave. And another thing. He was mature enough to know what marriage is about. He didn't up and leave me at the first flash of some floozy in silk stockings ... Like some people's husband did!"

"You always have to get personal Flo"

"Are you taking the Mick? You've just sat there waffling on about my husband's private affairs and you tell me I'M getting personal"

"Aw lets not have a daft argument. I'm glad she died"

"Come again? Are you saying you're glad that Bob's first wife died? You're not normal!"

"I don't mean it like that Flo. I mean, you might have gone back to Sheffield if you hadn't met Bob. Then I wouldn't have met you and we wouldn't be best mates"

"You daft apeth. You don't half have a 'funny' way of showing you like someone"

"It's just the way I am. You should be used to me by now. Can I have a brew? Licking these stamps has took the lining off me tongue"

"Yeah. Do you fancy a walk down the lane after? I've seen a lovely nightie in the shop next to the Post Office. I'm having that Twin tub if it's the last thing I do"

ALICE GETS NEW NEIGHBOURS

The poor sods!

"Gawd they drive off before you've even got your foot on the pavement. I'M A PENSIONER YOU KNOW"

"Don't waste your breath Flo. It's never been the same since they got rid of the conductors. Anyway, do you fancy popping to mine for a brew? Seeing as it's nearer"

"This Bus stop has been here since the year dot. It's ALWAYS been nearer Alice. Have you won 'Spot the ball' or something? You're not a woman who likes to waste tea. Especially when it's going free somewhere else"

"You go on like I'm a proper Scrooge. I'd give a dog me last biscuit. I bet you don't half call me behind me back"

"How long have you known me? There's nowt I would say behind your back that I wouldn't say to your face. That's why we always got so much to talk about"

"Cheeky madam"

"Just get your key in that door and put that kettle on before I die of thirst. Ooh whats going on over the road?"

"The new neighbours are moving in"

"Well that solves the riddle of your sudden hospitality!"

117

"Shurrup! ... I think we'll have our brew in the front parlour"

"Too bloody right Alice. Don't you just love nets? You can see out but they can't see in. Well in the day anyway"

"Who's being nosy now Flo?"

"Hurry up with that cuppa ... Should I shift the chairs nearer the window?"

"Only if you can manage. You being a Pensioner an' all"

Tut! "You're a cheeky mare"

A brew is made, and Flo and Alice settle down to watch the entertainment

. "She looks alright, dunt she Flo? A bit thin, and no way is that her natural hair colour. I wonder which one is her husband?"

"I'm not sure Alice. But I'd guess it's the one who's NOT wearing an overall saying 'Jackson and Son Removals ... I don't like that lamp"

"I know what you mean. I'd get an headache every time I switched it on. Who the 'eck chooses an Orange and Purple lampshade?"

"Our Joyce is a bit like that. Says it 'fashion' Well they can fashion off! I get queasy when I'm in her Living room for more than five minutes. But don't you dare tell her I said that?"

"As if I would?"

Hmmph! "Like you didn't tell her, I'd told you about me catching her kissing a picture of Victor Mature when she was a teenager?"

"I didn't mention your name"

"There was only me and her in the house at the time. She didn't need to be bloody Sherlock Hemlock to guess who'd told you. She didn't speak to me for a week ... That Settee's nice"

"Get your eyes tested Flo. It's an eyesore. I've had mine since the thirties...Dead comfy. That one won't last five minutes"

"You could be right. I've had mine for ages too. They don't make stuff to last nowadays. Our Joyce has been through about three sideboards since she left home...Nice tea, this"

"Brooke Bond. Proper tea, none of that cheap rubbish for me ... I tell you what? We'll have another cup. Give it half an hour or so, then pop over with a pot for the new neighbours. If she hasn't sorted out the living room by then, we'll know we're dealing with lazy sods, and if I get rats up my entry cos they can't keep their house clean, there'll be murder"

STRANGE RELATIONS

Alice's of course

"Flo. Thank God you're in"

"Where else would I be at this time? Our Bob's due in any minute. I'm just making his 'tea' what's up with you?"

"Any tea in that pot?"

"Is the Queen posh? Help yourself. I'm just putting these sausages on. Eeyar have a bit?"

"Ooh I've not had a bit of raw sausage for years. But I'd better not. It'll play havoc with me insides. I wouldn't say no to a custard cream though. I need the sugar, the shock I've just had!"

"The Grandkids love raw sausage, and the rind off the bacon. The biscuits are in the tin. Help yourself, but leave the ginger nuts for Bob. He doesn't like anything else ... So go on then? What could have happened to shock a woman of the world like you?"

"There I am sat in me house minding me own business"-

"That makes a change!"

"Sarcky cow. Let me finish. Like I said. I'm sat down, just me and the budgie, and I thought I'd have a sort through me knitting patterns"

"Well that's shocking in itself. I didn't even know you could

knit"

"I do have other friends you know"

"And by the time you get to the point, half of them will be dead!"

"Well stop interrupting then. So there's a knock on the door - *Who could that be?* I said to Joey"

"And what was Joey's reply? A cheeky buggar?"

"Shurrup Flo. You know what I mean. I goes to the door and there's this lad about six foot tall, just stood there smiling - Put your face straight. I'm not talking Clark Gable. *Hiya Aunty Alice'* he say's. *It's me, Charlies son*"

"Who's Charlie, when he's at home?"

"Me brother"

"I didn't know you had a brother?"

"Well first of all you never asked. And secondly. We don't talk about Charlie ... Black sheep and all that"

"Why? What did he do?"

"Married a Catholic"

"Married a Catholic? That's it?"

"We're tenth generation Methodist in our family"

"And very 'Christian' with it, I see"

"Each to their own Flo. It was the talk of the town when he brought Bridie O'hara home for 'tea' Me Mam went downhill after that. I blame him for her early death"

"She got killed when they bombed Picadilly gardens. How's that his fault?"

"I'm not saying he flew the plane. But if it hadn't been for the worry about him, she might have been concentrating a bit better. But anyway. There he was, Charlie's son. Stood on me doorstep, bold as brass"

"Could you see the 'Catholic' in him"

"Are you being 'funny'?"

"To be honest Alice. I don't know what the fuss is about. Anyway I hope you didn't leave him stood on the pavement"

"Well I wasn't letting him in. I'd got no stockings on. And he'd could have been anyone! Mind you, he's got the same shifty eyes and two faced look about him that our Charlie had"

"Are you and Charlie twins?"

Tut "I said I had the chiropodist in, so I couldn't let him in. I'm gonna meet him by Simpson Memorial next week, and if he thinks there was anything in Mam's will for him, he's got another think coming. She left everything to me. *I don't want nowt of mine, falling into papal hands.* she said on her deathbed"

"I know! Just think what diabolical dealings the Pope could have got up to with your Mam's sideboard"

"I think I'll go home and come back when you're less sarcky"

"You may have a long wait. Be careful out there. There's a few

Nuns walking about"

"Don't be surprised if I don't come back"

I bet you do!

FRIENDSHIP AT ITS FINEST

Move along please. No sarcasm here!

"Aw, have you got to go Beryl? There's a cup and half left in the pot. We can have half a cup each"

"Ooh I'm tempted but little Wilf's going to the match tomorrow with his dad, and I've got twenty rows to do before I finish his balaclava. I've made one for his dad too. They're like two peas in a pod are big Wilf and little Wilf. Anyway I'm off. See you tomorrow Flo. Bye Alice"

After a chorus of 'bye-bye luv' Flo and Alice remain at the table. They purse their lips, and look skywards.

Silence except for the clicking of heel in the hallway. Followed by the sound of the front door closing

"Did you hear THAT Alice?"

"I had to hold meself back Flo"

"Two peas in a bloody pod? She forgets we went to them G.I dances with her, whilst her Wilf was away fighting the war. That kid should be lassoing 'Trigger' not watching football"

"I just concentrated on me slice of cake. I didn't know where to put me face. Has she no shame? If she was a Catholic, she'd be choking on that wafer, of a Sunday"

"He's just as bad. Red headed, with a kid who looks like Mario Lanza. Well you know what they say? There's none so blind, as them that don't want to see"

"It'd break his heart if he ever found out. He idolises that kid. And they've never had another, have they?... Has HE had one at all?"

"ALICE! Don't be wicked"

"You're still laughing though"

"Well he'll never hear it from my lips. I don't carry gossip. That's how I was raised ... Pass us that pot. I can't have good tea going to waste"

"Ooh I love a strong cuppa" *Ew. It's stewed*

"He has got bad eyesight though"

"Who has?"

"Big Wilf you daft apeth! My Bob says he's rubbish at Bowls. I wonder he's not lost his hearing as well. All that bombing when he was abroad. And no way did his tin helmet cover them massive lumps he calls ears ... Have you seen little Wilf's ears?"

"Petite"

"Exactly! ... Pass us that last piece of cake. Unless you want it?"

"I've had loads thanks. You have it" *Next time, try putting more margarine in it. I've eaten moister sawdust.*

"That'll keep me going til tea ... Mind you, I knew she was on to a winner, when little Wilf was born three months 'premature' weighing nine pound, four ounces, and nowt was said"

"Don't you think we should have a word with her? in case the 'worst' should happen. He's growing up is little Wilf, and you've got to admit, he looks very 'Latin' Not everyone is as discreet as you and me, and half of Manchester was in the Alhambra that night"

"How do you know it was THAT night?"

"Oh come on Flo. That wasn't a parachute round her ankles, when we found 'em down the entry, and they were NOT Jitterbugging"

"I wonder the fifth column didn't try to recruit you for your marvelous memory. *'cept when you have a borrow* I'm saying nowt. It's not for me to judge. And she's me best pal ... After you"

FLO HAS VISITORS

"Have I got my days wrong, Flo?"

"What day do you think it is, Alice?"

"Wednesday"

"Well you're not wrong. Why?"

"Why what?"

Tut "Why are you asking about what day it is?"

"Because you've got your good tablecloth on. For a minute I thought it was Sunday"

"I told you ages ago. Me brothers Ted and Tommy are coming today"

"I mustn't have been listening"

"You never do!"

"Aw ... You'll want your privacy then?"

"That'd be nice" *But I'm not holding me breath.*

"Have I got time for a quick brew, before they come?"

"They're due in half an hour"

"Plenty of time. And I might as well stay to say hello. You don't want them thinking your best mate is rude"

Sigh "just don't mess up the table. And don't touch them chocolate digestives. You can have a custard cream if you're desperate"

"How long has it been?"

"How long's WHAT been?"

"Since your brother's were here? It seems like years"

"Twelve months ago! They come every Christmas. As well you know!"

"I forget more than I remember nowadays.What are they coming for?"

"EASTER! -What the bleedin ell do you think they're coming for, in the middle of soddin' December? -Christmas, you daft sod!. They're coming to see us for Christmas"

"No need to bite me head off! You forget stuff as well"

"Not bleedin' obvious stuff I don't. Has the Doctor put you on new tablets or summat, I've not had a sensible word out of you since you walked through the door. Mind you, when do I ever?"

"The tablecloth threw me. I came in thinking it was Wednesday and saw your second poshest tablecloth. And got confused"

"Well put an extra sugar in your brew and get unconfused... You're shorter than me. Do my skirtings look clean? -Have you eaten one of the chocolate biscuits? And don't lie, cos I counted them"

"I did, but it was before you said don't. And your skirtings look fine to me *for once! Eh?* They never got married, your brothers, did they? - I don't mean to each other! I'm not implying anything" *But there's summat 'funny' going on.*

"I'm glad you cleared that up, Alice *Stupid woman!* NO they never got married. Mainly cos of the War"

"You've mentioned this before, but never said anything further. Is it a delicate subject? Did they get their 'bits' bombed?"

"NO!"

"Did they have sweethearts waiting for them. But they didn't 'wait' if you know what I mean?"

"Not everyone's your Eddie! You're not gonna shut up, are you? I'll tell you why, but you breathe one word and me and you are done"

"I wouldn't dream! You're my best friend. I'll go to me grave with what you tell me now" *I bet they're both a pair of Liberaces.*

"Well our Ted had a bad time of it. Took a direct hit on the advance to wherever it was they were advancing to. He ended up, having to have a glass eye, and he's had nightmares ever since"

"Aw. I thought going abroad, had gone to his head, cos he always wears sunglasses. Like he's a film star. And all it is, is a glass eye? Can I just ask, is he not scared of it falling out? I wonder what you can see through the hole when he takes it out? I bet you can see through to the back of his head. Or is it glued in? I'd be scared of it falling out and I don't know how I'd cope only seeing half of everything. I don't blame him having nightmares"

"And THIS is why I didn't tell you! - It's not the soddin glass eye that bothers him. It's the things that happened and caused the glass eye, that give him nightmares. have you got that?"

"Loud and clear. No need to be so nowty"

"Well you do my head in, with your daft questions ... I'm just glad they've got each other. Now that I've moved away, and Mam and Dad are gone. Him and our Tommy have always been close. Tommy looks after him. That's why HE never got married"

"So they're not queers then?"

"ALICE! No they are bloody not. And if they WERE, it wouldn't be anyone's bloody business!Have you been thinking that, all these years?"

"NO!" *Yes.*

"Good! Anyway they'll be here soon. I'm warning you!"

"My lips are sealed, Flo. I'm a bit hurt though. All these years and you never thought to tell me. We've been through all sorts together. I was maid of honour at your wedding. I danced with your Ted. If I'd known I'd have walzted instead of charleston'd. No wonder he sat the rest of the night out"

"He didn't have it then, you daft sod. He didn't lose his eye til 'forty three"

"I still feel a bit tight though...I've misjudged him"

"I bet you've said that more than once!"

"I'd rather think less of a person and be pleasantly surprised. Then be little miss 'ray of bloody sunshine' like some. *You!* And be constantly disappointed"

"You kind of 'make sense' *For once* Anyway, at me wedding, he thought you had designs on him. That's why he didn't want to dance"

"OH DID HE? Well I like my men with TWO eyes, thank you very much"

"Are you calling MY brother?"

"He was calling me!"

Give me strength. "Have you not got a home to go to? I'm too busy for this nonsense"

"I'm going! ... Aw, do you know what?"

"WHAT?"

"I've not got any butter. I used the last of it last night on me crumpets, and the lump I got cos one of 'em fell off the toasting fork and I banged me head on the fireplace, getting it out. Can you see a lump?"

"No" *Go away!*

"That butter worked a treat. Butter's what I come out for in the first place. And it's half day closing. I've missed the shops"

"I'll lend you some"

"I thought you always say its 'BORROW'?... Why's your face like that?"

"Because you're getting on ME NERVES! - There's the bloody door now. It'll be the boys. One word, Alice - ONE. SODDIN. WORD!"

After half a day's travel from distant Sheffield. Tommy and Ted arrive at their big sister's home

"Aw Ted ...Tommy. Let me have a proper look at you both. I swear you've grown since last I saw you both. I know I've said it before but you both get more like our dad every time I see ya. Come here and give us a hug"

"You're looking well yourself, our Florrie"

"Aw Tommy. No one else calls me that anymore. Mainly cos I hate it - But you two are allowed. Get them coats off or you won't feel the benefit. Get a warm by the fire. You can sit in our Bob's chair. You too, our Ted. You sit in mine ... I'll stick the kettle on. I've got tongue butties and tomato soup. Tinned, but it'll still warm your cockles. You remember Alice, don't ya?She's not stopping. Are YOU Alice?"

"No. I've got tons to do. But when your FLORRIE said you were coming, she insisted I stop for a bit and say hello. Didn't you ... Florrie?"

Crafty sod! "Yeah"

"So how are you Tommy? Has your head grown? or is your hair going?"

"A bit of both Alice. I'm surprised you can see. Didn't you tell us last time you wrote, that she'd gone blind, our Florrie?"

"Gawd, my handwriting's terrible. I said 'Blonde' She'd gone blonde"

"You tell people I dye my hair?... In LETTERS?"

"Well you're like FAMILY! I say other stuff too. like you've had one of your knee afflications, or how you show me up. I told you didn't I, our Tommy.? About Alice fainting on Halloween, when I told her about the 'murder'?"

"You did, our Florrie. I nearly choked, on me pipe"

"FLO? Is that all your letters consist of? My doings?"

"You wish! Anyway aren't you going?" *You'd better be going sharpish. And I know, that YOU KNOW what I'm saying, in me head.*

"I will do in a minute. Just let me say a proper hello to your Ted. *You're fretting now, aren't you?* Hiya Ted. Can you see me ok, luv? Eeyar, let me get a bit nearer. Can you see me now?Which is your 'normal' side?"

Oh my God! "Ted luv. Alice found out about your eye, and she's been dead worried about you. So I put her mind at rest, by telling her, it doesn't bother you. But then, she felt bad for all the times she didn't put anything in the big dog money box outside the shops. So she's told me to give you the box of black magic I've got her for Christmas. Haven't you Alice?"

What an absolute cow! "Yeah, of course. What do I want with a box of black magic when I've already got a giant box of Thorntons. *And TWO eyes!* Ooh I do think you're brave though,

Ted. Can I ask you something? "

"I thought you was getting off, Alice?" *Get out. Now!*

"Leave her be, Florrie. She's harmless"

"She'll be headless in a minute!"

"Go on Alice, what did you want to ask?"

"Does it hurt? Ted"

"Not really. I sometimes get a bit sore when it's gonna rain"

"My knees do the exact same thing. They get creaky when it's damp. Don't they Flo?"

"You're a walking miracle, Alice. Any more daft questions before you get off?"

"Ted doesn't think I'm daft. Ted knows I'm genuinely interested. How do you keep it clean Ted? Is there summat like Steradent, but for eyes?"

"A bit of salt water's all I use"

"Well that's handy. You can go anywhere. Everybody's got salt!"

"He can go anywhere, anyway you daft apeth. It's only a glass eye. It's not like he's in a polio machine, is it?"

"Well Flo, if you don't know, all you can do is ask ... And I did. So now I do! Anyway it's time I was making tracks. It's been lovely to see you both. You can see me properly, can't you Ted?"

"OF COURSE HE BLOODY CAN!"

"I wasn't asking YOU, Flo. I was asking your Ted"

"I can see fine Alice. Shut one of yours and you'll see exactly what I see"

"Oh yeah ... Eh! Don't wink. You'll go blind for a bit"

"I'll see you to the door, Alice" *Get your bloody skates on.*

"No need, Flo. I know where it is. Look on the bright side, though. Your Ted's thrice as lucky as Helen Keller"

"THRICE?"

"Yeah, 'thrice' Flo. It means three. The library book I'm reading, is set in Victorian times. They said it a lot in them days. I'm just pointing out to your Ted, that even though he's afflicted, he's got one more eye, and two better ears than Helen Keller. And she had a full life. I've read the book. Ay Ted? It's a pity you've not been to America. You could sing 'I left my eye in San Francisco' *Chuckle* Do you get it? Do YOU get it, Flo?"

WHAT have I done to deserve this? "You're as funny as corn clippings, Alice. Now shift yourself. I want to give the boys a bit of dinner before they have to get back off for the coach. They're only here for the day"

"I'm going! Eh lads? If your Christmas card has Candles and Baubles on it. It means she doesn't like you"

"ALICE!"

"I'm gone!"

Alice finally leaves

"Bloody 'ell, lads. Sorry about that. I'm sure she should be on tablets"

"COOOEEEY! Only me! You forgot to give me the butter, Flo"

"HERE!"

"A full packet? Are you sure? I only need enough for two slices of bread"

"YES! SEE YA?"

"Every cloud and all that. See you tomorrow"

Not if I bloody see you first!

FLO'S REVENGE

NO ONE MESSES WITH HER BROTHERS

"Hiya Flo. I wondered who it was when me door knocked"

"Most people do. Are you letting me in then?"

"Course I am. What's up? Did you wet the bed?"

"That joke's as old as you. Nope! I've come to 'have a word'"

"I was coming to yours anyway. I just thought I'd wait for the sun to rise! Shove the kettle on whilst I make meself decent"

"I don't want a brew, Alice"

"YOU DON'T WANT A BREW? IT'S THE CRACK OF DAWN! Has summat happened? Is it your Bob?"

"It's half eight! And NO it's not Bob...It's YOU!"

"WHAT'VE I DONE?"

"You showed me up"

"WHEN?"

"Where to bloody begin. But the particular showing up I'm referring to, was yesterday"

"YESTERDAY?"

"Gawd, can your voice go any higher? You sound like Maria Callas. Stop acting all innocent. You KNOW what I'm talking about"

"You mean when your brothers were here?"

"Spot on Sherlock! I've never been so embarrassed in my life. And I was with you on VE day, so that's saying summat!"

"Bringing THAT old chestnut up, are we?...Have I touched gin since?"

"I specifically told you NOT to mention me brother's eye"

"Which one?"

"The soddin' one he hasn't got"

"No, I meant which brother"

"Don't play clever with me, Alice!"

"I'm getting the Police"

"YA' WHAT?"

"Whose got the high voice now? Yeah, I'm calling the bobbies, cos it's obvious someone's nicked your sense of humour. What's wrong with ya? I was only having a laugh. Your Ted didn't mind. He told me to ask"

"Just cos he was polite doesn't mean he wasn't mortified. I swear there was a tear in his eye, after you'd gone"

"Can a glass eye 'water'?"

"God you're hard faced. Well let me tell you summat! I can get friends anywhere. But I'm not gonna get anymore brothers"

"Well not unless your mam is a walking miracle. And actually alive"

"ALICE! Is nothing sacred to you. Now you're calling me mam"

"I'm not calling your mam. I'm just not taking it as seriously as you. I'm SORRY FLO. It was just a bit of banter. I didn't take offence at you telling them I dyed me hair"

"YOU thinking you're Lana Turner is not the same as my brother having his eye bombed out"

"I said I'm sorry. It won't happen again ... Promise"

"Oh, I know it won't. Cos you're banned"

"What do you mean, banned?"

"You can't come to me house anymore. Our Bob said. And he's sent you to Coventry as well. So don't try saying hiya when you see him"

"Your Bob said that?"

"Are you deaf?"

"Oh! ... But Bob wasn't even there when I was"

"I know. But how do you think he felt, when he walked in to see my brother sobbing all over the arm of his chair? First thing he said, was *Has Alice been round*?"

"I feel awful now"

"You look awful an' all. Go and put your teeth in. I'll put the kettle on. I might as well have that brew, cos it's not like you can come round to mine for one. I'm not one for holding grudges as well you know. But our Bob? Ooh, that's another matter"

"Can't you have a word? Your Bob's known me longer than he's known you. He knows what I'm like"

"That's why he's banned ya! He knows you won't change"

"Well what're we gonna do about the things we do?"

"Such as?"

"Post office day?"

"I'll meet you outside the Post office"

"What about going shopping?"

"Bus stop"

"What if something happens and I need to tell you?"

"Pop a note through"

"It's daft this! Julie Barker asked your Bob, if she could watch, when he died. And he still speaks to her"

"Julie Barker is FOUR! What've I told you? Time and time again. That gob of yours, is gonna get you in serious trouble one of these days. Haven't I always said that? I'll eat the Sunday Post, if you can swear I've never said that. Well, thanks to your rudeness about my Ted's lack of an eye. That day has come. He's not been this fuming, since 'City' signed that German fella. And you're lucky, he's a gentleman. Or he'd be round here with me. Giving you a piece of his mind"

"He'd get a piece of mine back. I don't care how old he is!...Well if that's how you want it"

"It is"

"So it's like that, is it? Well I'm not one to go where I'm not wanted"

"Since WHEN?"

TUT!" I've said I'm sorry. But it's obviously not good enough... You'd better go, if you've got to go. And don't worry, Flo. That 'thing' that you did, with the 'thing' when we went to 'Thingy' that time. It's safe with me. My lips ARE sealed. If anyone ever finds THAT out, it won't have come from me.I'm just saying .. .I wouldn't want Bob not forgiving me for summat that wasn't my fault"

"You can't not forgive someone, if you're already not forgiving them for something else. So don't even try 'that' with me. Anyway,What are me and you arguing for? I haven't fallen out with you. Even though it's MY brother you took the mick out of. It might NOT be hopeless though. I know my Bob. There's ONE thing you could do, to get him to forgive you"

"I'm not paying for him to go to Football"

"You've got more cheek than the butcher's. I'm throwing you a lifeline here"

"I can't help it. Go on, what could I do to put things right with Bob?"

"Give him your Twin-Tub"

"GIVE HIM MY ! Are you winding me up? ... You are though, aren't ya?"

"Your face is a picture. Bob dint say owt. Our Ted and Tommy had to get off, before he got back. But one of these days, Alice, you'll go too far...Did you enjoy that dose of medicine?"

"FLORENCE HOLDEN! You proper had me going. I even got a bit sad, cos we 'get on'... I don't get on with a lot of people"

"Don't I bloody know it. C'mon. Get dressed and come round to mine. I don't like your cups. They make the tea look watery. Oh! And one more thing"

"Those cups are bone china. What's the 'one more thing'?"

"If you ever mention that 'thing' when we went to 'thingy' again. You're DEAD!"

WHO INVITED THE 'KID' FOR SUNDAY DINNER?

"Oh! hiya Alice. You'd better come in"

"I've come for me Sunday dinner. You invited me, remember?"

Yeah, but I didn't say come for breakfast as well "Course I remember. Get your coat off and wait in the back room a minute. I'm just going in the parlour to check the Trifle. I'd invite you in, but our Bob's in there, with his leg"

"I'd be worried if he was in there without it"

"You know what I mean! We've had to bring the spare bed downstairs. He can't make it up them anymore. Anyway our Lesley's in the back. She'll keep you company whilst I get sorted"

"Great!"

Alice enters the back room. A child sits at the kitchen table.

"Nana? can I - Oh! - It's you...Hiya Aunty Alice" *Don't touch me. DON'T touch me!*

"Hiya. Are you here AGAIN? Give us a kiss then?"

"I'm not allowed. *I am. But I'm not kissing YOU.* I've got a cold sore and mam say's I can't kiss strangers" *And YOU missus, are the definition of strange.*

"I'm not a stranger. I knew your mam before you did. But never mind. I wouldn't have thought you could get cold sores? Being half tropical"

Weirdo!

"What are you up to anyway? Hadn't you better clear all that rubbish off the table so your Nana can set the table for dinner?"

"It's not rubbish. It's me Bunty dolls. I'm cutting them out. And it's not time for dinner yet"

"It say's One o'clock on my watch. That's always been 'set the table for Sunday dinner' time in this house. I knew your Nana before you an' all. A woman of routine is Flo"

"Did you forget to put your clocks back?" *You stupid woman.*

Flo enters the room

"Bloody ell! I DID. Eh Flo. I forgot to put me clocks back. And there's me queuing outside the Paper shop at Five this morning, thinking it was six. I went back home fuming. I thought they'd overslept. Very unprofessional. When I went back in at what I thought was ten. I cancelled me papers. Told them I was going with the other shop. The one on Kenyon Lane. No wonder she gave me a strange look. I'll go back in tomorrow and say me medication made me funny"

"Why don't you just tell them the truth. You daft sod. I thought you'd wet the bed, turning up so early. Never mind you're here now"

After taking a tray in to Bob. Flo, Alice and Grandchild sit down to Sunday dinner.

"That was a nice bit of roast beef, Flo. Some might say it was overdone, but I like my meat cooked"

"That's what I like about you Alice. No one can make a compliment sound like an insult the way you do. WHO would say it was overcooked?"

"I didn't mean it like that. You're over sensitive! I meant, some would have it still mooing on the plate. Rare? I don't call that rare. I call it 'raw'"

"Well I hope you've saved room for some trifle. Our Lesley made it all by herself. Opened the box herself and everything. The only thing I did, was boil the kettle for the jelly, and mixed the blancmange when it was hot. But everything else, she did. Dunt it look lovely? She's even done the hundreds and thousands to spell me name"

"Your name isn't 'Nana'"

"it is to her!..Pass us your bowl"

"Do y'know what? I think I overdid it on them spuds. I couldn't eat another thing. *I'm not eating anything, them crayon stained hands have touched.* I'll have a bit of that cake though, with a cup of tea. Why are you looking at me like that? Cake's not as filling as trifle"

"Suit yourself. Is that small enough?"

"Just a tad more...Perfect"

"Our Lesley made that an' all. Go on, eat up!"

8: OUT AND ABOUT

FLO AND ALICE VENTURE INTO THE BIG WIDE WORLD...WELL, THE MANCHESTER BIT OF IT

A TRIP TO THE LIBRARY

"Alice? You took your books back yesterday. Why didn't you get some more then? We've been in here for an hour. I'm getting fed up"

"I didn't have time to choose yesterday. If you don't want to stay with me, you can go"

"Right I will! I'll see you later. I need to go to the Butchers"

"Aw don't go, Flo. I'm nearly done"

Tut! "Don't you get embarrassed about all them bodice rippers you borrow, Alice?"

"They're historical novels Flo. I like history"

"That's cos you've lived through most of it. Look at this one? *THE FLAMING DESIRE OF LADY ANN* What's historical about that?"

"It's about Georgian times. She's a lady in waiting at Buckingham Palace"

"To who? "

"What do you mean?"

"Which King or Queen is she a lady in waiting to?"

"The one who was in at that time!"

"Well, I can see you've learned LOADS of historical stuff. Mind you, looking at the front cover, so have I. Who knew they had Jane Russell brassieres in them days. Anyway, hurry up. I haven't got all day - And don't be getting dead heavy ones, it's a bit uphill on the way back"

"It's alright for you. You've got Bob to keep you company. I need me books"

"You've got a telly!"

"It's rubbish though, especially on a Saturday"

"Is it eck! Saturday's the best day for telly. You've got the wrestling, and Morecambe and Wise in the evening. It's a bit rubbish on Sundays but I listen to 'Sing Something Simple' instead. I can't stand that Jess Yates and all the godly stuff. I get enough of god when I go to church"

"You don't go to church"

"Yeah I know. Have you finished choosing your books yet? I need to catch the Butchers before they shut"

"I've picked five, and I can have six. I'm just choosing whether to have this one or that one"

"They both look the same to me"

"Well this one's set in Portugal. This girl called Laralou goes to work for a widower called Rahool or summat like that. She hates him at first but they fall in love after he stops her falling off a cliff. And this one is about a girl called Sasha, who's blind til she meets brilliant and handsome surgeon Brett"

"Go for the second one"

"Why?"

"His name's daft, but not as daft as Rahool. I swear they make these names up. It's not even spelt right r.a.u.l? what kind of name is that? I bet it's 'Paul' and they've made a mistake"

"You might be right Flo. Well I've chosen. I'm having this one *UNBLINDED BY LOVE*"

"I'll stick to me wrestling. Come on, If I don't get some Prem me life won't be worth living. Our Lesley's staying for the weekend. She's going through a phase. won't eat nowt but Prem and the odd iced bun. She's at home with her grandad now. Helping him prepare for checking his pools. He has a routine. About an hour before the results come through on Grandstand, he starts shifting stuff off the table. Me vase ends up in all kinds of places. Then, he has to make sure there's not a single crease in the bit of table cloth where he's going to sit. He'll bloody check it every five minutes whilst he's waiting, just in case it re-creases itself. Even the budgie suffers. The poor mite gets dead confused having the cover thrown over his cage at four o'clock in the afternoon. Bob gets on me nerves with his faffing about sometimes. Then they'll both settle down at the table, with their coupons, waiting for the score draws"

"Does your Lesley do the pools?"

"No you daft apeth. She colours in the boxes, whilst she waits for her granddad to start swearing cos he's lost again. She gets the giggles when he swears. Her favourite one is 'buggar'"

I'm not surprised. She's one herself "Oh! It dunt take much to amuse your grandkids does it?"

"What do you mean by that?"

"NOWT! *Nana Hitler!* Aren't you going in the butchers?"

"Bloody 'ell! I nearly walked right past. Are you staying for some tea?"

Is it worth being stuck in a room with that kid? "Go on then. If you've got enough"

"Well, I will have if I get another two ounce of Prem. And keep your gob shut whilst the results are on. I'm not having Bob tutting his way through the rest of me weekend"

IN'T IT HOT?

"Alice. I am not going into town with you dressed like that!"

"What's wrong with me?"

"You could fry an egg on the pavement, and you're wearing a Gaberdine. You look daft"

"So! It might be sunny now, but it COULD rain. You know what the weather's like round here Flo"

"Well take a brolly then!"

"Oh! and someone wearing a summer frock and carrying a brolly doesn't look two butties short of a picnic, to you?"

"No, they don't"

"I'll take it off if it gets too warm"

"It's eighty eight degrees already and it isn't even dinner time! I know what's going to happen. You'll get too warm and then moan your way round the shops, cos your coat is too heavy to carry"

"When have I ever done that?"

"Last summer, the summer before that. The summer before. Should I carry on?"

"Oh you don't half exaggerate Florence. So are you coming to town with me or not?"

"Yes I'm coming, but I meant what I said. And don't try being clever, by sneaking it on to my shopping trolley. I'm carrying spuds in that. Coats are NOT allowed"

"I don't understand you Flo. My coat's got the same exact tartan lining as the cover of your shopping trolley, yet for some reason it offends you"

"YOU offend me, not the bloody coat. You think my shopping trolley is your personal butler. *Just pop this heavy item in your trolley. Oh, I might as well get a ton of shopping cos muggins Flo has got a trolley* Why don't you get your own soddin trolley?"

"Ew no. They're for old people"

"Do you know WHAT the main thing for 'old people' is Alice? A BLOODY COAT IN SUMMER!"

"Have you got a cardi I can lend, then?"

"You don't need a cardi. It's boiling"

"Yeah but me dress doesn't have any arms, and I couldn't be mithered putting a brassiere on. I've got a bit of arthritis in me shoulder. It's murder trying to do up hooks when you've got arthritis ... So I'm a bit bouncy. The Gaberdine covers it all up"

"The woman thinks she's too young for a shopping trolley. Then can't put on a bra cos she's arthritic. You're not normal Alice. Come on or we'll miss the bus. I don't want you bruising your shins trying to run for it"

"I'm coming. And I'm keeping me coat on ... OY! You cheeky cow. What do you mean 'shins?!'"

THEY ARRIVE AT THE TOWN HALL

"Oh my god Flo. Look at the size of the queue!"

"We should have brought some butties and a flask of tea. Why have we had to come to the Corporation anyway? You own your house"

"I need to see about something, and we're in town, so I might as well"

"Alice. What 'something' do you need to see them about? I'm not gonna stand here for hours. I remember that eternity we waited in the Doctors and how shown up I felt when he said you needed to see the dentist if your dentures didn't feel right"

"Me MOUTH was hurting. How am I supposed to know the dentist could give me something. I thought he only did teeth. And why were YOU so shown up?

"I work there Alice. I don't want people thinking I go around with idiots"

"WORK THERE? WORK THERE? You're the Cleaner. You just want people in the queue to think you're a Doctor"

"I don't care what people think as long as they don't think I'm an idiot. Mind you, I'm stood next to the real thing, so I might get judged by association. And I'll say it again. WHAT are we doing here?"

"Me Rates are not right. Her next door doesn't pay a penny"

"Int that cos she renting from the corporation? You don't pay rates on a rented house it's in with the rent, I think"

"Oh I SEE! Not only do they lower the tone of the place by turning next door. A beautiful house when the Brennans had it, into a Corporation house. But they make it cheap just to attract riff-raff! They might as well have took a lump hammer to it. I swear they've replaced the wall where it joins on to mine, with Formica ... Aw the Brennans...Horrible couple, lovely three piece suite in the parlour. I never let them know that though. I only seen it once to be truthful. I just tutted and pretended I hadn't even noticed, but it was gorgeous. Like them ones in the posh hotel suites Fred and Ginger were always in. You don't just want to sit down in it. You want to waft"

"What ARE you bloody wittering on about? I told you to take that coat off! You sound like someone with heatstroke"

"How would you know what someone with heatstroke SOUNDS like? I must have misheard when you said were born in Sheffield. You must have meant the Sahara"

"Alice? Why are we here?" *Sigh*

"Should we come back when it's cooler?"

"Yeah. Me corns are throbbing like mad. We need a hot drink to cool down, should we go to yours?"

"Yours is nearer to the bus stop" *If we get off at the next stop to our usual one. And walk back on ourselves*

"I've not got the strength to argue. Come on then. There's a bus due in five minutes. And I'm burning that coat, next time you take it off!"

JUMBLE SALE MADNESS

"I'm not sure if that was a jumble sale we just went to,Alice. It felt more like a riot at Strangeways. Shove that kettle on for us. I'm just popping to the loo"

"I'm not sure I'll make it to the stove Flo. That was a bleedin' nightmare. I'm shattered!"

"I'm telling ya! You don't know people til you've seen them at a

Jumble Sale. Did you see Bessie Calverley when she spotted that Fur Stole? I thought she was gonna takes someones eye out waving that white stick about"

"Well she saw the Fur stole didn't she? I swear she only pretends to be blind"

"Ooh I don't know Alice. When I picked it up, it smelled like a dead rat. Could have been her nose that led her to it"

"Don't let her fool you Flo. I was stood behind her in the Doctor's the other day. And it was that foghorn receptionist on duty. You know the one? Her mam works at Conran street. Likes to broadcast your ailments for the world and his wife to hear. I'm tempted to go in one day and tell her I've got a rash from wearing knickers off her Mam's stall. See if she's shouts that out!... Anyway she's got a cataract"

"Who has?"

"Bessie Calverley! Keep up woman!"

"What's a bleedin' cataract?"

"I don't know. But I know she's got TWO eyes. So I don't know what she's complaining about. She wants to try living with my knees"

"We all have our crosses to bear, Alice. Anyway, let's have a look at our goodies. What did you get?"

"Not clothes! You know me. I'm not wearing someone's cast offs"

"You and our Joyce, you're a right pair of snobs! I saw some lovely jumpers for the kids. But I know she won't have 'em, so I got the little 'uns some jigsaws and a couple of cushions to sit on, when they're playing in the backyard. You can get all sorts when you sit on a cold step ...Show me your stuff then?"

"Some 'Evening in Paris' perfume. The bottle's almost full. And this ornament thingy for that empty space on me mantle-piece"

"What's in the other bag? looks like material to me"

"Oh that's just some old cloth for the dog's bed"

"Let me see?"

"Flo! it's just rags. OY! stop rooting through me bags. That's RUDE!"

"Paisley print? You love Paisley print. Nice dress is that. Your size an' all. Too nice to waste on the dog"

"WELL IT'S FOR THE DOG. Honest"

"I believe you. Though thousands wouldn't. Oh well. At least you'll match ... I wonder if they've made enough to fix the roof yet?"

"They would if the Vicar's wife didn't keep helping herself to the best stuff. I know for a FACT that they had a coffee table donated. I saw it being dropped off. We were right at the front of that queue. So how come we didn't see it?"

"Alice! You can't say things like that"

"I just did! It's her husband that works for God, not her. Now where's that brew you promised me".

FLO AND ALICE INVESTIGATE

AND MISS MARPLE NEED HAVE NO FEAR!

KNOCK, KNOCK

"I knew it was you Alice. By your 'knock' You know the door's never locked til late. Why didn't you just come in?" *And save me the walk up this lobby.*

"Cos I want you to look at something. Have a butchers over there"

"Over where?"

"Eyes right...Two o'clock"

"Bloomin eck. A few months in the Land Army and you think you're a Dambuster. WHERE?"

"THERE! Right behind me, but a bit further up. All them boxes on the pavement"

"Oh yeah. I've seen it now. *Hmm* I wonder what's going on there?"

"Looks like a moonlight flit to me"

"At eleven o clock on a Sunday? How 'moonlight' is that?"

"Have you ever seen a rent man on a Sunday?"

"You've got a point. let me get me coat and we'll have a walk past. I need to pop to the shop before it closes, anyway"

"The shops are the other way"

"Well no one else knows that, do they Sherlock?"

Flo and Alice casually stroll up the street. Alice overdoes the casualness. Flo feels tempted to 'lamp' her one

"Alice! Stop that stupid whistling"

"I'm being casual"

Bloody idiot. "Oh hello Mary. Me and Alice were just passing. Do you know there's a load of boxes on your pavement?"

Nosy cows "Hiya Flo. Yeah I do. I'm just having a sort out"

"Oh! For some daft reason Alice thought you was moving. Didn't you Alice?"

She's 'dead' when we get back to hers. " Well it looks that way. But pardon me for being wrong ... When you say 'sorting out'? Are you getting rid of that telly?"

"NO! I'm lending it to me brother for a bit. He's coming to pick it up any minute now"

"Are you lending him that radiogram too?"

"Alice! Don't be nosy ... Are you?"

"Sorry ladies. I've not got time to chat. I've got to put the dinner on. Are you two eating out?See ya" **BANG!**

"Well! The cheek of some people. She practically shut that door in your face Flo"

"Yours too! There's something fishy going on there. Mark my words. Let's get to the shop before it shuts"

They continue on to the shop. And the mystery of Mary's stuff, remains unsolved. Until a few days later. When Flo and Alice meet up at the bus stop, for a trip to 'Town'

"Alice. What did I say the other day? I'm not often wrong. And I'm right again"

"What the bleedin' 'ell are you talking about?"

"Her, over the road, with all the boxes. Remember? last Sunday?"

"Mary? Ooh go on. Spill the beans?"

"The bailiffs came round. Left with nowt but an Hall Mirror and that horrible black leatherette three piece suite she has in her parlour"

"The crafty cow! She must have known"

"Of course she knew. Her sister works at the Courts.

"Are you saying she got 'tipped the wink'?"

"I'm just saying her sister works at the Courts. You read into that, what you want to"

"It makes me laugh, when you try to be discreet, Alice. You're rubbish at it"

"Well I'm not rubbish, at not having me goods repossessed"

"What are you waffling on about?"

"HER! That Mary. And all that bailiff nonsense. That's what happens when you get everything out of the catalogue and pay back fifty two weeks at nowt ... Here's the bus"

A TRIP TO TOWN

FLO AND ALICE BICKER ON THE BUS

"The bus is taking ages ... Gawd look at that house over there. Another idiot's got their lights up I see"

"They won't be our age group, Flo. It'll be the young un's. I wonder sometimes why we even bothered winning a war, for the ungrateful little sods. I blame pop music for a lot of it. The other day I was stood behind someone I thought was a woman, and when they turned round it was a fella. One of them hippies"

"All I know is they must have stopped doing sums in School. Cos there's twelve day's in December and none of 'em is in soddin' November. Here's the bus. Who's paying?"

"I've only got a ten bob note, til we get to town"

"Well I'll pay there, and you pay coming back"

"Someone's in our place!"

"Alice! You don't own the seats. Sit somewhere else. Other people want to get on. Get a move on ...There's two seats together near the front"

"I'll have to have the window. I get seasick in the aisle"

"I just wanna get the weight off me feet ...That's better. How long were we stood at that bloody bus stop?"

"Long enough for all the blood to go to me ankles. Have you seen how puffy they are?"

"You've never been one for having slim ankles - Here's the conductor ... Two to town please"

"Don't you mean two HALVES? Are you two wagging it from school?"

"Go on! you daft sod. Alright, you've caught us out. A half for me, and full fare for me mam"

"You're NOT funny Flo!"

"The conductor thinks I am ... Ay? it's better sitting here ... Warmer. It's too draughty at the back, in this weather. Nice in summer, though"

"I know, but you have to keep turning round every time someone gets on"

"Only if you're a nosy git. But then again, you ARE. So where are we getting off?"

"IN TOWN!"

"I know THAT, Alice. But I think we should get off at the bottom of Oldham street and walk up"

"WHY? I thought we was just going to Woolworths. The bus stop's right outside it"

"I know, but we could look in some other shops first"

"I tell you what? Why don't we skip the length of Deansgate whilst we're at it? We can even do two laps of the Town Hall, if

you want? These are legs, not bus wheels!"

"Bloody ell Alice. I've got corns too! But I don't let it ruin me life ... And come to think of it! I don't know how you've got the cheek! You're never in YOUR house. If you're not on Moston Lane, chatting somebody's business to anybody who'll listen. You're on your way round here. So FORGIVE ME for not believing your sudden walking problems"

"That's not proper walking. You only live two entries up. And we both practically live on the corner of the lane. That's not a 'walk'. That's a...a... A pop round"

"Well we're gonna 'pop round' the shops on Oldham Street. Or if you want? YOU can get off further up and wait for me at Woolworths"

"I'm not standing there on me own...People'll think all sorts"

"They won't think what you think they'll be thinking. And if they do, there's summat wrong with 'em"

"It's happened before! Remember when we were going to that dance near the town hall, and you were running late? So I was stood on the corner like a lemon, for ages. And that cheeky fella asked me 'how much'?"

"That was thirty odd years ago, Alice. Believe you me. It isn't gonna happen now"

"Well I'm not taking chances -Look! there's Monsall Hospital ... Ooh it gives me the creeps. That's where your Bob's first wife had Consumption. And DIED!"

"Yeah I know!" *You stupid sod!*

"If they ever knock that place down, they'll have to fumigate it proper"

"They're not gonna knock a hospital down. What sort of idiot knocks an hospital down. We've not long had a national health service. What use is it without hospitals?"

"Stranger things have happened at sea ... Eh? we're in Collyhurst"

"AND?"

"Keep looking out the window. You might see your Joyce"

"you keep looking. You might see 'sense'"

"Once, when I was on the eighty eight, I saw my Eddie, walking near Lily Lane. With some tart!"

"Did you get off, and have a word?"

"Did I 'eck. I'd already got the measure of him by then. I just put senna pods in his Cocoa. He dint leave the house for days. Someone got stood up! ... What're you getting from town anyway?"

"A Bunty annual for our Lesley. A doll each for the next two, and summat for the babies"

"You can get all THAT in Woolworths"

"I KNOW. But I want to look around. I might see something I didn't know I wanted"

"Oh go on then Flo. But if you go on the veg stalls, I'm not carrying spuds"

"I've not come all the way to town for proper shopping. I can do that on the lane. I can guarantee you, no spuds. Just Christmas stuff"

After a few hours shopping. They get the bus back home

"Bloody 'ell Alice. Weren't it hectic? I didn't know, there were that many people round here. Have you ever seen Woolworths more packed than that? And it's not even December til next week. Are you coming mine for a brew, when we get off?"

"I'll have to won't I? Unless you can manage the two ton of veg you just bought! You said -"

"I know what I said Alice. But at tuppence a pound cheaper than our grocer, I'd be daft ... Aw stop pulling your face. When we get off the bus, I'll pop in the cake shop and get a couple of iced fingers"

"To be honest. I'd prefer an egg custard"

"With what I've saved, by getting me spuds in town, you can have two"

"Oh I couldn't manage two. But get 'em. I can save the other for me supper"

Nowt like cheek!

LEAST SAID, SOONEST MENDED

HOW TO SURVIVE THE POST OFFICE QUEUE

"This queue gets longer and longer every week. Dunt it Flo?"

"Our Lesley says it's because everyone in the Tuesday pension queue, has a trolley"

"Your Lesley is a kid! What do kids know? -OW!"

"What's up?"

"I just stubbed me toe on me trolley ... The one with a corn on it, an' all"

" Alice? Are you telling me, your trolley's got a corn?"

"Don't give up your day job Florence! - Hey! look whose just come in? -The cheek of it! Talk about 'brass neck'"

"Who ARE you talking about?"

"Gawd, talk louder. Them at the counter can't hear you ... It's Goria Bellini"

"Italian Gloria?"

"NO. Welsh Gloria!"

"Ooh! someone's had an extra spoon of 'sarcky' for breakfast. And what's your problem with her?"

"Do you never listen to a word I say? She's the cow who let her grandkids chalk all over me pavement"

"Bloody 'ell, are you still going on about that? THAT was ages ago"

"It was HER that went on. All I said was *Gloria, when you've got a minute, can you get your grandkids to clean up the mess they made outside me house.* It was her that took it too far"

"She told me you called them scruffy little gits"

"The LIAR! I said Them little gits have made me house look scruffy. Talk about exaggerating"

"It was only a chalk arrow though, Alice. All the kids round here play 'Treasure trails' or whatever it is they call it. I sent our

Lesley to the Paper shop the other day, an' she took ages cos she spotted an arrow on the corner. She ended up on kenyon lane. You don't understand, cos you're not a Nana"

"I understand big trouble making Gobs. And that's what SHE is. Any normal person would have gone mad and made their kids clean it up. But she tried squaring up to me. All four foot, bloody nowt of her!. Saying how it wasn't even my pavement. It was EVERYBODY'S pavement. It's people like her who let Mussolini come to power"

"She was brought up in Monsall!"

"So!"

"Ooh You are petty sometimes Alice. Anyway, she seems to have forgotten it all now. She's already nodded at me twice whilst you've been prattling on"

"I hope you dint nod back"

"Why not? Cos I DID!"

"Some best mate you are! Well I won't be talking to her. Look at her. Smiling and chatting to people, like she's it!"

"You're offended she's even breathing, aren't you? I look forward to the day you've finally fallen out with everyone round here - Which shouldn't be too far off now. So you can change the bloody subject. Anyway it's us next. Have you got your pension book ready?"

"I'm not getting mine out this week, Flo. I'm saving it"

It's alright for some! "Well I'm getting mine. I want to do exciting things with it. Like 'eat' and pay bills"

Gloria approaches the pair

"Hiya Flo luv. Not seen you for a while. How are those beautiful grandchildren of yours? mine are coming round in the Christmas holidays"

"Hiya Gloria. They're fine luv. And there's another on the way. Mine are here every weekend. You can send yours round to play if you want"

"I will do. Are you sure your daughter isn't italian" *chuckle*

"I'm starting to wonder meself. But the more the merrier I say"

"They're a blessing aren't they. Hello Mrs Clough ... How's your pavement?"

Alice storms off. Flo tuts and waits to get her pension.Before sprinting up the lane to catch up with her.

"ALICE! That was downright rude! The way you walked off like that, without a WORD! Hang on whilst I get me breath back. Don't ever go on about your knees to me, again. You ran up the lane like Roger Bannister"

"I TOLD YOU. It'll be a rainy day in hell before I speak to her again! Did she say anything about me?"

"Least said, soonest mended. That's my motto"

"She did, dint she? Go on? I can take it"

"Oh leave it alone now Alice. Are you coming to mine for a brew?"

"Why? So you can laugh at me behind me back? Thinking of the way your bezzie mate Gloria was slagging me off?"

"How would I be laughing behind your back? We both sit facing each other, you daft sod.If you really want to know, she said you're too quick to take offense, and she's not even mithered about it anymore. She was just having a joke, when she mentioned the pavement"

"Well if that's her idea of a joke, Morecambe and Wise won't be fretting ... Is that all she said?"

"YEAH!" *No point mentioning she asked if you'd got the deeds, to prove the pavement was yours.*

"Alright then. Let me just shove me trolley in mine, and we can go round to yours"

"Why did you bring your trolley if you weren't even getting your pension?"

"Cos you never know"

"That's true"

ALICE MEETS HER MATCH

THERE'S NEVER A DULL MOMENT, IN THAT POST OFFICE QUEUE

"Flo. Try not to look like you're looking, but look at the state of that"

"Where am I supposed to be not looking?"

"Straight ahead, but a bit to the right"

"Bloody 'ell. What IS she wearing?"

"Not HER in the Poncho. HER with the hair!"

"The one with long blonde hair? It looks alright to me"

"Wait til she turns round again, and steady yourself"

"Crikey! I see what you mean Alice. I thought she was in the queue to get her mam's pension. Til she turned round. Talk about 'mutton' You know who she is don't ya?"

"Not got a clue. I don't mix with Trollops" *You're a special case*

"It's Kenny's mam"

"Who's Kenny when he's at home"

"The window cleaner. Not our window cleaner. He mostly does the houses in New Moston"

"New Moston? Aren't they nearly all council houses?"

"They've still got windows! I suppose looking at his mam sets him up for all the sights he must see on his rounds"

"I don't understand women who try to be younger than they

are - Ooh this girdle is killing me - Especially when they do such a bad job of it. She wants reporting"

"Nowt so queer as folk, Alice. Eeyar, she's coming this way. Try to keep your thoughts from running all over your face - Hiya Maureen, not seen you for ages. Did you change doctors?"

"Hiya Flo. Yeah I did. We moved to Nuthurst road. Didn't make sense trudging up the lane and if truth be told I'm one of them people who never gets ill I mean, I can't lie about me age, not with a son in his forties but people are always telling me I look young"

"Your hair certainly does!"

"Alice! I've not even introduced you yet - Maureen? this is my mate Alice. Alice? Maureen"

"Hiya Alice. Thanks. It's my pride and joy, is my hair. Nice blue rinse you've got yourself. Not my cup of tea, but each to their own ... I must say, your face DOES look familiar. Have you ever been in the Golden Garter?"

"NO I HAVE NOT!"

I meant as a cleaner "Hang on, it'll come to me ... What school did you go to?"

"Lily Lane" *Not that it's any of your business*

"That's it! You were in junior four with my big sister Joan. Do you remember Joan Cummins?"

"Can't say I do. I don't remember you either" *So stop going on like you're famous.*

"Oh you won't remember me. I was in infants two -Anyway I can't stop. I'm off out tonight. Are you sure you don't remember our Joan? I'm sure she battered you, one dinnertime, for being mean to the little kids. I'm dead good with faces. Even when they've aged - See ya"

Maureen leaves a gobsmacked Alice. And a 'laughing her head off' Flo

"The cheeky cow! She only got cocky cos she knew I couldn't leave the queue"

"Your face was a picture Alice, and you DID go to Lily Lane with her Joan. You know Joan? She worked in the pet shop on Kenyon Lane. You got a dog from there ... Just after she retired"

"What are you trying to say?"

"NOWT *But it's odd, how you never went in there, whilst she worked there.* Did she really batter you?"

"No she bloody didn't. I tripped and she took the glory ... Are you smirking?"

"NO! I'm just smiling. Int it a small world? Are you coming mine for a brew?"

"Are you gonna keep going on about this?"

"NO" *Well not much.*

The ladies return to Flo's

"Come on in Alice, and mind the step going into the scullery - I know it's always been there, but I don't want you tripping... People will think I've battered you"

"I'm going home!"

THE PARCEL

"Flo? Do you fancy coming to the library with me?"

"Not really. I need to unravel these jumpers, and the wool keeps getting stuck on the chair back"

"If I help you, will you come with me?"

TUT! "Go on then. Stick your arms out ... Have you finished the ones you got the other day, ALREADY?"

"I only got SIX"

"It'd take me a year to read six books. What with housework

and sorting out our Bob. And telly in the evening ...You're like our Lesley, you are ...She reads the cornflake box"

"I think you'll find there's a BIG difference between her Janet and John books, and what I read"

"It's Peter and Jane, actually. And YEAH, I'd certainly have summat to say if I caught her reading *THE LUST OF LADY LEMINGTON*'"

"That's an HISTORICAL book...It's about Queen Victoria!"

"So why's it not called the lust of Queen Victoria, then?"

"FLO! Don't be blasphemous. You can't say 'lust' and a member of royalty in the same sentence!"

"WHY NOT? She had umpteen kids. There must have been SOME lust in her life! No one loves the royal family more than me - Keep your arms up!- Look at that cabinet over there. What's it full of? ... ROYAL STUFF. And do you see that jug on the top shelf? That's King George and Queen Mary, that is -KEEP YOUR BLOODY ARMS UP! - It was me mother's and I treasure it. I wouldn't dream of ever using it. Even if all me other jugs broke. I'd sooner put the milk bottle on the table then use that"

"You'd be that 'common'?"

"That's not common. That's patriotic!"...

"Me arms are hurting me now, Flo"

"I'll be done in a minute"

"What're you unraveling all this wool for, anyway?"

"Waste not, want not. As well you know. They're old cardies. I've already took the buttons off. I'm teaching the older grandkids how to knit"

"I give mine to the Jumble. You can get a decent cardi for next to nothing, nowadays. And it doesn't look handmade"

"What's wrong with handmade. This cardi I'm wearing now is handmade. It only took a few episodes of Ivanhoe to get it done. Cos I use my time wisely. What've you got at the end of a book?"

"Knowledge!"

Don't make me laugh. "But will it keep you warm?"

"Well I don't know what was going on in Ivanhoe, but by the

amount of dropped stitches I can see on your sleeve, you must have been very distracted"

"It's meant to be like that, you cheeky cow. You don't know nowt about patterns. There's more to knitting than 'knit one, purl one' He is a 'dish' though, that Roger Moore - Ooh! I'm having a 'flush' just thinking about him"

"You might be on the 'change'"

"Am I Alice?...Well you'd know!"

"I'm not on it!"

"REALLY? So can you remember what it was like when you were?"

"I've NOT been on it yet, you cheeky mare! You can unravel this last bit on your own. My arms are killing me. I'm sure I'm getting arthritis"

"Dead common, is arthritis ... In women who've been on the change"

"How many bloody times, Flo? I'm NOT, nor have I BEEN, on the bloody change!"

"Keep your knickers on luv! I'm only kidding *I'm not!* I'm done now. I'll get me coat and we can go to the library. I need to pop in the Post Office anyway. So whilst you're looking at your 'history' books, I'll pop in there"

"You can have a very annoying tone of voice sometimes, Florence. I don't care what you think, I know for a fact, that I know me history. Cos I read and learn"

"Funny that. Cos you never 'live and learn'"

"Ask me any question about summat that happened in History? ... Go on! Ask me?"

"Who invented the Pyramids?"

"Not foreign stuff! I don't read about Foreign stuff! English history, that's what I know about. Go on! Ask me a question about anything in English history - Anything to do with Kings and Queens"

"I'm trying to think of one"

"I tell you what. Ask me anything at all to do with Queen Victoria. Anything at all"

"Did you go to her christening?"

"You're only funny in your own head. When WILL you grow up!"

"When I get to your age... Right, come on before the shops shut"

A chuckling Flo. And a frosty faced Alice, make their way to the shops.

"It dunt matter what day you go in that Post Office. There's always a queue. Are you sorted out now, Alice?. It's pitch black outside. Our Bob'll be home before I've so much as unwrapped his Kippers"

"Yeah. I'm all done now. I'm only getting four out, cos I've got double bingo next week, to make up for not going this week. What did you go to the Post Office for, anyway Flo?"

"I had to pick up a parcel. It come when I was out. And so it seems, was half the street! That's why I've had to pick it up meself. I'm bloody glad it wasn't heavy"

"A PARCEL? Oooh! What's in it?"

"Mind your own business!"

"Have you sent for summat out of the TITBITS?"

"NO! ... Not for ages"

"Is it a surprise from Bob?"

"He'd be a bit daft posting it to me, wouldn't he? When we live in the same house. No Alice, it's not summat from Bob. I know what it is, and when I'm ready I'll tell you what it is. Which won't be tonight, so don't think you're following me back to mine. I'll see you tomorrow. And NOT at the crack of dawn!"

"I wouldn't dream. Flo. I'll see you about eleven-ish" *By which, I mean nine-ish*

THE NEXT DAY. SLIGHTLY BEFORE NINE

KNOCK, KNOCK, KNOCK

"HOLD YOUR HORSES. I'M COMING"

KNOCK, KNOCK, BANG!

"I'M BLOODY COMING. Someone had better be dead, or they bloody will be. Alice! What an absolute soddin surprise! Have you seen the time? It's only a bloody quarter to nine. You'd better come in before the world and his wife see me bits"

"Is that all it is? Aw. Do you know what I must have done. This watch has been in me jewelry box for ages. And when I took it out last night - Cos I always get me outfit for the next day, ready the night before. Do you do that? - Anyway, I must have put it forward instead of back. I'm thinking it's coming up to eleven" *Alice Clough. YOU are a soddin' genius.*

You're a lying so and so."It's lucky for you, our Bob's left out early to go fishing. Or you'd have been getting told to sod off. He's not one for visitors before he's had his breakfast. And we have a lie-in at weekends. When the kids are not here"

"It was a GENUINE mistake. And your Bob's too much of a gentleman to say owt like that to me"

"It wouldn't be Bob, saying it"

Hmmph! Fishing? How can you have fish for your tea, on a Friday then go fishing, first thing Saturday morning? It seems like a bit too much fish for me. I don't really like fish. I've started having a cheese and onion pie on Fridays. I know what's gonna happen though. I'm gonna get sick of cheese...I wonder what else you can have instead of fish? Chippy fish is alright. But look at the price of it?"

"STOP TALKING ABOUT FISH! I've not even had a brew yet"

"Well put the kettle on then, Flo - I tell you what? You go and get yourself sorted and I'll brew up. Should I make you a round of toast? I'm fine me, I had porridge before I come round here. But I don't mind making YOU some toast?"

"I can't face food before I've had a brew and a cig. And what's wrong with your head?"

"NOWT! ... Why? Does it look funny? Have I got a lump?"

"No, it's just the way you keep looking round me room. Like a demented budgie. Your head's not kept still since you came in. Are you looking for summat?"

"NO!...No. Guess what? I went to bed early last night and started reading one of the books I got from the library, yesterday, whilst you were in the Post Office *Hint, hint* It's by Barbara Cartland. I've never read one of hers before, Have you heard of her?"

"I've more than heard of her. I've seen her, at the Chiropodist's"

"Having her FEET DONE?"

"No, you daft sod. There was an article about her, in a magazine I was looking at whilst I was waiting. Apparently, apart from the ton of multi coloured make up, she slaps on, she doesn't wear nothing but pink. which strikes me as downright daft, if you don't favour Shirley Temple. And she certainly doesn't. Fair enough, her colours'll never run. But what would she do , if she had to go to a funeral? Stand there like the Sugar Plum Fairy? Bringing mirth to an occasion you're meant to be morbid at?"

"Never trust someone who's happy at a funeral that's my motto, Flo. Although, having said that. I wanted to laugh me head off at me husband's. But I held it in. The 'afters' is a different thing. You've still got to remain miserable, but you can be a bit cheerier. I've got a special funeral smile. Where, I kind of smile, but stop quickly. Been using it for years. It's served me a treat"

"Oh the one, where you look like you've just picked up a piece of dog's 'do' thinking it was a cream cake?"

Cheeky cow. I'll get you back for that, when I've found out what's in your parcel "She does wear a lot of make-up, dunt she?"

"It's like Annie Walker's had her make up done by Coco the Clown"

"Ooh you are funny, sometimes, Flo. Coco the Clown! Very good, is that"

"Am I? You're not usually this impressed, Alice *I'm not as daft as I look, luv.* Anyone would think you were creeping to me for summat?"

"Well EXCUSE ME! I'm only trying to be a good pal"

"Yeah, right. Where's that brew then?"

"Get dressed *You slut!* And It'll be on the table waiting for you"

A FEW MINUTES LATER

"Is that a new Pinny?"

"Alice! FOR GOD'S SAKE. You must think I'm daft! You want to know what was in the parcel, don't you?"

"What parcel? Oh! The parcel you got yesterday? I'd forgotten all about it til you just mentioned it. But seeing as you have?" *And about time too!*

"Let me clear the pots away and I'll get it out"

"Do you want a hand?"

"With the pots?"

"No! With getting the parcel out"

"There's no end to your nosiness, is there, Alice. You're alright luv, I'll manage. I've already opened it. In fact you're looking at some of the stuff that was in it, as we speak"

"Where? what? where? I thought you might have had to hide it, cos I know Bob doesn't like you sending off for stuff"

"Well, we all know what 'thought' did! don't we? It wasn't summat I sent off for. It was summat someone sent me. From abroad"

"ABROAD? Who do you know from abroad?"

"Have a guess, Sherlock?"

"Well, there's your Joyce's husband. But he's here!"

"He does have family, you daft apeth .He didn't just hatch from an egg left under the lonely tree! I've been writing to his family for a while now. And one of his sisters sent me a parcel for Christmas"

"They do Christmas abroad?"

"No. It's only us in England that do it, cos Jesus came from Marple! - Of course they do Christmas, you daft lummox! She sent me loads of stuff. What do you think of my embroidered place mats? They've been staring you in the face, for the last half hour. our Joyce's sister in law made them"

"Them are from abroad? They look just like normal ones. What else did you get? Cos it was a biggish parcel"

"Don't miss nowt, do ya? A bottle of Rum - for me when I have a cold! Some photo's of the family - I'll show 'em you later. A set of plastic, but they look like glass, fruit bowls...And this, for Bob"

"Hang on while I put me sunglasses on. What the 'eck is THAT? It's certainly bright"

"They call them Afro shirts"

"I didn't know there were that many colours in existance! Your Bob'll never wear that. He's never wore nowt but brown"

"YEAH HE HAS! He's got a couple of grey jumpers. I know what you mean though. When I write the thank you letter, I'll say he wore it on Sunday, but no one had a camera. Which no one will, so it's only half a fib. Innit lovely of her, though? To think of us"

"You'll have to send her summat back now"

"I already do. Every now and again I send me old copies of Titbits. She loves em. I'm gonna put a postal order in her card this year"

"Ooh! proper best mates aren't you?"

"Are you jealous?"

"What of?... I don't even read Titbits anyway. It's COMMON! And what do I need with a postal order? I've got a cheque book"

"You're jealous.. And anyway, she's NOT me mate. She's me ... What IS she to me, if she's me son in law's sister?"

"Well over here she'd be your neice, I think. But I don't know how it goes for foreigners. Some of them get married to each other when they're babies, so they might be called different things, to what we've heard of over here. A fella at the bus stop said they eat cats. Are you gonna show me the photo's?"

"Have I just heard, what I think I heard! Do you think I've got time to sit here all day, showing you pictures so you can come out with daft remarks like THAT, about so called foreigners. You love that word, you do. Every time me son in law's name comes up. It's foreigners this, and foreigners that. Do you know what's 'foreign' about YOU? Bloody common sense!"

9: A BREW AND A BIT OF BIGOTRY

FLO AND ALICE DISCUSS FOREIGNERS AND 'FUNNY' PEOPLE

A GERMAN AT MAINE ROAD

"Flo? I heard the news! How is he?"

"What news? and how's who?"

"Bert Trautmann. And your Bob"

"I'm going to go in the scullery and pop the kettle on. When I come back you'd better be making sense ... Right! Come again?"

"City have signed Bert Trautmann as a goalkeeper"

"Have they? Should we have a parade? WHY would I or YOU for that matter, be the least bit interested in football?"

"Don't you know?"

"Obviously bloody not Alice. And you're not helping with the soddin riddles. Speak up woman!"

"City ... Your Bob's beloved City,have signed Bert Trautmann ...Who's a German" *Alice smirks, and takes a sip of her tea.*

"A GERMAN?"

"Yep. A German. And we all know how much your Bob hates them"

"I'm not overkeen meself. And you can't blame our Bob. he fought in two world wars against them"

"Technically he was too old for the last one"

"HOME GUARD Alice! If they'd ever landed it'd be men like my Bob waiting for 'em"

"He'd have had to wait a while. I'm sure they were coming in from Dover way. That's miles from Manchester"

"Shurrup! What did your Eddie do for the war effort?"

"That's a tad mean Flo. You know the Army wouldn't take him because of his leg"

"Oh yeah. Must have been all them times he 'got it over' Must have shortened it"

"Flo! Have some respect. The philandering son of a...GUN! is dead"

"I do know! You bought cream cakes to celebrate. Very respectful!"

"Can you not remind me of HIM? I get a rash. Where is Bob?"

"Where any man of worth is...At work"

"Does he know about the German?"

"Well if YOU do, I'd say it's highly likely. I'd better make him a Shepherd's pie. That'll cheer him up. He HAS been quiet for a couple of days, but we don't really talk about sport. Mainly cos I can't be mithered with it. And he has the sense to know ... A GERMAN? What's the world coming to. Who signed him? Mengele?"

"Nowt would surprise me Flo. Look what they did to Winston once the war was over"

"They? Did you vote Conservative? What's wrong with ya? the amount of times you're at that doctors, for FREE treatment, and YOU voted conservative?"

"Me mam would have turned in her grave if I'd voted Labour"

"Them lot are the reason she's in it! Anyway I'm not arguing politics with you. There's no cutting through that daft snobbery of yours. A bleedin' German playing for an English team? Bob is gonna be fuming. They were trying to kill us, just the other day"

"Ooh I remember the bombing. Pat Morrison's Mam got killed in Piccadilly. Strange set of affairs was that. She'd told her husband she was only popping to Newton Heath. To this day people talk about it"

"YOU talk about it, cos you're a nosy sod"

"It's not just me! Beryl from the wash house was talking about it, last Wednesday at the bus stop"

"I was THERE. You started it!"

"Well never mind that. He might have to start supporting United cos I can't see your Bob EVER having owt to do with one of 'them'"

"Alice! Say summat like that when Bob's in the house and you won't be coming here anymore. He's gonna have to live with it. He's 'Blue' through and through. But he won't be best pleased"

"Should I stay and be here with you when he gets home"

"WHY?"

"In case he gets ...Y'know?"

"My Bob? Not in a million years. But like I said, he won't be happy about it, and you get on his nerves at the best of times, so I don't think it's a good idea for you to be here"

"Has he been saying summat behind me back"

Plenty! "No he hasn't Alice. You know what he's like. He thinks we go on daft sometimes. And he int wrong" *About YOU.*

"Well I've got loads to do anyway. I only came round to tip you the wink. Forewarned and all that. I have known your Bob longer than you, and there's a man who doesn't forgive when it comes to Germans"

"You're not wrong. I'd better get some mince. There's nowt my Shepherd's pie can't make better"

It dunt help my indigestion "Alright luv. You know where I am if you need me"

I'M NOT EATING OWT FOREIGN

"Oh it's you, Alice. From the top of the street I thought it was a munchkin sitting on me doorstep. Budge up then, so I can open the door. How long have you been waiting? I told you I was going to our Joyce's didn't I?"

"Yeah you did, but you're also going to the library with me today, we arranged it, remember?"

"We said two o clock dint we?"

"Yeah"

"Well It's only five to one now!"

"Me watch must be slow"

And the rest! "Well it's a good job I came home early, or you'd have been welded to me step. How did you get down there?"

"It wasn't easy. Not with my knees, but I didn't have the strength to go back home. These books weigh a ton"

"I don't understand you. You've lugged them books to mine cos they're too heavy for you to take back on your own. But you live nearer the library than I do!"

"I made two trips Flo - What? Why's your face like that?

Why don't you just move in! "Never mind - *you can't teach the daft* - Put the kettle on, whilst I get me coat off. We've got plenty of time. Or have you booked a special appointment to hand your books back?"

"You're being sarcky aren't ya?"

"Noooo! whatever gave you that idea! Anyway, have a butchers at this?"

"What is it? It smells lovely"

"It's Chicken and rice. Our Lesley's dad made it"

"RICE?... Foreign food? Are you gonna eat it?"

"Well I'm not gonna display it on the mantle-piece am I, you daft sod. Course I'm going to eat it. You can have some too if you want?"

"I THINK NOT. When have I ever eaten foreign muck?"

"It's not technically foreign. I was with our Joyce when she bought the chicken. The butchers is under her flats"

"Yeah but it's cooked foreign. And I'm not eating rice that isn't in a pudding. It's not normal"

"Suit your bloody self. All the more for for me. It's bloomin' lovely"

"Are you gonna give your Bob some?"

"Bob?... Bob's set in his ways. It's Thursday and Bob always has a Shepherds pie on Thursdays"

"Plus he won't eat foreign muck either. Will he?"

"Are you telling me what MY husband does and doesn't like?"

"Well I have known him longer than you have"

"Not in the biblical sense you haven't! Never you mind what my Bob eats ... Aw just have a taste. Honest to God it's delicious. It's not dead hot either.just pleasantly warming on your tongue. Put your face straight! Anyone would think I was asking you to try sh*t with sugar on"

"I'm not being funny Flo, but I can't eat foreign food"

"And I'm not laughing, Alice! Anyway, how do you know you can't eat it? You've never even tried any!"

"That's a LIE! Who made the Coronation Chicken for the street party? That's got curry in it!"

"You didn't know that though did you? YOU thought it was mustard powder"

"YOU told me that!"

"I couldn't have took the constant moaning about foreign stuff. I knew you'd be put off, and I was tied up making the paste butties and jelly. Why should you stand around watching people work. And you ate enough of it dint you? Even AFTER you found out it was curry"

"SO! It wasn't foreign curry powder anyway. It's as English as the queen, is Coronation chicken"

"Bob says she's a German really"

"Who's German?"

"The queen"

"Well Bob is daft, Flo"

"He is, int he. We'd better shift our socks before the library gets full of kids coming home from school. You know how your nerves get when there's too many of 'em around you. You carry half the books and I'll carry half - Oy! divide 'em properly. No way am I carrying the hardbacks whilst you swan up the lane hugging three mills and boons ... Are you sure you don't want some of this food for your tea?"

"I couldn't Flo. Me stomach can't take strange food. I've got some tripe soaking in vinegar on the windowsill. I'll have it with a bit of brown bread and butter. I tell you what. So you're not offended, I won't take the 'Chicken' *Cos it's probably Cat!* but if you want you can give me a slice of your Hovis, and a bit of that Adam's best butter. I've only got Mother's Pride and a bit of Stork at mine"

"If there were prizes for 'Cheek' Alice. You'd get the soddin Oscar!"

MAKING ASSUMPTIONS

"Are you putting on weight, Alice?"

"When have I got time to put on weight! I'm always on the go"

"You're always here"

"I have to get here don't I? It's not like I live next door"

"You're only a couple of streets away. You don't exactly have to cross the Sahara to get here"

"A couple of streets is a couple of entries and you know what my knees are like. Them cobbles are like razors to me. Every step is agony. I don't complain about it cos I'm not one of them who moan all the time - I saw that look! - And I'm only here cos I was worried when I didn't see you passing mine this morning. I had visions of you lying on the floor dead. *She always passes mine, on a Monday. When she's going to clean at that posh house near Lily Lane school* I said to meself. And you know you do, cos it's the quickest way to get on kenyon lane. So when it came to eleven and you hadn't passed, I started to fret. So I came round, cos that's what friends do, Florence. I bet I could be dead for weeks before you bothered to look for me"

"One no show on pension day and I'd have the fire brigade out, so shut it! You obviously wasn't listening to me last night. I told you I wasn't working today cos it's wakes week and they've got a caravanette in formby"

"You never told me that Flo or I'd have saved meself an hour at the parlour window fretting. It's freezing in there 'an all. So if I catch my death I'll know who to blame"

"It'd be your own bloody fault for being such a nosy cow. Hovering behind your nets. And I did tell you. But you were too busy being mortified by what the Tiller girls had on. I wish you'd get your own telly"

"You only have to say! I'm not one to stay where I'm not wanted -But did you see the state of what they had on? I've got doily's that would cover up more. An' on a Sunday too. What is the world coming too? In my day you didn't even talk on a Sunday til your dad said you could. Never mind prancing on stage in your underwear"

"You should lend 'em your knickers, Alice. Now the army doesn't need any more barrage balloons"

"You're not funny! And If modesty is a crime, let them 'hang' me. You wouldn't understand anyway, not with your father being the way he was"

"And what do you mean by that!?"

"Oh come on Flo! It was you that told me, in the first place"

"Me that told you what?"

"Y'know? About your dad ... Being 'you-know-what"

"Jewish?"

"Yeah. Don't get me wrong. I'm not saying YOU are. You always get eggs in for Easter, and you're the first one to put up a tree at Christmas. I know proper Christians who don't do that. And that's why I can understand when you're lax about 'Christian' values. 'They' have different ways don't they?"

"Who's 'THEY'?"

"Aw Flo. You're getting the hump now. I can tell by your voice. I wasn't saying anything untoward but ...y'know? I mean...erm - They have Sunday on a Saturday. That's not right is it? - And they cut bits off. If God gives it you it's cos he wants you to use it. AND - They killed baby Jesus"

"Listen luv. I'm proud of my heritage. Me dad was born a Jew but so what! An' you want to get your history right. It was the Romans who killed Jesus. I don't see no one blaming the Pope. Gawd! It was bigots like you that made Oswald Mosely think he had a chance"

"Aw don't let's fall out. Like I said, I only came round cos I was worried. But if I'm not wanted?"

"Well take your coat off then. You look like you're waiting for a bus, and last I heard, they don't stop in my living room - Bloody 'ell Alice. How many coats have you got on?"

"I put me summer coat on cos it looked warm but when I stood on the step it was freezing, so I slipped my woollen jacket on under it. A chill could be the death of me"

"That big tweed thing is your SUMMER coat? What do you put on in Winter? A leather one, with the Cow still attached? No wonder I thought you'd got fat"

"Oh! - Who's the bigot now?"

I bloody give up!

IT'S ONLY A GAME

"What's up with your Bob? He nearly took me leg off, barging past me in the hallway"

"City lost the derby"

"Who did they play?"

"Alice! Are you naturally 'thick' or do you practice? and stop exaggerating about your leg. Why don't you try knocking? before YOU barge in. How was our Bob to know you were gonna suddenly appear whilst he was tantrumming up the hallway. The daft sod. 'It's only a game' I said to him"

"He's a man. They're like kids when it comes to sport. What did he say when you said that? - Why don't you tell me after you've put the kettle on"

"Sod off you daft cow. Why don't you bugger off back to where you come from"

"FLO! Are you on the change? I'm practically offended. Why would you say that to me?"

"No, that's what Bob said to ME -Someone's getting no supper - *Give me my fare to Sheffield* I shouted back. *And I'll get off.* I half meant it, too' "

"He wants to count his blessings having a filly like you, at his age"

"I don't know what I'd do without you Alice. Everyday I wake up not even thinking about the age gap between me and Bob. Thank God I've got you to remind me!"

"I was only sayin'!"

"Well change the bloody record and say something else. He'd still be a stroppy sod about the football if me and him were twins"

"Ew. Twins getting married to each other? That's one I've yet to read in Marji Proops, but the way the world is going, I wouldn't be surprised. I tell you what did surprise me though. Your Bob marrying you - I'm NOT talking about the age gap, so put that butter knife down - I'm talking about you being from Yorkshire. Anywhere further than Wythenshawe is foreign to him"

"First thing he brings up, any time we have a row. I dread the cricket. He told me the other day -When Lancashire were behind, that I'd let him marry me under false circumstances"

"Did he not know you was a Yorkshire lass before he took you up the aisle?"

"Of course he did! He just can't take a loss in the football or the Cricket, and he takes it out on me. Apparently he thought me Sheffield accent was posh Mancunian and the fact that the first meal I made him was a Lancashire hot-pot was all part of me 'cunning plan' to catch him"

"The daft sod. Who'd have you down for 'Posh'? - What've I said? Why are you looking at me like that? "

"With friends like you, Alice"

GUESS WHAT

HOW ALICE CAN OFFEND HALF THE WORLD, IN ONE CONVERSATION.

"Ay Flo. Do you remember whatserface from Arran Street?"

"The one with the funny legs?"

"No! Anyway SHE'S dead"

"No way? When did that happen?"

"About twenty years ago. Are you going senile?"

"We're not talking about the same person are we? I thought you was talking about Rita whojamaflip"

"What's so funny about her legs?"

"She couldn't keep 'em shut Alice *chuckle* Eee. I should be on the stage. So who are YOU talking about?"

"Her name escapes me. I'm sure it's Mavis or Murial. I'm positive it starts with an 'M'...NORMA. That's it"

"That dunt start with an 'M'"

"It's got one in it. Anyway. Guess what I heard?"

"The sound of the men in the square wheeled ambulance coming to take you away?"

"Sarcky aint something to be proud of Florence"

"Well what have you heard then?!"

"You know she had a Son?"

"Hasn't she still got him?"

"There ARE other places I could go!"

"Aw, I'm sorry Alice. I'm just in one of them moods. Right. Go on. I promise I'm listening"

"Well this Norma's son ... He's got a 'special' friend"

"Aw, is he courting?"

"You could say that. You could also say, Norma needn't hold her breath waiting for a Grandchild"

"Oooh! Are we talking Liberace?"

"Nah! more like Larry Grayson, if he wore denim"

"Doesn't bother me anyway. We're all God's children. Live and let live, I say"

"I know what you're saying Flo, but what would you say if it was your Joyce?"

"What a daft question. She's already got four kids. I think she'd have realised by now if she batted for the other side. But if you want an answer. I'm glad she's not, cos I love the bones off them grandbabies. But if she was, I wouldn't care"

"You're very 'liberal' aren't you? Mind you, how could you be anything else with your family background"

"What do you mean by THAT?"

"Nowt Flo! Just ...You know? Your dad being a *mumble, mumble* and your Joyce marrying a *mumble*"

"You don't have to mumble. The world and his wife know me Dad was a Jew. And I'm dead proud of my West Indian Son-in-law. Them that don't like it can stick it in their pipe and smoke it! - Now do you want a brew, or are you late for your Brown-shirt's meeting?"

"Gawd you always take things the wrong way"

"So does Norma's son by the sound of it"

"Bloody 'ell Flo, that's near the knuckle. Give me an extra sugar for the shock ... I'm sorry if I offended you. You know I didn't mean it"

"You'll offend the pall bearers at your own funeral, you will. Come on drink up and let's nip to the shops for a bit. I've heard

the butcher's got a special offer on 'Prem'"

ALICE 'CALLS' THE DOCTOR

"Flo. Put the kettle on and listen to this"

"You put it on. Can't you see I'm doing me skirtings. I always do me skirtings on a Tuesday. You'd have me living me in a hovel, you would. As long as I brewed up every five minutes for you"

"Well pardon me for breathing! Anyway I had to have the doctor round this morning, and guess what?"

"The doctor came round?"

Tut! "YES But it was a new doctor"

"And?!"

"It was a WOMAN!"

"So! Gladys Riley has a woman doctor. At that surgery on Rochdale road. She says she's brilliant. Just like a proper doctor. It wouldn't bother me having a woman. What's up with you anyway?"

"Oh, you know. Downstairs stuff. I practically slept on the toilet all night"

"Well all the better Alice - Having a woman doctor. At least she's familiar with your bits and bobs"

"Yeah I know, but you just get used to things the way they are. Men are doctors. Women are nurses. It's always been that way. And she was a bloody nowty cow an' all. Cos I wasn't expecting 'her' I thought she was being a bit previous when she asked me what the problem was' So I said 'Aren't we gonna wait for the doctor? Nurse 'whoever you are'"

"I bet she's crossed out YOUR name on her Christmas card list"

"Well I'll tell you what Flo. Even if she was on MINE, she'd be getting one with 'Candles and baubles' on it. I always give them ones to people I can't stand"

"Oh yeah? I've still got all the ones you ever sent me. Some of them have got candles and baubles on!"

"That was when I first knew you. You grew on me. I give you Nativity or Victorian village ones now"

"I'll let you off then. So what did she say?"

"She said 'Mrs Clough, I AM the doctor' Then she pursed up her lips like she was sucking a lemon"

"I meant, what did she say about your toilet troubles?"

"Oh that! She gave me some 'oinkment' and waffled on about thrush or something. Do I look like a newborn baby? I'm gonna pop in the surgery later and make an appointment to see a 'proper' doctor"

Sometimes I wonder how you get through a day "Ee-yar here's ya brew. I've put an extra sugar in" *Hopefully it'll rush some sense to your head.*

BEING MARY

"Alice. Have you got any stripey sheets you don't need?"

"I'm a pensioner. I need everything I've got. Why?"

"If you haven't got one it doesn't matter"

"Well I might have something in the Ottoman. I wasn't saying no"

No!. You were just being a cantankerous sod "It's for our Lesley *I saw that look!* They're doing the Nativity at school, and she's got her heart set on being Mary. If we send her in with the outfit, she's halfway there"

"Your Lesley? Being MARY? With her skin colouring?"

"What are you trying to say?"

"Everyone knows Mary is Blonde Your Lesley's half-caste"

"Well you know what Alice. I won't lie, I always thought the same thing meself. But when you come to think of it. Where IS Jerusalem?"

"Somewhere down south"

"SOMEWHERE DOWN SOUTH? Did you not go to school Alice?"

"Yeah I did! and I'm almost offended by that remark Florence Holden. I remember every word of that song - *And was Je-ru-sa-lem founded there. On england's green and* - I've forgot the rest. But there you go. I'm not an idiot"

"You do a bloody good impression of one. I was having a chat with Lesley's dad the other night. He might be a bit of a buggar with the ladies but he knows how to hold a conversation. Anyway, he was telling me that Jerusalem is in the Middle East. Where that Lawrence of Arabia fella went to. And they're all brown over there. So it stands to reason that Mary would be too"

"What bloody utter tripe Flo. There's loads of pictures of her in the Art Gallery. And you practically live on top of that Grotto in Moston Cemetery. I wouldn't exactly say your Lesley was the 'spit'"

"None so blind as them that don't want to see Alice. You can stick your stripey sheet. I'm gonna nip to the material shop and see if they've got any oddments. Our Lesley's got as much right as any other kid in that school to be Mary. In fact she's got more when you think of it. Jesus wasn't English"

"I'm not standing near you when there's thunder and lightening. You get done for blasphemy"

"Are you playing daft, Alice? You don't really think Jesus spoke English do you?"

"I've read me Bible and I've watched 'King of Kings' How much more evidence do you need"

"I'm going home before I lose the will to live"

"Are you still going to the Market on Friday?"

"Yeah"

"I'll meet you at the bus stop then"

THE 'JOKE'S' ON ALICE

LIFE, LOVE, AND THE ODD BIT OF RACISM.

"That step's looking a bit grubby Flo. Did you not have owt to give the rag and bone man?"

"You cheeky sod! I did it just the other day. Anyway our Lesley's here so I got her a windmill. You might as well sit down seeing as you've just walked in uninvited. I'll put the kettle on"

"I'm not sure I'm welcome but go on then. Two sugars in mine"

"I've only known you for thirty odd years. I'd have been fretting over how much to put in if you hadn't told me!"

Tut! "Anyway where is she?"

"Who?"

"Shirley Temple! Your Lesley? She doesn't like me. I can tell"

"She's in the back entry with her friend from next door but four, and she does like you. She's just got one of them faces.

Her dad calls her a long streak of misery"

"Ooh Can't he speak English good?"

"He's been speaking it all his life you daft apeth. He come from the British West Indies...They speak British"

"Yeah but not the same way we do"

"Well I'd have never bloody known! Thank heavens for you"

"You know what I mean"

"Yeah I do. And you'd better not let our Joyce hear you. You know how sensitive she gets"

"Remember when your Bob's family came round? Your Lesley was just born then, and with things the way they were, you asked her to wait in the parlour til they'd gone. And then out of the blue, she just come swanning in with the baby"

"I didn't know where to put me face. Mainly cos I was laughing so much. Our Joyce was right though. Why should we have to hide? I've got lovely grandkids and I don't care WHERE their dad comes from"

"Flo. I was in stitches when she waltzed through to go to the kitchen saying *Don't mind me. I'm just getting a bottle for me Monkey!*"

Chuckle "Don't Alice. I'm choking on me tea. Horrible people. They told our Bob if he had anything to do with his own child They'd never talk to him again. Their faces when he said *Well you'd better sup up, Cos that's the last brew you're getting in MY house.* They soon scarpered after that. Not seen head nor tail of them since ... Ooh, here she is. Mind what you say in front of her. That child has got a memory like the fella we saw in Blackpool"

"Can she recite every winning horse since eighteen ninety six?"

"Shurrup. Hiya sweetheart. Do you want something to eat? and say hello to Aunty Alice"

"Hello Aunty Alice *you smelly cow* Nana can I go to the cemetery with Julie?"

"On your own?"

"No her Mam's going as well" *Not with us though. And maybe not even on the same day.*

"Okay, just remember what I said about not stepping on the graves"

"Do they have graves in your dad's country?"

"Alice!!!"

"I'm only asking. How can you learn if you don't ask?"

"My dad said to tell you-"

"Er - Never mind what your dad said. Run along now if you're going to the cemetery. I'll do Ham butties for tea. Give us a kiss?"

"Bye Nana, Bye Aunty malice - I mean Alice" *I MEAN malice.*

With a skip in her step. And a furtive 'dirty' look thrown Alice's way. Lesley goes out to play

"Light of my life, are them Grandkids"

"Not exactly 'light' though are they?"

"Alice Clough! I swear I'll lamp you in a minute. If you've got a problem with my grandchildren being half-caste. You don't have to come round here"

"Don't be daft. You're me best friend. Can't you take a joke"

Tut "Well there's no point letting good tea go to waste. Pass us your cup ... By the way. I've heard that just before he left you. Your Eddie's was doing a foreigner. Some Italian Woman from Ancoats"

"What're you trying to say? Who said that about my Eddie? He would never...."

"I meant she was paying him cash in hand for cleaning out her gutters. What's the matter? Can't you take a joke?"

A BREW AND A BIT OF BIGOTRY

"I wish I had some privets"

"Do you Alice? I wish I had a million pound note. But if you're idea of heaven is privets?... Pass us the sugar "

"Shurrup Flo! - You're gonna get worms. I'd already put two sugars in - You know what I mean. Just a little front garden with a privet hedge. Like the houses on Hinde street. Should we move?"

"WE? I don't think my Bob would be impressed if he came home and his dinner was in another house. Plus I'm used to me own cooker and there's no way I could take it. It hasn't been moved for thirty years - Well it has when I've cleaned behind it *I saw that look!* But apart from that"

"I didn't mean 'WE' as in 'live in the same house. We're not them 'funny' people. I was just dreaming out loud"

"What 'funny' people?"

"You know!? Women ...Who live together"

"Nuns?"

Tut! "NO! Women. Who. LIVE. Together"

"Sisters?"

"NO FLO! Stop acting daft. You know what I mean"

"Let me just get something straight Alice. If I was going to be 'one of them', it wouldn't be with you!"

"Why? what's wrong with me?"

"Where to begin! Anyway it's Wednesday I need to catch the shops before they shut. Our Joyce is bringing her fella for tea"

"Does Bob know?"

"Does Bob know what?"

"Y'know? About him coming to tea, and being foreign an' all. I thought he wasn't best pleased about her being with a coloured man"

"Bob thinks I'M foreign cos I come from Yorkshire, and he can be as unpleased as he wants. She's been with him long enough now. He can just like it or lump it. At the end of the day, she's our only child and if that lad makes her happy, we have to be happy too. Anyway he's a lovely young man. Handsome, got beautiful manners and he's dead intelligent"

"Ooh! Do they have schools in his country?"

God give me strength, but still keep me from strangling her "Yes Alice, they DO! He's actually came here to go to University"

"Is he gonna be a doctor? Kath from the cobblers was telling me they've got a coloured doctor at her surgery and you wouldn't even know he was coloured, if you closed your eyes cos he speaks dead good English"

"Like what we do?"

"Yeah!"

Sometimes, sarcasm goes right over your head "No he's doing law"

"LAW? Well I'll go to the foot of my stairs. Whatever next?"

"Is there summat wrong with you ? He is a bloody human being. Anyone would think I'd just told you that a talking dog was gonna be the Pope"

"Aw I don't mean it like that Flo. It's just ...They're different aren't they? More physical than brainy. Whereas us white people are more leaderish like. I've read that book 'Mandingo' - by accident! I thought it was summat else"

"I know you mean well Alice, but you have some daft notions in that head of yours. Mind you I'm not surprised, the daftness we get shown at the 'Pictures' and in the Papers. Meeting our Joyce's fella has certainly opened me eyes. He comes from a very wealthy and highly educated family. He grew up in a house that had an inside toilet - I've seen pictures! And don't give me that tripe about Mandingo, I've seen the cover...and your face has gone red"

 "it was a bit rude"

 "Get your coat on or we'll miss the shops. Never forget Alice, Hitler was white, and look where he was leading the world to!"
"Yeah but he was a German. You can't judge us English by a GERMAN!"

 "Well DON'T judge my future son in law by a daft book set in slavery days. He's never even been to America"

 "Son in law? So if they have kids, what will THEY be?"

 "MY GRANDCHILDREN! Any more daft questions?"

 "Gawd. I was only asking! AY Flo? Is it cos you're a bit Jewish, that you're not as bothered about foreigners as some people?"

 "A BIT JEWISH!? *God. Take me now!* It could be Alice. Is it cos YOU'RE 'TAPPED' that you come across as an idiot?"

TALK ABOUT TWO-FACED!

"This country's not the same anymore Flo"

"You might be right Alice. After all, Victoria's not on the throne. Like she was when you were a kid"

"Why am I even friends with you? Is that how they raise you in Yorkshire? To drip sarcasm? And are you putting the kettle on? I've been here for minutes!"

"You weren't forced to come round here. We won the war remember. We're not Nazis. Anyway I put it on as soon as I heard you coughing your way up me lobby. You want to lay off the Senior Service"

"Hark at you. The Woodbine's queen"

"Me doctor told me to go on them. They're 'good for you' He smokes 'em"

"Does he? Let me try one. Ooh they are 'smooth' aren't they? *cough, splutter!* I bet they'd be perfect with a brew. If I had one!"

"Eeyar, how many lumps?"

"Ooh, have you got sugar cubes?"

"No. The bag's damp. So what were you moaning about when you come in?"

"Bloody Paper shop. Full of kids"

"And?"

"It took me ten minutes to get to the magazine rack for me Woman's Realm. When are they going back to school?"

"What're you asking me for?"

"You've got about a hundred grandkids. I thought you'd know"

"I've got SIX!"

"From an only child. Are you sure there's no Irish in the family? Mind you, the coloureds breed like rabbits 'an all. Your Joyce must regret the day she met a foreigner. Give it another twenty years and there'll be more of them, than there is of us"

"Well if you're an example of 'US' I'm glad! You're two steps away from getting thrown out of here, Alice Clough. What have I told you about making remarks towards my family?"

"WHAT'VE I SAID? You can't even mention population growth nowadays without someone taking it the wrong way"

"it's not what you say. It's how you say it. All this 'them' and 'us' nonsense. We're all human beings"

"I think you're being a tad unfair, Florence. You're going on like I'm prejudiced. How can I be prejudiced when I give crochet squares to OXFAM? You do it all the time"

"I don't crochet"

"Ha, bloody ha! I meant you change the meaning of what I'm saying"

"No Alice. I don't change it, I 'GET' it. Mind you, at least you're consistent. Man, woman, child, beast. You can't stand any of them"

"I LOVE animals. It's cheeky kids I can't stand. They're like bloody animals. Why's your face like that?"

"I just wondering what I did to deserve you, you daft sod. Let's have a gander at your magazine then?"

"Buy your own, you tight get - DON'T crease the pages!"

"What do you buy this rubbish for? I mean who has a bouffant and twin-set on when they're cooking"

"People with CLASS that's who. Anyway I buy this one, mainly for the patterns. They cost a fortune in the wool shop. Look at them doilies on page thirty five. Aren't they lovely?"

"I've got doilies coming out of me ears, ever since I taught our Lesley to 'French knit'...Can't stand 'em"

"Well that's what you're getting off me for your birthday, Flo"

"Ideal for you innit? Giving someone, something they hate for their birthday!"

"I was just testing you. I was gonna get you some perfume. But you're definitely getting doilies now. That's what happens to ungrateful people"

Well you'll be getting 'em back for yours "There's the door!. It'll be Jim, come to do me feet. Are you stopping?"

"To watch you have your corns cut off? Ew, I don't think so.Come round to mine later. If you can walk. You know he got sacked from the surgery? Ruined Martha Hodges feet. She's in a wheelchair now. He knows as much about Chiropody as I do about Timbuktoo - Oh hiya Jim. You're looking well. I was just saying to Flo, not seen you at the surgery for ages. I was wanting to book you for me hard skin. But I'm sorted now. Anyway, I'm off. See you later Flo - If you can make it"

Alice leave. with an air of triumph

"Catching flies Flo?"

"No, Jim. Just gobsmacked at the barefaced cheek of some people. *TUT!* I saved some old newspapers for your clippings. Should I sit on our Bob's chair as usual?"

10: FOOD FOR THOUGHT

RANDOM DISCUSSIONS AROUND FOOD AND DRINK

GETTING THE TEA IN

"Alice. You're gonna get corned beef legs, standing that close to the fire. And you're blocking the heat. But whilst you're there, make yourself useful and give it a poke.Then MOVE!"

"You wouldn't believe it was June, would you Flo?"

"I can't believe the amount of coal I'm going through, at this time of year. We haven't had a decent summer since Moses went to school ... With you! It's all this modern rubbish. Like Cars. And all that stuff you have to plug in. That's why we keep having loads of thunder storms. The used up electric has got to go somewhere - Our Joyce has got a plug in kettle. Have you ever heard owt so daft. Water AND electricity. Did none of them watch THE PERILS OF PAULINE? And then. When it's what 'it' calls boiled, you don't get a whistle. You get a 'click' Who can hear that? You'd die of thirst if you was deaf"

"I've always thought your Joyce made an horrible brew. Now I know why"

"You're a cheeky cow you are. Don't stand in my house calling MY daughter. If there's anything about my daughter you don't like, please feel free to sod off!"

"What did I say? I don't know what I'm supposed to have said ?" *what?*

"You're hard faced. I'll give you that"

"But I didn't mean your Joyce was horrible *I'm saying that with me fingers crossed* I said her brews were. It's like you said, no whistle. How are you supposed to know the water's boiled properly without a whistle?"

Hmm"Anyway we'd better get our skates on if we want to catch the shops. It's half day closing"

"Innit funny how we always forget stuff on half day closing. Last week I ran out of butter and couldn't get none for love nor money. Me crumpets for tea were horrible with just Jam on"

"You should have knocked on mine"

"I did, but you wasn't in"

"You should have asked her next door to you then"

"Are you mad?! She's filthy! Last time I borrowed summat off her it was covered in Cat hair"

"What did you borrow? The Cat" *Chuckle*

"Ha ha Florence. Very bloody funny. What do you need from the shops, anyway? Your kitchenette looks full to bursting"

"The only thing that's bursting is the hinge on the pull down. The grandkids keep sitting on it. I've told 'em. *One day, the whole thing is gonna collapse on you,* I said - *And then we'll have to bury you, and you won't get no toys for Christmas*- But they still don't listen. I need some cooking cheese. I just fancy a cheese and onion pie for 'tea' tonight"

"I can only eat white cheese. That cooking cheese takes the roof off me mouth"

"Well lucky for you Alice, I'm not inviting you to stay. The roof of your mouth will be safe tonight. What are you having for your tea?"

"Oh I don't know. It's hard to be bothered when you're all on your own. 'Specially at tea-time. Sometimes I think, why bother Alice. Who'd miss you? I'd be better off six feet under"

"Well if you're planning to commit suicide by not having any tea it'll be a long slow death, judging by the size of ya!"

"Oh thanks for bloody caring!"

"I tell you what. I'll get two ounces of 'Lancashire' and make you a little pie of your own"

"Can I not have cheese on toast, Flo? Pastry plays havoc with me ulcer"

"Nowt like cheek is there! Go on then ... Hey you cheeky sod. Your ulcer's on your leg!"

THE TRIFLE THIEF

"Alice?"

"Ooh I don't like that tone. What am I supposed to have done?"

"You're about to find out luv! When you came round the other day. Just as we'd finished our tea. And I said help yourself to anything from the table? Whatever possessed you to do what you did? I wondered why you got off so quickly"

"I didn't hear you say 'table' Are you sure you said 'table' Flo?"

"That's not the point - And YES I bloody did. What do you think I am? Some kind of idiot who walks around saying 'Eeyar I'm a right bloody fool me. I make trifles and give 'em away'"

"What do you mean?"

"Oh here we go. Acting daft are we? Well it doesn't wash with me, Alice. You nicked my trifle, and I wanna know WHY?"

"Well for a start Sherlock hemlock I didn't nick any trifle. You always do your trifle in a glass bowl. I took what was in the MIXING BOWL"

"I broke my glass bowl"

"Well how was I to know that. It's not like you said 'Oh Alice I've had to make me trifle in the mixing bowl so don't take that. Even if you have been told to take what you want, and it's staring you in the face'"

"And whilst you were staring back, did you not notice the hundreds and thousands? Was that not a cunning clue as to what it was? Why don't YOU name me, a pudding other than a trifle that has hundreds and thousands on it?"

"A Manchester Tart"

"YOU LIAR. THAT HAS BLOODY COCONUT ON IT"

"Not if you've run out, and all you've got is hundreds and thousands"

"You'd swear blind a mouse was an elephant, you would. Just to get out of something. I wondered why I didn't see head nor hide of you yesterday. For once I wish you had come round. Just to see the look on my poor Bob's face when I handed him an Eccles cake with custard for his pudding, cos that's all I had in. It's the first Sunday since the rationing ended that's he's not had trifle after his sunday dinner. And that's down to YOU"

"Oh it's like that is it Flo? You'd wished for ONCE that I'd come round? Well I know where I'm not wanted!"

"There you go again. Only hearing what you want to"

"And I think I've heard enough! No such thing as an honest mistake, in your eyes is there? Mrs Florence 'I'm so Perfect'. You seem to forget all the things I give you. You see that pile of 'People's friend' on your sideboard? Where did they come from? ME!"

"There's a big difference, Alice, between a pile of magazines you've pinched from the Doctor's and an homemade trifle. You must have a season ticket to that surgery. You could open your own Paper shop, the amount of magazines you nick from there. And you still haven't explained why you took me trifle"

"I took the so called trifle cos I thought it was one of your experiments gone wrong - Remember your egg-less cakes in the war? *shudder* - I didn't check what was inside. It was an honest mistake"

"And when you was eating it what did you think it was then?"

"Well I won't lie Flo. It did taste like trifle. Aw I'm dead sorry"

HMMPH! "And I want me bowl back"

"I'll run round for it now. I've just got a little errand to run. I'll be back in a hour

Alice leaves. And true to her word, returns in an hour

"Well thanks for me bowl back - What's this?"

"It's a Battenburg. Are you blind?!"

"I can bloody see what it is Alice. What's it doing in me bowl?"

"It's a peace offering to say sorry, although it WAS a genuine mistake"

"I believe you. *Thousands wouldn't* Put the kettle on - And don't nick the kippers on the window sill or Bob'll have nowt for his tea"

"You're never gonna let this drop, are ya?"

ONLY IDIOTS THINK STORK IS BETTER THAN BUTTER

"Where should we go for our Tea?"

"I've just put an extra boiled egg on! I thought you was staying here, to help finish off the last of the ham?"

"I meant when we go to Blackpool"

"Alice! That's not for another fortnight"

"Yeah, but remember last year? It was like eating old boots. And when you've saved for months it's heartbreaking to waste your money like that"

"YOU DIDN'T EVEN PAY. You only came with us cos Mrs Flynn died and her daughter didn't want the ticket to go to waste"

"Aw I know. Weren't that nice of her? She didn't even want it for herself"

"Yeah! It must have been murder trying to decide. Should I go on the 'Bobs' or grieve me recently departed mam?"

"Are you being sarcky, Florence?"

"Only where it's needed. Do us favour? Get the salad cream out of the kitchenette. Do you want a bit of salad with it? I've got some lettuce and cucumber. And I'm sure there's a tomato on the window sill"

"Ooh no. I can't stand rabbit food. Have you got bread and butter?"

"Is the Pope a Catholic"

"Is it proper butter though?"

"Adam's BEST! Why are you interrogating me over butter? You know I only have butter"

"I had me tea at that Wilma Holroyd's, the other day - What are you looking at me like that for? We got talking when I knocked on to tell her that she'd missed some man who'd been knocking at her door for ages. And he didn't look like a Club-man. So I thought it might be important"

"You knocked on to be nosy"

"Yeah, well that's by the by. Anyway She'd asked me in cos she was in the middle of 'tea' and she ended up asking me to stay"

"And you did! Cos she hadn't told you who the mystery man was, yet. You're a right hypocrite Alice. The last time you went in there you said there was more grease on the kitchen walls then there was in the chip pan"

"I like to give people a second chance. Nowt wrong with that is there?"

"So who did it turn out to be?"

"Who did 'who' turn out to be?"

"The fella at the DOOR?"

"Oh him? Turned out it WAS a club-man. He's new. He hasn't got got that haggard look yet"

"Ok, but where does the butter come into it?"

"Oh yeah, I was telling you til you interrupted me . Like I said, she invited me for tea. Kippers with brown bread and buttter"

"Give me white bread any day. I can't stand Hovis, and it's dead little. You're lucky if you get six slices out of it"

"I've seen them doorsteps you give your grandkids. I'm surprised YOU get more than one slice. But back to HER bread and 'butter' Which turned out to be bleedin' STORK. You got better during the War. I'd spread it dead thick an all, before I realised. The sly cow had unwrapped it and put it in the butter dish, so I had to sit there with a mouth full of dog's do and pretend I was enjoying it. It's an experience I'd sooner not repeat so I'm checking what you've got"

"Well don't worry about that Luv. I'm not one of those idiots Leslie Crowther's been fooling. He wants to stick to Crackerjack. Only best butter in this house. They'll be saying it's bad for you next! We've won two wars on butter and lard, and now some scientist is trying to convince us that something grown by

Frankenstein is better than summat what comes out of a real life Cow"

"You're not wrong Flo"

"I never am Alice - And they're all Nazis"

"Who are?"

"The Scientists. I read it in the Tit-Bits"

"Makes you wonder why we even bothered winning the War. Are them eggs boiled yet?"

ROBBED!

"I've been robbed Flo"

"What? Who by? Where? Did they get your pension? Was it one of them hippies? No way was it on Moston Lane? Was it in Harpurhey? It's getting rough round there? Have you called the Police?"

"Gawd! Take a breath woman! I've been robbed by the Government"

"THE GOVERNMENT? You nearly had me rooting for me Angina spray. What are you talking about you daft sod? I nearly had kittens"

"Well if you'd have let me get a word in edge ways I would

have elaborated"

"Elaborate then, Alice. You know I don't like mysteries"

"It's this new bloody money. They're robbin' us blind and there's nowt we can do about it. Last night - are you putting that kettle on?"

"It's on! Go on? I can brew up and listen at the same time"

"Last night, I just fancied a Mars Bar. Well you show me a shop round here where you can get a Mars bar at eight o clock in the evening. Anyway when I went for me pension today, I still had the craving - No I'm not pregnant?" *Chuckle*

"My Joyce is two months gone. I reckon by the time you get to the point with this story, the kid'll be drawing it's own pension"

"Sarcky! Do you want to hear the rest or not, Florence?"

"I'm slowly losing the will to live, but yeah. Carry on"

"Where was I? - Oh yeah - Mars Bars. So I popped in the Paper shop. Not the one near the Post office. I can't stand her behind the counter. The one up here"

"AND?" *Talk about loving the sound of your own voice!*

"I'm getting to it Flo. So I thought I'd get two. Eat one, save one - Why are you huffing?"

"I'm blowing me tea. It's hot. Go on?" *Before I hit you over the head with me tea strainer.*

"Guess how much they bleeding charged me? A SHILLING! Oh

they say it's five pence - Two and a half pence each BUT It's a soddin' shilling. After we risked life and limb during the war. They've got the cheek to rob us, now we're pensioners"

"I know what you mean Alice but we worked at Ferranti's during the war. We weren't exactly on the Front line"

"Our husbands did - Well not yours, he was too old. And not mine either, but he had special skills. He was exempted - And what were we making Flo? Bomb bits. Do you think the Germans didn't know where our factory was? Think about it luv?"

"You've got a point - And hey! you cheeky cow. My Bob served his time in the Great War - A shilling for two Mars bars? You could have bought the factory they make 'em in"

"I'm writing to me MP"

"I wouldn't bother luv. You'll probably have to dip in to your funeral savings for the stamp"

"Why do things have to change Flo? We knew where we were with proper money. When they do stuff like this they should wait til we're all dead"

"That's commonsense Alice. The government don't do commonsense. What we need is a Woman Prime Minister"

"Like that'll ever happen. Anyway do you want half a Mars Bar with your brew?"

"I thought you'd bought two?"

"Yeah I did, but at these prices I'm looking to eat it in more salubrious surroundings"

"Salubrious? What does that mean when it's at home? Are you insulting me and my house?"

"As if I would Flo"

"Give us half then?"

"Eeyar. Eat it whilst the brew is still warm"

"Is THAT what you call half, Alice? You'd be lynched if you were pulling pints"

"Some people have NO gratitude"

"And some people have no friends, but me! So they should be bleedin' cherishing them. Not half starving 'em"

"Remortgage your house and buy your own Mars Bars. Anyway I can't stand here all day. Me step needs doing. Are you coming to mine later?"

"Yeah. But don't worry I'll bring me own tea. Wouldn't want you having to give me half of yours"

"Ha, ha, bloody ha...See you later"

And it's pointless hiding the biscuit tin. I know all your hiding places.

I THOUGHT YOU WERE DEAD!

Bang, Bang,

"Hang on. I'm coming"

BANG, BANG, BANG,

"I SAID I'M COMING ... Bloody ell Flo. Give me a chance to get to the door"

"Oh Alice. Thank god for that. I thought you were dead"

"Dead? You don't do things by halves do you? It didn't cross you mind that I might be poorly? You just went straight for 'dead'. I bet you've already been in the Cake shop and ordered a few extra white sliced for the wake butties"

"Well pardon me for caring Alice 'Sarcky drawers' No one's seen hide nor hair of you for three days. I thought you might have gone to visit your sister, but then I thought, NO she would have told me. And when you didn't come out on pension day, I did start wondering. But I proper fretted this morning cos there was a big scrap on Stovell road - Redifussion trying to repossess a telly off the Nolans - If she was well, she'd definitely be here, I thought to meself. You're 'back to back' with the Nolans and no one can accuse you of being deaf! Anyway what's up with you?"

"I don't know. I just feel out of sorts. I can't believe I never heard a thing. Mind you I've been sleeping on the settee. Not got the energy to move"

"Right well get yourself to bed. I'm gonna tidy up and make you a soft boiled egg, and if you're still not feeling any better, I'm getting the doctor. Where's your hot water bottle?"

"Under the sink"

"Bloomin' eck Alice. You need to move with the times luv. Have you not got a rubber one. Even I've not had a stone one since Moses was a lad"

"Well you can buy me one for Christmas. Until then, I'll make do ... I'll go in the back room. You never know"

"It's all done now. They give em the telly back, and a few choice words an' all. You missed a good 'un Alice. I even sent our Lesley to knock on, but she said there was no answer"

"Oh was that her? One little tap on the door. Superman couldn't have got there in time. I thought it was kids playing knock-a-door-run"

"I'll be having words with madam. She said she was knocking for ages. That's why I ended up coming round meself. I had visions of your cold lifeless body lying on the kitchen floor"

"You watch too much Alfred Hitchcock you do. And I know she's your grandaughter Flo, but she can be a bit 'sly' can your Lesley"

"Yeah you're right Alice. She IS my grandchild, and we'd best leave it at that, don't you think? I don't want to be falling out with you. Not when you're half starved. She means well, she probably wanted to get back quick to see the rest of the row"

She definitely takes after you "Alright. Least said, soonest mended. Do y'know? I'm feeling a bit better already. Where's that chucky egg you promised me? I've just realised, I've not eaten for days .. And a brew wouldn't go amiss"

"Oy! what did your last slave die of? I'll be up with it in a bit. I'm just gonna mop that floor and tidy up a bit. If you do die, you don't want anyone thinking you were a slut"

SOME PEOPLE ARE NOT USED TO HAVING THINGS

"You know what, Flo? They're not used to things, some people"

"Why do you say that, Alice?"

"THEM! On the same street, as him, who has the same Chiropodist as you"

"I've not got a bleedin' clue who you're on about?"

"The fella that does your feet!"

"I KNOW what a chiropodist is! What I DON'T know, is who you mean when you say, him who gets seen by Billy, as well"

"Who's Billy?"

"ME BLOODY CHIROPODIST! Alice? Should we start again? *Before I'm tempted to slap you* WHO are you talking about, that ISN'T my chiropodist?"

"His name's on the tip of my tongue. Remember when we were in the Greengrocer's that time. With your Joyce,and there was this fella stood in front of us, waiting to be served. And your chiropodist came in, and you and the fella stood in front of us, both said, at the same time *Why do me feet always throb when i see you*... Remember?"

"Ah! I know who you mean now. Danny Roberts"

"Are you sure? That doesn't sound like the name that's on the tip of me tongue"

"Well you must have the bloody wrong one, on it then! It's definitely Danny. I remember that day well. We all cracked up laughing. All except our Joyce - I wonder if she's mine sometimes. So what about him?"

"If you're saying THAT'S his name, I'll have to believe you...But it's not him I'm talking about anyway"

How do you even get up in the mornings "So WHO, for the umpteenth time, ARE you talking about?"

"THEM! Down the street from him. Are you going senile, Flo?"

"I'm going 'something' I'll put the kettle on, whilst you get your brain into gear"

TUT! "I'll start from the beginning, shall I?"

"It'd be a good help, Alice" *sigh.*

"I was walking up Millais street, Cos it's a good shortcut, coming back from the cemetery .I went to see Bridget McCarthy. I'm not Catholic as you know, but we did get on, me and her when we were little. It was Polio that got her. Only about six or seven,she was. None of us found out she was dead, for years. They didn't want to upset us, I suppose. My mam told me she'd moved to Wythenshawe. I used to wonder, who with. Cos her mam and dad stayed on Kenyon Lane"

"The last time you told me this story. You said it was Marple, where she'd moved to"

"Did I? You might be right Flo. But the point I'm trying to make, is she was dead, but we thought she'd moved - Anyway, that's not what I'm trying to tell you"

"GOOD! Cos you've told me that one, a million times"

"Stop exaggerating! And it's not like you don't repeat yourself. I know the story, of how Bob fell in love with your Cottage pie, before he fell in love with you, inside- bloody- out. In fact I can't eat Cottage pie anymore, because of it"

"You ate one HERE, the other day"

"That was a Shepherd's you said?"

"You keep fooling yourself, luv. Have you seen the price of lamb? Anyway. Go on with your story" *Before I lose the will to live.*

"So I was walking past this house. The one three doors down from that Danny -or whatever he's called, and I couldn't help but notice, that the front curtains were wide open, and it looked like the nets had fallen down. Bloody horrible wallpaper.

Anyway, I've took a couple more steps, and the front door's wide open. And there's a Woman, in her lobby, with a feather duster. Just swiffin' it over the dado rails"

"Did you tell her, her nets were down?"

"What do you take me for? Course I did! *Eeyar luv* I said *Do you know that your front curtains are wide open and your nets have fallen down. Everyone can see right in.* Hear her, back to me *Ooh! Have they?*"

"Was she doing a posh accent like that?"

"Worse! *Let me have a look* She says -LIKE I'M LYING! - *Oh you're right. You can see everything. Even me Hostess trolley*"

"HOSTESS TROLLEY? How far is it from her kitchen? Has she got Buckingham Palace hidden under her stairs? What a bloody show-off. So what did you say?"

"I'd got the measure of her. The boastful tart! I acted like I hadn't even heard her. I bet she'd seen me coming from the bottom of the street and pulled the nets down deliberately. If I hadn't just thrown a penny in the grotto for Bridget, I'd have given her a few choice words.But guess what I DID say to her?"

"Go on"

"I said...'I'd put them nets up sharpish, if I was you. Your wallpaper is bloody horrible!"

"Some people just aren't used to having anything, Alice. Bessie Charlton was like that when she got her first fur stole. Wore it right through Summer. Looked a right idiot. And remember

Annie Beckett at her daughter's wedding? With the price tag hanging off her hat. Who pays two guineas for a HAT? Mind you, I heard she'd taken it back to Kendals after the wedding. So leaving the price tag on, makes sense ... I'd be wrong to call her a show-off. She's more of a 'swindling git. But like I said, there's plenty of people out there, who aren't used to having anything. And most of 'em are no better than they ought to be, anyway"

"You're not wrong, Flo. If someone told me now, they'd seen a woman pushing a Hostess trolley round the market. I just say 'Oh it's her from Millais street. She's one of them who's not used to having owt' ... I'd love one meself though. Wouldn't you?"

"Oh yeah. Especially at Christmas. All them compartments, to keep your food hot? I'm always meeting meself coming back on Christmas day. I'd feel like the Queen, with an Hostess trolley. I wouldn't take it to the Pictures with me though"

Chuckle "Shurrup you daft sod. Top up this brew for me. I called in the butcher's first, before I came here and got two ounces of Prem. Have you got bread? We can have a butty"

"When have I ever not got bread?"

SUPERSTITION

"Hello Alice. You got here safely I see"

"Well the wars over, so we're not being bombed. And it's only the two entries, I've got to come up. So, why wouldn't I get here in one piece?"

"The date!"

"Is it your wedding anniversary?"

"Why would I want you here for THAT? No, it's Friday the 13th"

"It dunt bother me, Flo"

"Well it does me"

"I'm not one bit superstitious. I've been walking under ladders and crossing black cats all my life. And 'touch wood' nowts ever happened to me"

"TOUCH WOOD! And you say you're not superstitious?"

"That's not a superstition. That's a Saying"

"Course it's a soddin' superstition. You say 'touch wood' in the hope that everything will go well for you!"

"I DON'T! I say it for luck"

You stupid woman! "Anyway you're here now...What do you want?"

"What do you mean? What do I want? It was YOU what told me to come round"

"Oh yeah. I need you to go to the shop for me. Me and Friday the thirteenth don't get on. So like i said, I'm staying put"

"I hope it's not for heavy stuff. I've got 'knees' you know"

"Well you'd have trouble sitting down if you didn't! Just get me a small hovis-

"Do they do a big hovis?-

"Shurrup! I can't stand it, but Bob loves his brown bread. And you can get me five pounds of spuds as well"

"FIVE POUNDS OF SPUDS? They'll weigh a ton!"

"No they won't. They'll weigh five pounds! And you're only going round the corner! But if it's too much for you, we can always have our tea without potatoes. If you can call that a proper tea"

Bleedin' blackmailer!" I'm going! Give me your list then?"

"You don't need a list. I only want spuds and an hovis"

"Well don't blame me if I forget something"

"Like what? your brain! I'm putting the kettle on, so hurry up. I'm gonna put us a couple of boiled eggs on. We can have egg and soldiers for our dinner"

"Don't make mine runny. It goes right through me when it's

runny. But not hard either. It binds me up summat chronic when I eat hard boiled eggs"

You're just getting toast! "Not fussy are we? Hurry up then! Before the shop shuts for dinner"

Alice goes to the shop. Upon her return...

"What's up with ya?"

"I'm just getting me breath back Flo. I'm sure these spuds weigh more than 5lbs"

"I wish. Where's the bread?"

"I told you to give me a list! I got talking to John behind the counter. So you can blame him for putting me off"

"You're as useful as a chocolate tea-pot sometimes. I've got some Nimble in the bread bin, we'll have to use that. I keep it in for our Joyce. She's forever on a diet"

"She needs to stop getting pregnant. That's what causes weight gain"

"You don't say, Sherlock. How many slices?"

"Two. Are we still having soldiers?"

"I'll try, but it's round bread. I'm not sure it'll go into proper soldiers"

"Leave it then Flo. I don't want to put you out. Just a scraping of butter on mine, and will you cut the crusts off. I've already got curly hair"

"Don't put yourself out, she says. I thought you weren't superstitious, Alice?"

"I'm NOT"

"So why did you just throw salt over your shoulder?"

"Tradition! which is an entirely different thing. This bread tastes like fresh air. And I'll prove I'm not superstitious. Remember before when we was talking about wedding anniversaries?"

"You was. I didn't say owt!"

"What date did I get married?"

"I can't remember that far back, Alice"

"The thirteenth of May"

"It wasn't a Friday though or I'd had said I'm not coming. And I was your Matron of honour, so I'm a hundred percent sure it wasn't a Friday"

"I've got me wedding certificate in me handbag if you want proof - Oh yeah, you're right. It wasn't a Friday. It was still the thirteenth though"

"Why have you got your wedding certificate in your handbag?"

"Just in case"

"Just in case what?"

"I don't know. Just in case I need it. Where do you keep yours?"

"In a Quality street tin, in the sideboard. Like normal people"

"In your button tin? What if the kids got hold of it, and coloured it in or summat"

"Me button tin's an old biscuit tin. Everyone knows I use the Quality street tin for important paperwork. And my grandkids don't go in tins without permission. They're brought up, not dragged up"

"You might have a point though Flo, about the thirteenth"

Don't ask. Don't ask "Go on then. Why?"

"Well Like you said, it wasn't a Friday, but it WAS the thirteenth I married that weasel. And only one of us is dead!"

"YOU DAFT APETH! But see what I mean? If you'd gone for the Friday it could have been the two of you in the cemetery"

"It wouldn't have been the same one. No way would I be interred any where near him!"

"Ooh, aren't we getting morbid? Come outside with me, whilst I sweep the backyard. I might see a magpie"

Daft sod!

A BREW AND A BARNEY!

"This tea's a bit funny, Flo"

"Funny 'ha, ha' or funny 'peculiar'?"

"Can you see me laughing?"

"Only if summat bad happens to someone you can't stand"

"I'll pretend I didn't hear that! Look at the colour of it?"

"It looks fine to me"

"It looks too orange to me"

"Well it doesn't look one bit orange to me. And I'm not begging you to drink it. Why don't you go to your own house for a change. I bet your tea caddy's got cobwebs on it!"

"God! Aren't you touchy? It tastes fine -ish. It just looks a bit funny that's all. Is it proper milk or stera?"

"When have you ever seen a bottle of stera on my kitchen window sill? We only have real milk in this house. I'm from Sheffield. I grew up with cows. I'm not like you, jumping up and down like a demented whatsit cos you've seen two cows and some sheep, out of the sharra window. Every soddin' time we've been to Blackpool, you've done that"

"You're just as bad on Tib Street. D'ya know what'd be nice? If we could walk down Tib street, just once, without you having to sing 'How much is that doggie in the window?'"

"You're offended by a sense of humour, aren't ya? It could be your eyesight"

"What ARE you talking about Flo?"

"I'm talking about you, saying the tea looks orange. The reason why the tea looks orange could be because your eyes are going?"

"Me eyes are going nowhere. Thank you very soddin' much! There's nowt wrong with my eyes. I've got perfect vision. The only reason I wear glasses, is for reading. Looking at tea is NOT reading, is it? I've seen orange jelly, less orangey than this tea"

"Let me have a look. I'm taking it, you've took the cup into account?"

"What's that supposed to mean?"

"The cup! It's new. Well almost new. Our Joyce bought a set of six, with matching saucers. She got 'em to go with her kitchen - She's gone all orange. She's even got a real plastic colander. In orange. Anyway when she got home, these weren't the 'right' orange, so she gave them to me. She's only had a brew in one of 'em.To test it. So they're practically brand new"

"It's Brown! This cup and saucer you've given me is BROWN"

"Is it eck! Are you trying to say my daughter's blind now? She's the one who bought it. As an ORANGE cup and saucer. She didn't give it me cos it's brown. She gave it me cos it was the WRONG ORANGE. Eeyar, what colour is that tea-pot?"

"All colours"

"Take the bloody cosy off first" *How do I put up with you!*

"It's brown. But name me a tea-pot you've had, that wasn't brown?"

"I've got the stainless steel one, from the set our Joyce bought me, last Birthday"

"Yeah but you'll never use it, will ya?"

"Ew, will I eck. I'm not drinking tea out of metal. I'm not a night watchman. But don't breathe a word to our Joyce. It's the thought that counts. Anyway, you agree with me, that the tea-pot you're looking at, is brown?"

"Is Perry Mason back on? Yeah, I agree the tea-pot is Brown ... Like the cup!"

"Put the cup next to the tea-pot - I saw that shudder! - Go on then? What colour's the cup?"

"Well my giddy bloomin' Aunt! Have you got David Nixon hiding behind the curtains? The cup looks orange-ish now"

"Never mind the 'ish' It's orange innit?"

"Well yeah it is. It's like summat Tommy Cooper would do - He's dead funny though int he? Mind you, he'd have to be. He'd get booed off the stage if his tricks were all he had. He's RUBBISH at magic"

"It's what they call a two-tone effect. *You've never heard of it. I can tell!* It gives the pottery a shimmery effect and it flits between colours"

"Do ya know? I watching that programme UFO the other day - I was waiting for the news to come on and I couldn't be mithered turning it over - This is the sort of 'in the future' stuff they have on there. I'm not sure i want to live in nineteen eighty. The hairstyles are horrible, and cars fly. But what's any of that got to do with me saying the tea looked orange?"

"Do you practice being THICK?"

CHICKEN IN A TIN

"You can get bacon in a packet now. I was in the co-op and I couldn't make me mind up whether or not to buy one. But then I thought, Oh go on Alice, treat yourself"

Shurrup waffling "Good for you. I prefer mine from the butcher's. You can see what you're getting. And you get more rashers for your money. You're just paying for a bit of plastic"

God! Dunt she drone on "It looks loads nicer when you display it in the fridge"

"DISPLAY IT! Mine gets unwrapped and straight in the pan luv. Who the 'eck displays food?"

"Erm if I recall rightly. When your Bob's sister came to visit, you got all your Christmas stuff out. And you borrowed my four tins of Chicken in a tin. She wasn't daft you know. Who has a tin of Quality Street open in November? And as for the Peek Frean assortment casually loitering on a doily where you normally keep a fruit bowl filled with your fags and pools coupons - Well all I'm saying is pot, kettle, black"

"Shurrup! I only did that because she's a snooty cow. Thinks she's the only person in the world who eats Battenburg on a week day. Anyway, are you ever gonna eat that tinned chicken?"

"Ew no! There's summat not right about chicken in a tin. But ever since I started getting a hamper - cos I can't do a big shop with my knees. Plus people get on my nerves. There's only so many times you can say 'And a Merry Christmas to you, too' without your face starting to hurt - Where was I? -Oh yeah. Every time the hamper comes, there's a tin of chicken in it. So What am I supposed to do"

"Why don't you give it to the church for Harvest Festival?"

"Are you mental, Flo? I'm one of the pensioners they give the food to. If I start giving them tins of Chicken, they'll think I can manage"

"You can! I mean look how lucky you are. Your husband died when you were in your twenties and had proper insurance. A two bedroom house all to yourself. No mortgage. A tidy sum every month to live on. You're laughing!"

"Oh yeah. It's dead lucky being widowed!"

"Alice Clough. Don't let me and you, be falling out. Did you or did you not, hate his guts? DID HE OR DID HE NOT. Leave you, 3 months after the wedding? WERE YOU OR WERE YOU NOT, celebrating cos you heard he was ill, a week before he died?"

"That's not the point. It was still a sad time in my life ... For a bit"

"Is that why you were cutting the head off a peg doll? A peg doll with clothes you made from his pyjamas. On one of your wedding anniversaries"

"As he sowed, so he bloody reaped. You don't leave me for some 'Tart' from the library and expect me to do nowt. I told you I had special powers. Sometimes someone just has to get on me nerves and the strangest things happen"

"Are you saying you 'thought' him to death?"

"I'm not saying anything til Perry Mason gets here"

"Oh shurrup you daft sod. I still mean what I said. You can manage"

"Barely. And it's not just me in the house is it? And I'm Electric throughout. Unlike some *sniff!* Running a modern home doesn't come cheap"

"Oh yeah, I forgot about Mrs Tiggywinkle. I think I read it in the 'Titbits' Something about Poodles being notorious for leaving the 'big light' on *Sniff on that, cowface!* Why don't you save some money on dog food and give her the Chicken in a tin?"

"You don't give a dog of my Poodle's pedigree, that rubbish. She has them 'Pal minced morsels' everyday, like that posh dog Henry and Clement Whojamaflip. And a Winalot bone as a treat! I don't give her rubbish . Only the best for my little precious"

"I bet she'd love a massive bone from the Butcher's to chomp on. My Roger used to love a bone. Daft sod never gave up trying to bury 'em in the backyard. That's why his claws were always dead short"

"Tiggy's teeth are too delicate for a bone"

"She's a dog!"

"She's not THAT kind of dog!"

"Can she talk?"

"Well not in English, but I understand everything she's trying to tell me. Why?"

"I'm surprise you haven't shunned her for being foreign. My Budgie can talk"

"Your budgie CAN'T TALK. Your budgie can 'copy'"

"No luv! My budgie says recognisable words IN ENGLISH. You just put your own meaning on your dog's yapping"

"I'm not gonna sit here arguing with you about my dog"

"Go home then!"

"I will!"

"GOOD!"

"Are you still coming to the Jumble with me, tomorrow?"

"Course I am"

11: TRIALS AND TRIBULATIONS

YET MORE STUFF FOR FLO AND ALICE TO HAVE A MOAN ABOUT

THE GLASS EYE

FLO GETS HER REVENGE FOR TED

"I can't stand that Cliff Richard"

"Don't let our Lesley hear you say that Alice. She'll have your good eye out with her skipping rope. She's planning on marrying him, when she grows up"

"What are you trying to say about my other eye? We've had this conversation before, Flo. It's a real eye! Why would I have a glass eye and not tell people?"

"Cos you're embarrassed. Remember how you went on about my brother's? Anyway, it never moves. No matter what direction you're looking in. That eye looks straight ahead. I'm not mithered mind. I'm not one to turn me back on someone with an affliction ... That's probably the reason why we don't often see, eye to eye" *Chuckle*

"It is NOT GLASS! Next time you're round at mine, look at that photo of me mam, on the sideboard. It's the family squint. We've got the exact same eyes. I get my looks from her"

"I'd already noticed. And I'd presumed her 'look' had been left to you, in her will - 'To our Alice, I leave ten bob ... And me glass eye'"

"You're not funny"

"I think I am!"

"Anyway, why's your Lesley swooning over a man old enough to be her dad? - Oh! I forgot. May to December weddings run in your family, don't they?"

"Bringing up that old chestnut again? You're just jealous"

"What of? his pension? or his stick?"

TUT! "Mind how you talk about my Bob. Your under HIS roof remember. Sitting on his chair, supping tea out of his pots! ... Come to think of it, what's Cliff Richard got to do with anything?"

"I was just reading the Radio Times. He's representing us in the Eurovision song contest at weekend. He dunt represent me, he sets me teeth on edge with that caterwauling. They should have someone like Perry Como. That's what you call proper singing"

"Perry Como's not English"

"Int he? Well Val Doonican then"

"He's not English either, Alice"

"Of course he bloody is, Flo. He comes from Ireland and he's always on the BBC"

"How you lived long enough to get a pension is beyond me!"

"Cheeky sod! And it's a widow's pension. I've got years to go before I get an old age one"

"So you say ... Do you want another brew?"

"Well I was planning on doing me skirtings, but go on. You've twisted me arm. And seeing as everything in here is your Bob's. Does he have any biscuits to go with it? - OY! Watch where you're throwing that tea-towel. You nearly had me eye out"

"Aw sorry. I wasn't thinking. You walked in here as Nelson. Don't want you leaving as Helen Keller, do we?"

"IT'S NOT GLASS! *You're getting on me nerves now!*

DEAD LEG

"I literally can't move, Flo"

"Well how did you get to me house then?"

"You know what I mean you daft sod"

"What's up with ya?"

"I can't feel me leg"

"Well it's still there, Alice - Are them new stockings?"

"Tights actually. American Tan, they're called. I got them from Kendals"

"KENDALS? Where've you got 'Kendals' money from?. You were moaning that you're half starved the other day, cos of your rates bill" *Not that you look it.* And wasn't there talk of you having to go in the Workhouse and have a pauper's grave?"

Tut! "I never said none of that - *You jealous cow* - January sales. Less than half price. I did knock on to see if you wanted to go to 'Town' with me. But you were too busy being a slave to your grandkids ...You know what Flo? They are dead comfy. You get what you pay for in this life and nowt says 'Class' like kendals... I couldn't even bring meself to throw the packaging away. It's dead posh. I'm displaying it on me dressing table"

"Who's gonna see it there?"

"The Window cleaner for one. He's a big girls blouse him. Tells his wife everything. She'll be livid with jealousy"

"You're not normal you. I prefer me stockings. Our Joyce wears tights, they look too complicated for me"

"Oh you just pull 'em on and you're done. None of that faffing about with suspenders, and looking for a ha'penny when the buttons pop off. Snug as a bug in a rug I am in these"

"And do you still wear knickers and a girdle with them?"

"Of course you do! What sort of woman walks round with no knickers?"

"I could write a book. Starting with her at number forty four. And not even a fur coat to make up for it"

"Oh her? You're not wrong Flo. But like I was saying, you just pull them on. They're like a second skin. And no draughts, if you know what I mean?"

"Ah! well that explains your dead leg Alice"

"Ooh I'd forgotten about that. What do you mean?"

"You're all closed in. You're not getting any air to your parts and your groin's seized up. And another thing. if you get a run in one leg you've got to throw the full pair away. False economy Alice. keep the packet though. I might borrow it off you when our Bob's snooty sister comes to visit. Thinks she's better than people cos she lives in Cheadle Hulme"

"I'm gonna nip home and change Flo. You might be right - *For once!* - I'll keep 'em for best. Stick that kettle on, I'll be back in a minute. And I'll treat you to a piece of the luxury shortbread I got as well. It's no more than you deserve. I could have ended up with my leg off"

"Well there's no danger of you ever getting it 'over'"

"You cheeky mare! You can have Rich tea for that"

IT'S THE LITTLE THINGS, THAT LEAD TO THE BIGGEST ARGUMENTS

"You'll never guess what I've just seen, on me way round here?"

"Well it won't be 'sense' So you'll have to give us a clue, Alice?"

*TUT! "*Christmas decorations!"

"They're getting greedy buggars at that co-op. I went in the other day, on the off chance they had candied peel, for my pudding. And they did!"

"Probably last year's Flo - But I didn't mean in the shops. I meant in someone's house. Dangling down off the ceiling. And a tree. With tinsel on it. They'd left the curtains open a bit and you couldn't help but see in. It's people like that who'd have had us getting shot during the war"

"Come again?"

"Leaving the curtains open a bit. You couldn't have gotten away with that during the blackouts. I could see right through to the far wall. They've got a massive picture of the 'Blue Boy on it. And hung straight underneath, three of them plaster heads'"

"You see a lot, for someone 'just walking past'?"

"What d'ya mean by that!?"

"NOWT! ... Your new glasses seem to be working a treat!"

"They are good, Flo. What do you think of me frames? I went for the Cat's eye ones, like Marilyn Monroe wears in that film. What do you think?"

"You could be twins! So whose house was it where you saw the decorations?"

"Three doors down from me. That youngish couple. He works all over the place and she does God knows what, cos her nets are filthy. They've got kids but you hardly ever see them. Mind you, when you do, all you want to do is give em a good scrub"

"I think I know who you mean. The poor little mites got taken off em a few months ago. Our Joyce was at the clinic and someone was telling her the welfare had taken them"

"You never mentioned it to me!"

"Well Alice. Knowing how much, you can't stand kids, I didn't think you'd be interested" *Plus I was watching Dixon of Dock Green, and couldn't be mithered with you and the million questions, if I'd mentioned it*

"I DO LIKE KIDS! In me own way ... I certainly wouldn't hurt one. Are you sure though? About their kids? I'm positive I saw one of the little gits climbing on my back gate a few weeks ago"

"Well it was our Joyce that told me. And she dunt gossip. Jack and Rita they're called aren't they"

"Oh! You've got it wrong. Jack and Rita live three doors down. The ones I'm talking about live three doors up"

"That's what you said! Three doors DOWN"

"You might want to get your ears tested Flo. I said UP"

"No you never"

"Yes I bloody well did"

"I'm gonna start making notes when you come round. You're always saying you said summat, different to what you actually said"

"Such as WHAT?"

"Such as what you just said, five bloody minutes ago. Anyway I've not got time to argue with you. Have you got a sixpence for two thruppenny bits?"

"I might have. Why?"

"For me Christmas pudding. I need to start getting me bits and bobs ready to go in it. I always start me pudding the last week of

November"

"Nowt wrong with that. But decorations though? In November?" *The world's gone mad*

"Oh yeah, you were saying - *Before you got it wrong!* - About them on your street putting theirs up already. Are you sure they wasn't just getting them sorted out?"

"If you call tacking paper chains to your ceiling and dangling a bell off your big light, sorting out. Then YES they might have been"

"They've really put them up? Properly?"

"That's what I've been trying to tell you, ever since I got here. Their front room looks like C and A's grotto. They've even put balloons up!"

"They'll have popped before Christmas eve. I only put mine up, a week before and I'm sick of the sight of 'em by Twelfth night"

"I'm sick of 'em too, Flo"

"You don't put any up?"

"I meant yours ...Why's your face like that?"

"It's how I always look, when I'm staring at BARE FACED CHEEK! I bet you weren't just 'walking past' when you saw them decorations. I bet you was stood there staring in - You're BRAZEN you are. I wouldn't be surprised if you'd nipped back to yours for a kitchen chair and a flask! Have you finished that brew? I don't want yesterday's pots on the table when our Bob comes home for his tea. And I definitely don't want YOU getting sick of the sight of me furniture!"

"Well I know where I'm not wanted!"

"Our Bob's due any minute, anyway. I'll see you tomorrow"

"I might be busy doing something tomorrow. If you see me, you'll see me. But I might be DEAD busy ... I might go to Kendals"

"I'll SEE you tomorrow"

"Might? Might not?"

You'll be here. I'll bet me mam's dressing table set!

DISEASE!

"What's with the big smile Alice? Has someone you can't stand died?"

"You're not normal you. Why would I be happy about someone dying? 'Cept one or two round here.. I've just seen a massive scrap on my street. Talk about airing your dirty washing in public. I learned things I didn't even know existed"

"Go on then, Gordon Honeycombe, spill the beans"

"Let me get me coat off then. It's freezing outside and I won't feel the benefit. A brew wouldn't go amiss either"

"Well that tea-pot isn't sat on me table for fashion. Help yourself"

"Is that milk fresh?"

"The Cow's still trying to get out me back gate. Course it's bloody fresh. Look? there's a feather from the bird that was pecking the top off this morning - Put your face straight, I'm only kidding. And when have I ever given you sour milk?!"

"I can still taste the brew I had at Joan's the other day. It was proper on the 'turn' But she was coming to the Bingo with me so I didn't like to say anything"

"Ew, and you drank it?"

"Did I buggery. She dunt have any house plants so when she went in the kitchen I tipped it in the coal scuttle and rearranged the coal on top"

"Well she'll know about it when she goes to top up the fire, with yoghurt. Our Joyce eats that rubbish. I've told her it's just sour milk, but she won't listen. So go on then. Tell us about the scrap?"

"Oh yeah. There I am, minding me own business and having a little chat with the dog, when I heard raised voices from the front of me house. Time to wash down me window sills, I thought"

Nosy cow! "As you do"

"Ooh! Don't be going all 'holier than thou' Florence. If I recall, it took you two hours to donkey stone your step, when them across the road had the bailiffs in"

"Utter coincidence luv. Now go on, before I lose the will to live"

"Well you can't wash down your window sills without a bucket of water- Why's your face like that? If you just want half a story?"

You just like the sound of your own voice, you do "No. You go on. I wasn't pulling me face - *I WAS!*- I had tea leaves stuck under me 'plate' - Now what's wrong with YOUR face?"

"Are 'Dentures' the sort of thing to talk about at the table? - *You're SO common!* Anyway, I've got me bucket and I've gone outside. Some young woman looking like she got dressed in the dark is banging on the door of number fifteen. And she's screaming out, *I know he's in there*"

"Who lives at number fifteen?"

"Y'know! Him who takes a briefcase to work with him. Who he thinks he's fooling I don't know. It only has butties in it. He's called Brian or Bernard. Summat like that. Always come across as a bit wishy-washy to me"

"Aw you mean Barry Riley. They call him Barry 'Nearly' behind his back. Nearly went to grammar school, nearly got an office job. That's why he carries that briefcase"

"You've lost me!"

"His mam bought it for him when he passed the Eleven plus. But his dad wouldn't let him go. So she put it aside. Then when he left school, he went for an office job, which he 'kind' of got, cos they took him on as tea boy. And his mam whipped out the briefcase again, saying, *It'll bring you luck, will this briefcase, son. You'll be running the company in no time* ... He's still the Tea-boy to this day"

"He must make a bloody good brew - *He should teach you* - How many scoops did you put in this pot?"

"Three! And one for luck. Why? What's wrong with it?"

"NOWT! it just tastes a bit - *'Orrible* - What's the word I'm looking for? - Bitter! That's it. It tastes bitter. Have you bought a different make?" *A cheaper brand, I'll bet.*

"It's proper Typhoo, is that, Alice. There must be something wrong with your mouth - Anyway, never mind the tea - *You ungrateful sod* - Finish off telling me about the scrap"

"Well. By this time, I've done a dry dust of the window and the sill, and she's still bangin' and shoutin' I'm just going on like I don't even know she's there"

"She must be easily fooled. You could spit from your back room and hit number fifteen's parlour door"

"Do you want to hear this story or not, Flo?"

"Yeah. Course I do"

"Well stop interrupting. I've lost me thread now"

"You were dusting. She was banging!"

"Oh yeah - She's practically got her head through the letter box. And she's screaming by now *I KNOW you're in there* -

257

Which he was, cos I could see the bedroom curtains twitching like mad. Then all of a sudden, the front door flies open"

"Was it him?"

"Was it 'eck. It was his mam. Don't ever let her tell you she's got Rheumatism again. It was like watching Henry Cooper in a dress!"

"What did she do?"

"Well she didn't invite her in for tea! I'm slapping suds on me glass by this time and trying not to look. But when an handbag crashes into your bucket, what you supposed to do? I turn round to say 'EXCUSE ME!' And she's dragging the girl by her hair and the girl's screaming *He's given me a disease*. I didn't know where to put me face"

"Did she name the disease?"

"I know what you're thinking Flo, cos I was thinking it too. But we're talking about Barry. He's as much chance of getting a you-know-what, as the virgin Mary. Apparently he's got Impetigo and she works in the typing pool"

"I didn't even know Adults could get it. But what's her working in the typing pool got to do with anything?"

"He brews up for 'em, dunt he? He should have stayed off work. It's dead contagious is Impetigo. All the brews were tainted with it. And she must have caught it ... As his mam was swinging her round, I could hear her screaming, *I'm supposed to be going to Blackpool at weekend. Look at the state of me!* I tried having a look, but Barry's mam was like a whirling dervish. She'd dragged the girl to the end of the street by this time"

"And where was Barry during all this?"

"Hiding in the bedroom probably. Didn't see sight nor sound of him. But a few people had come out by now and Gladys who lives right next door to them, was telling me she'd seen him the other day, in his back yard, covered head to toe in Gentian Violet"

"How did SHE see him in HIS back yard?"

"She'd have been nosying from her back bedroom window"

"Gawd. You can't do owt round here, without some nosy buggar broadcasting your business"

"You're not wrong Florence. Makes me want to 'move' sometimes"

"Should we have another brew?"

"Go on then. But put an extra scoop in it. You'd better tell your Joyce about grown ups getting Impetigo"

"WHY?"

"Well she's always getting pregnant. If one of the little ones picks it up at school, it might get on her, and taint the baby"

"My grandkids DON'T GET IMPETIGO. She keeps 'em spotless.

But I know what you mean... Just tip them leaves on me 'wandering jew' and I'll make a fresh pot"

EVERYONE HAS 'TICK'

"Flo! I let meself in. Your door's wide open. Flo?, Flo luv, have you been crying?"

"Can you see any bloody Onions in front of me? YES I've been crying. It's Bob ... He's gone"

"Oh Flo luv. You knew day this would come. It's the price you pay for marrying a much older man"

"He's not dead you daft sod. We've had a row...He's walked out"

"Oh thank God for that! - That he's not dead I mean, not that he's left you - *Ooh! if looks could kill* - Anyway he won't have got far, not with his leg. Did he take his stick and scarf?"

"I don't bloody know. I was too busy being devastated and offended. Look behind the door"

"He's took 'em. He'll only be in the 'Ben' or the Bookies. I'll put the kettle on and you can tell me all about it" *I love a kerfuffle*

"Nowt to tell. But all I will say, is when God was giving out stubbornness, that big lummox went back for seconds. He's not getting any younger, as YOU'RE always quick to point out. And we've had this three piece suite since Moses was a lad. It's getting dead uncomfy. There's a spring keeps popping out of HIS chair. Anyway I popped into Beddoes with our Joyce, the other day. She needs a chest of drawers for the little 'uns"

"You never told me you was going shopping?"

"Are you my MAM? *tut!* Anyway, they had a lovely modern one. Real leatherette with orange cushions - they're in material, the cushions, not leatherette. Lovely sunny shade of orange it was an' all. It'd brighten this room up no end. and only two and sixpence a week. That's not even two pints of Double Diamond. Get your husband to sign for it, they said, and we can have it delivered in time for Bonfire night"

"You asked your Bob to get HP? ...YOUR BOB?"

"Yeah well I thought he might have mellowed. I even made his favourite stew and dumplings. With extra dumplings. Suet dunt come cheap"

"But Flo? You've only had Electric lights for the past few years, cos Bob wouldn't have it done on the 'never, never' and he insisted on saving up for it. If his sister hadn't died and left him a few quid, we'd be having this conversation by gaslight. But going back to what you said before. You mentioned summat about being 'offended' What did he say?"

"Oh I knew YOU'D latch on to that! It'd better not go beyond these four walls"

"I wouldn't dream, Flo"

"Oh yeah? The other day I told you I wee'd a little bit when I coughed, and two days later, Miriam Hayes is asking me how me waterworks are!"

"Aw Flo, that wasn't gossiping. That was concern. She works in the chemist. She's practically a nurse. I was just asking her if she could recommend summat for you"

"At BINGO? You asked her at BINGO!"

"It was half day closing. I wouldn't have seen her otherwise. So what did he say?" *WHAT DID HE BLOODY WELL SAY?*

"He started off saying people had warned him I was a Gold digger before he married me"

"He's right. They did - WHAT?... I'm not saying I DID - *I did a bit* - But he's not lying. I mean look at it from their point of view. A Teenage girl, not long arrived from Sheffield, marrying a Widower of almost fifty. With his own house. A lot of people said it wouldn't last five minutes" *I was one of 'em*

"Yet here we are thirty odd years later. *hmmph!* - There's some cheeky sods round here. I hope they choke on a piece of Tripe. Anyway *Gold digger?* I said. *You must think you're Busby bleedin' Berkley! The only bit of gold I've ever dug out of you, was me wedding ring. And after getting to know how 'tight' you can be, I wouldn't be surprised if THAT was second hand.* Then I took it off, and threw it at him. Along with some other stuff"

"D'ya think it was hers? His first wife's?"

"Well I must have touched a nerve, cos he started putting his collar on. He never puts his collar on, unless we have visitors. And then he said, *Don't you DARE bring Mary up!"*

"Aw! So what did you say?"

"Well I'm not proud of it Alice. But I said, *If I wanted to bring Mary up, I'd be stood in Blackley cemeter, with a shovel!*"

Gulp! "You never?"

"I did - *sob* - Aw Alice, I didn't mean to be so horrible. And as soon as it had come out of me mouth, I regretted it. But there's no getting through to him. He's so pig headed. Everyone has 'tick' nowadays. I just wanted summat nice. And NEW, for a change"

"He's pushing eighty. He's not gonna change"

"I KNOW! And I don't want him to. He's the love of me life. I just wish - Oh never mind. I'd better pick up that broken plant pot"

"I never even noticed that! Did you have an actual fight?"

"Not really. Like I said, I threw stuff at him ... You're slacking aren't ya? You're usually the first to spot summat out of place" *And gloat about it.*

"I suppose I was too busy fretting about me best mate" *So swivel on that!*

Gawd I'm gonna have to be grateful now "Sorry luv. I shouldn't be taking it out on you"

"Never mind. Hey! Why don't I crochet you some arm and back covers to freshen the suite up a bit? And you can invite that fat cow Sandra from number nine, round for a brew. Whilst she sat on the chair and the spring is pushed in, I can sew up the hole.

You know I'm a whizz with a needle and cotton"

"What are you gonna tell her you're doing? Praying at her feet?"

"No I'll tell her her hem's come down and I'm being neighbourly"

"I think she'll faint at the thought of YOU being neighbourly"

"All the better if she's unconscious. The dead weight'll hold the spring down better"

CHUCKLE "You're a rum buggar Alice Clough - *And under all that 'attitude' A bloody good friend* - There's the door! It's him coming back. Just act casual and ignore him"

"Should I moan about me back when I get up from the settee?"

"NO! - Mention that suite and I'll have your guts for garters. Least said, soonest mended"

EVERY CLOUD...

"Did you think I was dead, Flo?"

"Why would I think you were dead, Alice?"

"Cos I've not been round for a while"

"I don't call TWO days a 'While' It was weekend anyway. I just thought - *And was extremely grateful* - that you were having a bit of a rest"

"And you weren't even worried? Well God help me if I fell and broke my hip. I'd have started eating the lino before anyone found me"

"I tell you what, luv. If you do ever have a fall so serious that you can't get back up, like normal people do. Fall on a Tuesday. Because if I don't see you in the Post office queue for your pension I won't hesitate to call the ambulance"

"You're not funny!"

"Yeah I am. So go on then. I know you're dying to tell me. WHY haven't you been round?"

"Cos I was having a bit of a rest - WHAT? Why are you giving me that 'sucking lemons' look?"

"Never bloody mind...Do you want a brew?"

"Does it rain on Bank holidays? Of course I want a brew ... I wasn't just resting though. I got one of them thingummjigs from Ronco. Or was it K-Tel? It was on sale, at the back of Woman's Realm. So I wrote a cheque, and sent off for it. I was trying it out to see if it helped with me knees"

"And you call me, for buying stuff out What is it? Summat medical?"

"No. It's a mini vacuum cleaner. They call it the 'Miracle broom'"

"So how does it help your knees? Did you Vac 'em?"

"Florence! Are you daft?"

"Pot, kettle, black luv!"

"I got it to save me getting the Ewbank out. It's murder pushing that thing, with my arthritis, and I never got 'the hang' of a broom. In the advert, they tip an ashtray full of dimps onto the floor and it picks the lot up, but it's small enough to fit in your hand. I'm hoping it'll fit in me pinny pocket. You know, the big front one on me frilly pinny. The orange and green one with fruit round the edge. Are you rationing the sugar? This tea int sweet enough"

"Eyar, help yourself - *And get worms, for all I care* - You NEVER got the hang of a broom? I don't think I've ever heard owt so daft in my entire life!"

"That must be saying something. The amount of time YOU'VE spent alive! I was a delicate child. The seventh of fifteen. Nine of us died though - I wasn't one of them! But it was touch and go for a while. I ended up being the youngest of the ones left. Spoiled rotten I was"

"The more I know you, Alice. The more I wonder about you! So is this 'Miracle Broom' any good?"

"Load of rubbish! I tipped me ashtray onto the hearth rug and I swear there were more dimps after I'd finished using it. By the time I'd swept it properly and put it on the washing line to beat the deep down dust out of it, I was fit for nowt!"

"Well what are you gonna do now? Haven't I said, if you're gonna buy rubbish, buy it from a proper shop. At least you could have taken it back. I've certainly learned my lesson since I sent for the Colour telly transformer, from the back pages of the Sunday Post"

"Oh Yeah. That sheet of see though plastic. Tinted Blue at the top for sky, green at the bottom for grass and pink in the middle for people. It'd be great that ... if Coronation street was set in a field"

"Like I said, lesson learned. You'll just have to chalk it up to experience. Expensive experience"

"Every cloud and all that Flo. Where are we going next week?"

"You've lost me?"

"The wedding! Her, two up from them scruffy gits who live across the road from me. If she doesn't have a premature baby weighing eight pound odd, in about seven months. I'll eat the hat I'll be wearing to the church... CHURCH? The little tart!. You know what she's getting off me? A Miracle Broom"

"Aw, put my name on the gift tag too"

"Are you gonna give me half towards it? I spent nearly ten bob on that"

"What! And throw good money after bad? MY good money. I think not! Keep you're miracle broom. I've got enough Green shield stamps to get 'em a fruit bowl"

12: CONVERSATIONS AT THE KITCHEN TABLE

MAINLY AT FLO'S BUT OCCASIONALLY AT ALICE'S - WHEN IT SUITS HER!

ALICE GETS A TELEPHONE

"Flo, are you going to come round to mine tomorrow?"

"I might have a bit of spare time, in between washing down the windows, scrubbing the kitchen floor, and making our Bob's breakfast, dinner and tea. Why?"

"Have you forgot?"

"Have I forgot what, Alice?"

"You've forgot!"

"How am I supposed to know if I've forgotten something? It might be something I've remembered. But I won't bloody know, til you tell me what it is you think I've bloody forgot. Then, I can see if I did forget it. Or not"

"I can't believe you forgot. I told you loads of times. I can't come out of me house AT ALL, tomorrow. I've got the man from the Telephone Exchange coming round to put me a phone in, and they can't give me an exact time. I cashed in a couple of premium bonds and thought 'Why not' They were my Eddie's anyway. Nowt good ever came from him. If I don't include me Widow's pension"

"And what do you need me there for?"

So I can show off "He might be a murderer"

"A MURDERER! You've been watching too much Alfred Hitchcock luv. The copper's will be laughing their heads off when it comes to solving that one. They'll have worked out 'whodunnit' before Dixon's had time to say 'Evening all' ... We deduct that, because she couldn't come out of her house, AT ALL. And the man who was installing her phone was the only person to go in *rolls eyes* You're a daft sod sometimes Alice. He'd be a rubbish murderer. You just want to show-off, don't you? And why are you wasting money on a phone, when there's a perfectly good phone box just across the road"

"So I can keep in touch with people"

"What people? You've got no kids and you hate your family"

"Who said I hate my family?"

"YOU HAVE! On many occasions"

"No I NEVER! I said I can't stand 'em. That's different to hating 'em"

"Do any of 'em have a telephone?"

"Them lot of idiots, have a telephone? Half of 'em can't even afford bedding. I'll be the first"

"So how are you going to let them know you have one?"

"Oh they'll find out. You know how news travels"

"Well I think it's daft spending good money on summat you don't need. Why don't you get a colour telly instead?"

"And how daft would that be! I only watch the Black and White minstrel show"

"You're not normal, you"

"Like you can judge! So are you coming round or not? I'll let you have a go as long as you're not gonna phone abroad"

"And who would I know abroad?"

"Your Joyce's husband is from abroad"

"I knew you'd be raising that old chestnut. He might be from abroad but he's in Collyhurst as we speak. Like I said before, you don't need me to come round. And I have got things to do, y'know"

"Aw go on Flo? It's a party line. We might be able to listen in, to the other people"

"I'll be there for twelve-ish"

THE NEXT DAY

"I thought he'd never finish, Flo"

"He was ready for the off, a good hour ago. He only stayed cos you wouldn't sign the paperwork til you'd inspected every inch of your skirtings for damage"

"Would you part with good money for a botched job? He only swept up his mess cos I gave him a dustpan"

"And what was you playing at checking the skirtings in the back room? He never set foot in there"

"Have you never heard of an echo?"

"Alice! What's a bleedin' echo got to do with it?... Got to do with it"

"Ha, ha! Bloody funny! You know what I mean. When he was banging like God almighty, I thought the entire house was gonna cave in. Remember that shop in town, during the war? When they bombed Piccadilly. it was nowhere near. The next day there was a massive big crack running down the sides. That's the word I wanted! Shock-waves"

"And yet every time you heard a siren, you hid under the kitchen table!"

"Oh shurrup. Anyway what do you think? Dunt it look posh?"

"Yeah, but couldn't you have gone for something a bit more modern? And not Black. Our Joyce has got one of them Trimphones in two colours of green"

"You never told me your Joyce had a phone!"

"Didn't I? *That'd be because she told me not to.* I don't know her number though. *I DO but she's go mental if I gave it to you.* Did you hear what the telephone man said about the party line? It'll ding when the other people pick it up"

"Yeah. And they'll get a ding when I pick mine up. The cheeky sods had better not think they can listen in to my private affairs. There'll be murders, that's all I'm saying"

Hypocrite! "Anyway is there any chance of a brew? All that dust has got stuck in me throat. Me stomach thinks me throats been cut. I'm spitting-

"Bloody 'ell Flo, you know where the kettle is"

"I'm a GUEST!"

"Remember that next time you're rooting through me kitchenette. How many sugars?"

"The usual - Oh I forgot. How would you know? It's usually me making you a brew. Two - and an extra one for luck"

"Eeyar. And use the saucer. I don't want drips on the Axminster"

"I wouldn't fret, Alice. It'd freeze before it hit the ground. It's bleedin' perishin' in here. Why didn't you have the phone put in the back room?"

"You don't know nowt about the finer things in life do you Florence? Have you ever seen anyone have a telephone in their backroom. We're not Americans y'know - Hey! did it just ding?"

"It sounded like a ding to me. Unless you've got musical mice?"

Tut! "You're mistaking me for someone that lives in a hovel! Should I pick it up?"

"Yeah. But do it quietly"

"Do I look stupid?"

"Well you are stood in a freezing cold room wearing a coat with a pinny over it.... Go on then! Pick it up"

Alice picks up the receiver. And both ladies hold their breath

"Why's your face like that?...What are they saying? Alice?...Alice?"

Clunk!

"I don't know who they are, but I'm getting this phone fumigated. Someone's asking someone else about Gentian Violet. For years I've wanted to get a telephone and what do the bleedin' Telephone people do ? - Make me share it with scruffy gits!...And why are YOU laughing?"

MY PET'S BETTER THAN YOUR PET

"Who's cheeky buggar, who's a cheeky buggar"

"Why would you teach a budgie to say that, Flo?"

"Because, Alice. Everyone teaches their budgie how to say it"

"I don't"

"You don't have a budgie. Why don't you teach your poodle to do something, other than snap at people"

"My Tiggywinkle does not snap! She's highly strung and frets if people come to near me"

"Not that I would, Alice. But if i wanted to go for you. I wouldn't be scared of a six inch tall dog called Tiggywinkle! What sort of name is that?"

"Sez YOU who's called her last ten budgies 'Joey' At least I'm original"

"One of a kind you are, Alice. Thank God! And how you can stand in front of me. ME! whose still got the scar on her baby finger, and say that dog doesn't snap. I don't know. You should get a prize for bare faced cheek"

"That was your own fault. She thought you was going for her Bone. You should never disturb a dog when it's eating"

"I gave her that bone. It was off a ham Shank. It was bigger than she was. The poor mite was struggling to pick it up. I was only trying to help. Anyway there's no such thing as a bad pet. Just rubbish owners"

"What are you trying to say Flo? That I can't look after me dog?"

"Well now you come to mention it, her coat could do with a bit of a comb"

"Why don't you concentrate on your filthy birdcage, and keep your nose out of me and my dogs business. There's nowt wrong with her coat. She's a rough haired poodle"

"You've just made that up. I can tell, and who do you think you are? My Joey gets fresh newspaper EVERY DAY"

"That bit of cuttlefish has seen better days"

"Buy him a new one if you're so offended, Alice"

"I didn't say I was offended. It's not my house, it's making look scruffy"

"I'll remember that when I come round to yours. Cos it's not my house that stinks of dog"

"Come on Tiggy. We know where we're not wanted!"

"Good! I need an hour to clean up the hairs she's gonna leave behind. AND DON'T SLAM ME DOOR. She slammed me door! As God is my witness she's never coming in me house again. Right Joey, say it after Mummy *Alice is a cow. Alice is a cow*"

RUDYBALD BOSENKWET

"Can't you just tell he's had a drink?"

"Aw sorry Alice. I'm not really watching the telly. I'm trying to find the end of this jumper, so I can start unpicking it. Me grandaughter's coming tomorrow and I'm gonna teach her how to French knit. And anyway the news is depressing. All wars and people getting killed. Like that poor luv, Martin Luther King, who wants buses for coloured people, or summat like that . Shot dead on his landing. Who are you talking about?"

"I'd make them share the bloody bus. If I was stood at the bus stop and a bus came along that was for coloured people only, I'd be fuming!. Anyway I only watch the proper news, about stuff going on over here - I'm talking about that Rudybald Bosenkwet who's reading the news. I say reading. I mean slurring. You never told me your Lesley was coming tomorrow?"

"Bleedin' eck! I nearly had the end then, til you put me off. Old news is that, and it's Reginald you daft sod. I read about him in the Sunday Post. You know that saying 'Any Port in a storm'? Well he's 'A glass of port for the slightest little thing ... And I didn't know I had to give you my grandchild's itinerary"

"Oooh! Stop getting catty cos I mentioned your precious grandchild. It's just that I thought we'd arranged to go to the Market?"

"We still are, Alice. I'm picking her up on the way back"

"But she lives in Collyhurst! We're going from Moston Lane to Conran Street. It's another six or seven stops to her house. I'M not paying the extra fare"

"You're not coming with me *Joyce and the kids will moan* I'm sure you can find your way home, by yourself. After all, you only need a couple more trips on the one, one, two, to get to your millionth. They might give you a prize or something - Like a go on the conductors ticket machine, or a date with the driver. Hey? play your cards right and you could have free travel for life"

"There's a touch of the 'common' about you Flo. I don't 'Date' I'm a widow. Plus have you ever seeing someone worth looking at twice, driving a bus round here?"

"I see you've looked then? And it's not like you ever mourned your Eddie. If I recall rightly, you did a lap of honour round the grotto in the cemetery when you heard he was dead"

"Well that's what happens to cheating sods. But I am still a widow. So I'm used to being abandoned. Yeah. I'll be fine going home on me own. Like a Billy no mates. Don't worry about me, it shouldn't be all that dark when I'm walking up the entries to me house. And I don't suppose there's that many sex fiends roaming about"

"You read too many of them 'True Detective' magazines. Walk on the street like normal people"

"That's the long way round!"

"Bloody 'ell Alice. What's the difference ? Two feet?

"It all adds up - Anyway, don't be mithering yourself over me, Florence. When you've got better things to do" *Like picking up Shirley Temple gone wrong - I can't stand that kid.*

"I tell you what. I'll go and pick her up first then me and her will meet you at the market. I think you'll be safe from the Boston Strangler, on Moston Lane in broad daylight"

"Aw you don't have to change your plans for me, but go on then. I'd better be getting off. I want to be settled before the ten o'clock news starts"

"You're obsessed with the news. Mind you, all that misery in one sitting, must suit you down to the ground - Right. I'll set off to our Joyce's at ten and meet you by the ice-cream van at Twelvish - OH! And if between now and then you decide you want me to change my plans again. Just to make doubly sure you're not ravaged by a short sighted sex maniac. Send me a telegram"

"Are you being sarcastic?"

"Not about the short sighted bit"

"I do have other friends"

"Not between here and Conran street, you don't"

"Oh shurrup Flo. I'm getting off"

"Hang on. Let me just check that Christie's not hiding in me hallway"

"You daft apeth. Ooh! You've given me the heebie jeebies now. Innit dark out there?"

Tut! "Let me get me coat. I'll walk you to the top of the street and watch til you get to your corner"

"Aw Flo. You don't have to. But go on then"

Sigh!

THE VOTE

"Sorry I'm late flo. I got held up by all sorts"

"What are ya talking about? I only said pop round for a brew when you're ready. I hadn't planned a time - I didn't bake a cake, 'specially"

"No, But you know me, I like to get here early"

Sometimes I wonder why you don't just move in "And who's been hogging your time today?" *I wanna thank them. I was glad of the rest.*

"Put the kettle on Flo and I'll tell you. I just need to take this coat and cardi off. It's roasting out there"

"Well it is almost Whitsun. Did the sunshine not give you a clue before you stepped out, dressed like you were going to meet Scott of the Antarctic?"

"Remember that time we went to Skipton Castle, Flo? I got heatstroke and frostbite all on the same day"

"No you didn't, you don't half exaggerate. We got caught in a bit of rain going from the cafe to the sharra"

"You don't have my chilblains. You can't judge. Is that brew making itself?"

Tut! "So what is it that's got you running late today?"

"Bloody politicians, knocking on me door with waffle. You don't see 'em from one day to the next and then they decide to knock on, just as you've sat on the toilet. I wouldn't mind if I had an outside one. Like SOME! But you know how steep them stairs are. I nearly broke me leg rushing to answer it"

"You could have ignored it? *It's your own fault you're such a nosy cow* - I don't have that problem, being one of the 'SOME' who have an outside lavatory. You don't hear owt from our outhouse. *Chuckle* Which one of 'em was it anyway? They'll be knocking on mine soon. I'm fuming about them binmen. They left me lid in the entry last week. They'll know about it when they knock on for their Christmas box"

"I know! lazy buggars. It was whatisface? the Conservative chap. We ended up having a nice chat. He's an homeowner, like me"

Is there no end, to your pretentiousness? "Oh! Well THEY can't do sod all about the bins round here. He's not bothered about the likes of us. I bet he doesn't even live round here"

"Do any of 'em? Flo. Who are you voting for anyway?"

"Who do you think I'm voting for Alice? Bearing in mind the fact that you've known me for ages"

"You might have fancied a change"

"I 'fancy' an egg custard every now and again. I FANCY Ronald Colman. What I don't think I'll EVER fancy, is saving up to be sick. Or trying to talk like Annie Walker *Like YOU do*. I'm voting Labour luv. Always have done, always will do"

"I used to think like that, til I became a property owner"

"I'm a property owner too. And it's an identical two up two down to yours. 'Cept my wallpaper's nicer"

All your upstairs is distemper "I THINK you'll find Flo, that it's your Bob's name on the mortgage - Which means it still belongs to the Bank. I don't even have a mortgage"

"And I THINK Alice, that you'll find the front door at the end of the hallway if you carry on your daftness!"

"Well it's true int it? Your Bob bought this house before you'd even met him. *Before you were even bloody born, I bet* Anyway you're making me go off on a tangent. What I'm trying to say is, my mortgage is paid off, thanks to me dead husband dying and having insurance. It's a different world when you own property outright"

"Oh do fill me in on the subject of being landed gentry Alice? hat's if it's not too common for you round here. Should I get me best china out or can you cope with a tin cup?"

"Hurts you when people want to better themselves dunt it?"

"Reach for the sky - like Kenneth Moore did. He was lovely in that film - I'm still wondering how they made his legs disappear though? He had some lovely hairy ones in 'The Admiral Crichton' - Anyway reach for the stars but don't look down on people when you get there. That's my motto in life, Alice. But YOU are a snob madam. And a daft snob at that. The Tory's aren't for the likes of you and me"

"Churchill won the war and he's a Tory"

"WE won the war cos our Son's and Father's got out there and whipped Adolf's backside. And whilst they were doing that us women ran the country. And THEN, as soon as it was done they expected us working class people to go back to tugging our forelocks"

"Well I'M voting Tory Flo. It's in keeping with my status"

"And I'M voting Labour luv. It's in keeping with reality"

"Suit yourself"

"Suit YOURSELF too. Just don't let our Bob hear you 'blaspheme' in his house. Like you said, it's HIS name on the mortgage. I might not chuck you up the hallway for your political views but HE will"

CHEER UP!

"Cheer up Alice, It might never happen"

"What are you wittering on about woman? There's nowt wrong with me"

"Well put your face straight then... I've been meaning to tell you this for ages, years in fact! You've always got a face like a wet weekend in St Annes"

"A lot of people have said that Flo. But I'm dead happy inside. Well happy-ish. I've just got one of them faces. D'ya know how when you see someone? And you think to yourself *I bet she's a right cow* And she's probably a mixture of Julie Andrews and Doris Day once you get to know her. Well I'm like that. People like you, who really know me, see beyond the regal stare"

"REGAL?"

"Yeah! regal. You see beyond that, to the funny and sociable person that I really am. People who don't know me think I'm standoffish"

"I've always found you to be a miserable sod and most other people tell me they can't stand you. To be honest, apart from me - Bob doesn't count - The only people who like you are those that have never met you" *Chuckle*

"I'm getting close to being offended, Forence"

"Let me know when you arrive. I'll get the iced fingers out to celebrate"

"I find you very sarcastic sometimes, and there's no need"

"Oh shut up. How long have you known me? - don't answer that! - You should know by now, that I'm only sarcky with people I like, and idiots. I'm not saying which category you come in to"

"You're doing it again!"

"I can't help it"

"If you're like this with your 'friends' all I can say is God help your enemies"

"I don't have enemies, Alice. Apart from Germans. And I'm not over keen on her at number forty four - Anyway, how did we get on this subject?"

"You was telling me to cheer up and I was saying there's nowt wrong with me"

"Oh yeah. You've just got one of them faces luv. Our Lesley is the same. Her dad calls her his long streak of misery"

"She does have a bit of a long face. I'm not sure I've ever seen her smile"

That's cos she can't stand YOU "Aw she's a little ray of sunshine when it's just me and her grandad here. She's shy"

More like 'SLY' "I wouldn't say she was shy. Snooty's the word that springs to mind"

"I'd 'spring' it back if I was you. That's my grandchild you're talking about"

"You brought it up!"

"I CAN - And who are you calling 'it'?"

"Flo! You take offence quicker than me dog takes a Bonio. He nearly took me finger off the other day"

"Well you WOULD go for a Poodle. They're known for being 'snappy' I've always preferred mongrels meself. Look at our Roger? Definitely got a bit of Lassie in him but God knows what else he is. Placid as anything. The budgie sits on his head sometimes. Not a peep"

"Why would you call a dog 'Roger'?"

"After Ivanhoe"

"Shouldn't he be called Ivanhoe then?"

"Not Ivanhoe after Ivanhoe. Ivanhoe after Roger Moore playing Ivanhoe. Look at my Roger's eyes ... Spitting image of Roger Moore's"

"Simon would have suited him better - *Cos that dog's simple*- After Simon Templar"

"We'd already had him for about three years when that came out"

"Oh! Do you know who I named my second dog after? - The one I got after the one I had when I met you"

"Of course I bloody do" *If they paid people for stating the bleedin' obvious. You'd be a millionaire*

"Go on then Florence 'know-it-all' - Who?"

"The talking horse"

"How did YOU know that?"

"His name is a cunning clue. Mr Ed!" *Daft sod!*

"Lucky guess. It could have been someone I know called Edward"

"But it wasn't. Bloody 'ell Alice, our Joyce is seven months pregnant. Her unborn child could have guessed that. You're not all there you"

"Speak for yourself. Anyway, I'm off. Can't sit about, like some"

"You know where the door is"

"Will I see you tomorrow? Are we still going to Town?"

"Course you will and course we are. It's your turn to pay the bus fare. You're not getting away with that one"

FLO AND ALICE 'RAMBLE' - WITHOUT A COUNTRY LANE IN SIGHT

"Do you know what just come in my head, Flo?"

"No I don't. But I'm betting it was something daft"

"I was just thinking. No one we know has died for ages"

"Your spells must have wore off Alice - And why are you so obsessed with death? Or do you just fancy a Ham butty without the expense?"

"You can be a COW sometimes, Florence. And I'm NOT obsessed. Death is a normal thing when you get to our age"

"Speak for yourself 'morbid Mabel' I'm still in me forties"

"Ya forties! I'm talking age NOT girdle size"

"So am I Alice. I'm forty-sixteen" *Cackle*

"You sound like Hilda Ogden when you do that laugh"

"And you look like her!"

"Sez you! wearing a Pinny and hairnet"

"I've got a table full of brass ornaments here to polish. What should I be wearing? A Norman Hartnell two piece, with matching hat?"

"Who's Norman Hart-i-bobs when he's at home?"

"He makes dresses for the Queen. God bless her"

"And how do YOU know that?"

"It says it here. On the magazine I've put under the brasses to protect me table .Just move that Cannon out of the way - See! I love the 'Tit-Bits' You learn stuff without it feeling like school"

"I prefer 'Cheshire life' meself"

"Only when you nick a free copy from the doctor's. And you only have them for 'show' I've seen your paper bill. The News of the World and the Sunday Post are the only things that pop through your letter box"

"Flo! It's not stealing when you take a magazine from the doctor's. That's why they're there"

"They are THERE for patients to read whilst they're waiting to see the doctor. And if you don't think it's stealing. WHY do you sneak it under your coat whilst you're humming 'We'll meet again' You have 'Guilt' written all over your face as well. Like you're just waiting for 'Gideon of the Yard' to burst in and say *Alice Clough I am arresting you for nicking posh magazines*"

CACKLE!

"You're sounding like Hilda again"

"Yeah - But I'm not wrong am I? *Cackle*

"I'm going home"

"Aw don't be daft. I've just put the kettle on. AND I was stood behind Mary Barlow and her mate from Ancoats, in the butchers. You know what big gobs they've got?"

"No sugar in mine. I'm dieting. But I can have a couple of biscuits if they're plain"

FACEPULLING

"Alice? Our Lesley says you've been pulling faces at her?"

"Your Lesley is a little liar!" *And a soddin' grass!*

"Well she knows she'll get in trouble if she tells fibs. And she crossed her heart and hoped to die, twice, when I asked her if she was telling the truth. TWICE"

"OHHH! I know when she means. Did she say it was when I was here yesterday, and you went in the kitchen to start the tea?"

"She did. She said you made a fist at her and screwed up your face like Willie Weasel"

"Aw she got it wrong - *The tell tale tit!* - Me arthritis come on dead quick, and stiffened up me arm. That was my 'in pain' face. Who the ecks Willie Weasel, anyway?"

"Don't you watch Tufty? Willie Weasel's his mate- Not a real weasel, a puppet. He goes for an Ice-Cream and gets run over"

"A puppet gets murdered?"

"I don't know. It's just summat they put on telly for the kids. Teaches them how not to get run over - So are you saying she got it wrong then? You wasn't picking on her?" *Cos if you was!*

"FLO? I'm getting a bit offended here! Why would I pick on a child? If she's watching weasels get murdered do you not think it might have addled her brain a bit? What did I say when Telly first come out? 'This'll all come to no good' That's what I said. And I'm not wrong. I went round to Beryl Jackson's daughter Linda's house, the other day. To pay me catalogue-

"What've YOU GOT from the catalogue?"

"The real china lady ornament I've got on me sideboard. The one in a pink crinoline that I've got displayed on me best doily"

"How many other pot dolls have you got displayed on your sideboard?"

"None, and it's not a doll. It's an ornament. A limited edition ornament"

TUT! "You told me it was an antique"

"NO I NEVER! I said it was UNIQUE. There's only ten thousand of them made"

"TEN THOUSAND IS UNIQUE?"

"You see that picture on your wall? Of that daft girl showing her bosoms and hugging a tree. There's a million of them round here. Let's go and knock on ten doors. I bet you every single one of 'em has that picture. But they won't have my crinoline lady. You can't 'buy' what I have"

"Is that why you had to get it on 'the weekly'?"

"I didn't mean like that, you daft sod. I meant 'class' And I got it out of the catalogue cos it was too dear to buy in one go. I can manage one and six a week. And it'll be worth a fortune in a few years. Anyway I was saying, I went round to Linda's house at one-ish in the afternoon and guess what she was doing?"

"Counting her commission from mugs who buy daftness out of her catalogue?"

"We'll see whose daft in years to come - No! she was watching telly. Watching telly in the middle of the day, and she's got pots in her sink. *What's this you're watchin?* I said. *Trumpton* she replied, bold as brass. I looked at her, looked at the state of her house, threw her me money, made sure she wrote it down in me payment book, and left. If she'd had even offered me a brew, I wouldn't have took it"

"The Slut! Her mam's not much better though. She's a stranger to a donkey stone is Beryl. Her front's a disgrace"

"Well her Linda's a chip off the old block. Them doors in her house, haven't been wiped down since she moved in"

"it's a council house 'an all int it? White doors throughout. I'd love some of them modern doors. People today don't know they're born"

"They're more like nicotine yellow now. You'll have to think of an excuse to go round, and have a look yourself. You'll be mortified Flo"

"I don't need an excuse. I can go round with you. You'll be going round every week for the next ten years to pay for your doll"

"Bloody 'ell Flo. How many times do I have to tell you it's NOT a doll! It's an investment"

"So you say. If I was gonna get summat out the catalogue, it'd be one of them twin tubs you don't need a mangle with. The bedding's starting to kill me"

"Why don't you get one then? My ornament's spread over fifty three weeks but you can have longer for big stuff. Myra

Bennett's paying for her three piece over a hundred and odd weeks"

"The way they make stuff nowadays, she'll be still paying for it when its gone to the tip! And Bob would go mental if I got owt on the never, never. A hundred weeks? That's bloody years! how does she know she'll still be alive? I'd die of shame if I died owing people money"

"Don't tell him. Say you got it cheap in the sales. Give it a kick, say they took money off cos it was dented"

"I'm not gonna pay money out of me pension every week for summat scruffy looking. Would you put a dent in something expensive you was paying good money for?"

"I would if me only other option was that monstrosity of a mangle that takes up half your scullery"

"Its good enough when I'm mangling your curtains every spring"

"Oh I didn't know you was counting things you do for me! I'll get me own twin tub shall I? Then I won't have to bother you!"

"You don't often come up with good ideas, Alice, but that one is brilliant. We could go halves and keep it at your house - But if I die first you've got to save my half for our Joyce- We could take in washing for people and go on like we're working ourselves to the bone..Then sit with our feet up watching telly whilst the twin tub does all the work. And the money we make will pay off the catalogue"

"There'll be a female Pope, before I take in any buggar's washing"

"Is that the 'face' you pulled at our Lesley?"

TOO MODERN FOR ME

"Do you ever look at all the modern stuff around us Flo? And wonder how we got by in our days"

"I'm still in mine, thank you very much. You talk like we're at death's door. But I know what you mean. You think my Ewbank's good? Our Joyce has got an Hoover. All you do is plug it in, and push. She was showing me, the other day. She tipped her ashtray out, onto her fireside rug. I thought she'd gone mental til she switched the hoover on...You couldn't see a trace of ash. And there must have been eight or nine dimps in the ashtray. I know that cos I'd been there long enough to have two brews"

"What colour's her rug?"

"Orange, with brown blobs. Or is it the other way around?"

"Do you think it would work on my sheepskin rug? I sweep it regular, but I think it might have some deep down dirt I can't reach. It is very plush. Cost a bomb. Straight off the sheep to my fireplace"

I can tell, by the smell! "By the time it'd finished, Alice. Your rug would be saying baa"

"Do you think she'd let me lend it?"

"BORROW! Have you ever seen an hoover upright? They're massive and they weigh a ton! Who's gonna lug that up here, from Collyhurst? Not bloody me! It's brilliant for our Joyce, cos she's all on one level in the flat. But you couldn't do the stairs with it. Not without putting your back out"

"I won't bother then. It doesn't sound very labour saving"

"Oh no! It most definitely IS. Once you've got it going, it's brilliant. She's got an electric kettle an' all. Dunt whistle cos it switches itself off once its boiled. People in the space age future will never know the pain of boiling a kettle dry. Even one with a whistle on. Like I did the other day. Although it was your fault really"

"How was it MY fault?"

"I left you in here whilst I answered the front door But you had to come trotting up me lobby, dint ya? Leaving the kettle I was boiling -to make YOU a cup of tea -to boil dry"

"I heard Joan's voice and thought she might have come for me. An' we both forgot, if you remember!"

"You heard Joan's voice and thought 'Juicy gossip' you mean. Why would Joan knock on here for you?"

"She might have needed to tell me something important about Bingo. She gets strange feelings about Bingo. One time she knocked on mine and give me barely a minutes notice to get ready. Although it was the day we'd planned to go - But later. She only went and won 'the line' And we go halves -I soon got me breath back. I wouldn't ask her to read me palm. But there's no doubt she's psychic at Bingo"

"You've got some strange things going on in that head of yours. I'm half expecting an ambulance with square wheels to knock on and take you to Prestwich!"

"Cheeky madam! Why don't you get an electric kettle?"

"Not in a million years! I like my brew to taste proper. Our Joyce has never been one for making a decent brew. It's like she just waves the tea at the water. And she's gone worse since she got that kettle - I didn't even think 'worse' was possible. I think it's something to do with the electrical bit that touches the water. It must affect it"

"Sounds like she's frying it instead of boiling it"

"You could be right Alice. The world's moving too fast. You mark my words. By the year 2000 we'll be eating pills for dinner and everyone's house will be run by them computers"

"COMPUTERS? Where will we fit 'em? Have you seen the ones in Man from Uncle? They're gi-bloody-normous. Like giant bus ticket machines. All that faffing for a bit of paper"

"Oh there won't be any houses. No pavements either .Everyone will live in massive flats, and they'll fly everywhere. Just like Flash Gordon"

"Well I'm not saying I want to be dead, Flo. But I'm glad I won't be around for any of that nonsense"

"You're not on your own, Alice. It's been getting too modern round here, since the war. Look at doorbells?"

"What about 'em?"

"Where did you see doorbells, when we were kids?"

"The Vicar had one .And some of the big houses near Bogart Hole Clough. But you wouldn't know that. Cos you lived in Sheffield then"

"It was exactly the same there. Doorbells were on the big houses. Bloody ell Alice, you go on as if I grew up on the Moon. Sheffield's only down the road. Not even half a day by Bus"

"If it's more than 20 minutes I get 'funny' I sometimes get wobbly when I've just gone to town"

"It dunt seem to bother you going to Blackpool"

"Sharra's are different!"

"So are YOU! Anyway, back to doorbells. I went round to Bessie Charlton's the other day, and guess what was stuck on her front door?"

"An eviction notice?"

"Where the bloody 'ell did THAT come from? - No! - A doorbell. Next to the Knocker. Talk about over egging the pudding. The houses on Scarborough street are EXACTLY the same size as the ones here. So I don't know what she's playing at!. There's nowhere in that house, you can't hear the door knock. And she's got an inside toilet. So she can't use that excuse! I was gonna pretend I hadn't seen it. But I was there to get me wages, and I knew she'd be already pulling a face cos I'd done an extra half a day putting up her winter curtains, and I made sure I was getting paid for it! So I pressed the soddin' thing"

"Beggar's belief Flo. Was it one of the ding-dong bells, or did it play a tune?"

"It played 'Oh Susannah' By the time she finally got to the door, it felt like she HAD come all the way from Alabama"

"I'm daft me. I've always sang 'I've come from the Alhambra' like the bingo hall"

"You daft sod! *chuckle* Shove that kettle on, and I'll make us a good old fashioned cuppa"

"We're a dying breed Flo"

"Gawd! Death's forever on your lips. Is morbid your middle name?"

"I didn't mean it like that! I meant normal people who get by on a brew. Your grandkids will probably be supping moon juice when they're our age"

"I'm not swearing you're right, but you could be, Alice. Our Joyce has got a mate who only drinks coffee"

"I bet you're talking about Brenda Clarke"

"How did you know?"

"War baby! Only blonde one in her family. Born three months premature, according to her mam. Yet STILL weighed in at nine pounds. She's not Bert Clarke's daughter. She's half G.I. Coffee's in her blood"

"Alice! You can't go round saying things like that!" *Even if it is true.*

"I'm not 'going round' I'm sat here saying it. And I can tell you know what I'm talking about. So don't be pursing up your lips

297

like you're shocked!"

"Do you think Bert's ever 'wondered?'"

"I went to school with him. He isn't capable of wonder"

"It's a true saying innit? 'Ignorance is bliss' - OY! Are you thick or summat? Put your cup on it's saucer before it makes a ring"

A FOND LOOK BACK

"Flo? Do you ever wished you'd gadded about a bit more when you were younger? I mean, who'd know?"

"Three quarters of Moston if you had owt to do with it, Alice"

"Don't be mean! I've kept loads of secrets in my time. As well you know"

"Oh yeah? Was it, or was it not YOU, that told my granddaughter there was no Father Christmas? I've still not forgiven you for that!"

"What on earth are you talking about?"

"Last Christmas. When you told her she wasn't allowed to go in the stairs cupboard"

"How is that, saying there's no Father Christmas? If I recall, it's me whose queued up with you for the past few years at Lewis' grotto. You risk life and limb with some of them kids -NOT YOURS! - *I saw that look!* - But some of 'em don't know how to behave in public. Do you remember that dead ugly one? About two Christmases ago? I had to catch me breath when he stared at me"

"Aw you're horrible, you. He wasn't ugly. There's no such thing as an ugly child. The poor luv must have had some sort of affliction?"

"Did you see his mam? I'm still trying to work out how someone even married her, never mind got her pregnant. That was no affliction. THAT was hereditary ugliness. Ken Dodd's got

better teeth"

"At least they were his own"

"Hark at you! The steradent queen!"

"Only for me top set, Alice. Anyway stop changing the subject. You roused her curiosity when you said don't go in the cupboard. And she found her Etch-a-Sketch, and all the selection boxes ... I tried to cover up by saying he'd popped in for the 'list' and left one of his sacks, but she's a clever little sausage. *Why was my Etch-A-Sketch already here, if he'd come for the list it was written on?* She asked me. She's a little Albert Einstein, that one?"

She's a little miss soddin' know-it-all! "Well she is pushin' eight. And be honest, Flo. In our day we wouldn't have dreamed of disobeying an adult. If a grown up had told us not to touch, we'd have chopped our arms off before disobeying. That's why we've won two wars. We had discipline. God help us if there's ever another war, with the namby pamby kids they're bringing up nowadays"

"Aw, I miss the war. Not the death and rationing bit, but the way we all rallied together, and got stuck in"

"Do you remember Maisie Reynolds? She certainly got stuck in. With half the American army. She had enough nylons to open a shop. And look at her now? Like butter wouldn't melt. I wonder that pew doesn't start sizzling when she sits in church of a Sunday. If I opened my gob about her, she'd be excommunicated. Her husband would return from the grave, just to change his will. Mind you, some people are just born daft. Four kids who look like strangers to each other and he never said a word. Think about it Flo? You're ginger, your husband's ginger, but two of your kids are blonde. And the littlest one looks like he should walk with the Italians at Whitsun"

"You can't judge someone cos of the colour of their kids hair"

"I'm NOT. I'm judging her cos she couldn't keep her gob, OR legs shut when she was younger. Thinking she was 'it' cos she had a few years on us. I mean don't get me wrong, I was never scared of her, but I can see why others were"

"I bloody wasn't!"

"I don't mean you Flo - I remember when you and her had words in the butcher's queue, that time during the war. When you said *Back off horse face, before the butcher makes you in to chops.* I nearly wet meself laughing"

"It wouldn't be the first time. Remember when we missed the last bus home from the pictures cos you fancied that lad from the queue"

"Oh yeah.I made you wait with me at the entrance so we could casually saunter by when he came out"

"And the he came out with one of the usherettes"

"Gawd. Don't remind me. I was heartbroken"

"You was bladder broken. Halfway up Kenyon lane and I'm trying to look casual whilst you're watering someone's privets"

"Just think though, Flo. If it wasn't for that usherette, he could have been my second husband"

"You don't half jump the gun, Alice.You never even saw him again"

"Neither did the usherette, so I heard. All she got from him,was a bun in the oven"

"How on earth do you get to find out this stuff? I swear the war would have finished years earlier if they'd asked you to find out Hitler's movements"

"I went to school with the girl who did Wednesday's in the kiosk.His name was Terry.Went on to emigrate to Australia. If it wasn't for that hussy, I could have been living with Skippy and sunshine"

"But would you have got a widow's pension?"

"Well. That was a silver lining in the cloud that was Eddie, I suppose"

"Skippy? good name that"

"For a kangaroo?"

"No. That Terry. He certainly skipped out on the usherette"

"I'd love to see her again. I'd wave Eddie's insurance policy at her. and laugh"

"You're a cow, you sometimes. The poor woman must have had a lifetime of devastation"

"Should have kept her knickers on then, 'shunt' she?"

"Let she who is without sin cast the first stone!"

"What do you mean by that?"

"Well you know how you was saying you wished you'd gadded about a bit more? All I'm saying is, VE Day. Or gin and sin, as we call it"

"Don't Flo! And who's 'WE' You swore to me you'd never say a word"

"I'm only having a laugh. I've never told a living soul. You're blushing?"

"NO I'M NOT! It's me rouge. Anyway. You've done worse!"

"When?"

"The 'thing' when we went to thingy"

"Oy you! SHURRUP!...Walls have ears"

"Ooh. Touched a nerve have I?

"No! You're just 'touched' Stick the kettle on and change the subject. Our Bob'll be home soon"

"Funniest day of my life, that was. Mind you, I wasn't faced with your predicament"

"ALICE! Change the bloody subject"

"I bet you wish you were still that supple"

"Alice! I'm warning ya!"

"How many times do I have to tell you?. My lips are sealed. If only summat of yours had been -OW! - Did you just throw your TV Times at me? Paper can hurt, you know. You could have had me eye out. Or given me a paper cut. I know people who've died from a paper cut"

V. E. DAY

OR THE DAY FLO AND ALICE, DID THE 'THING' WITH THE 'THINGYS'

"Innit wonderful news Flo? The war's finally over. Are you and Bob gonna come into town with me later. There's gonna be loads going on in Albert Square"

"I've not stopped smiling, Alice. Hitler dead and the war over. It's bloody brilliant. Bob's with his Home Guard lads. The war's still on for him til he get official notice. And it's his turn to do the night watch near the Prisoner of War barracks. But I'm up for a trip to town. What should we wear?"

"Well we'll need coats. It might be Spring, but there's still a 'nip' in the air. I'm gonna wear my Paisley dress. So don't wear yours, cos we'll look daft if we're dressed the same"

"I don't have a paisley dress" *I hate paisley*

"Yeah, you do, That one I bought you, just before the war started. I got it for your birthday" *And cos it was dead cheap*

Bloody 'ell. I made the dog a bed with it! "I wouldn't dream of wearing that - *literally!* - I'm saving that for best. I'll probably wear it when our Joyce gets married"

"She's barely started school! But I know what you mean. It is special. So what ARE you gonna wear?"

"Me green skirt and me white blouse"

"Good choice *-for someone with your shape* - Right, I'm gonna get off and do summat with me hair. It's a curse sometimes, having these beautiful curls. The time I have spend on my hair"

"You wouldn't think!"

Is she being 'funny' "You wouldn't know, with that straight hair you have. You can just brush and go. Born with ringlets, I was"

"Funny that. Cos you look bald on your baby picture"

"It's just the way the camera was set up" *Cheeky sod!* Anyway. Are you knocking on for me, or am I knocking on for you?"

"I'll call for you cos it's on the way"

A FEW HOURS LATER. FLO AND ALICE FIND THEMSELVES

AMONGST THE MASSES, IN ALBERT SQUARE

"Aw, innit wonderful Alice?"

"I can barely hear meself"

"Don't be bloody moaning. You're the one who wanted to come down here. It is a bit noisy though. I need to get me breath back from all that cheering. Should we pop in one of the Pubs for a breather" *And a cig. I don't know why people say it's common for women to smoke in public. I'm gasping for a cig*

"I need a wee, Flo. Let's go"

THEY MANAGE TO FIND A RELATIVELY QUIET CORNER IN A NEARBY PUB

"That's better. Look at us, drinking beer on a week day, Flo"

"Well it's not every day, we win a war, is it Alice?"

"That's twice now. Let's hope them bloody Germans have finally learned their lesson. Nice bit of stout is this ... Hey, Flo? Don't look, cos they'll know you're looking. But there's two fella's over there? They keep staring at me? - What're you looking under the table for?"

"Just checking you hadn't tucked your skirt into your knickers, when you went to the lav"

"You cheeky cow!. I reckon they're staring at me curls"

"Well you could pass for a giant size Shirley temple"

"I don't know why I put up with you - Bloody 'ell! I think they're coming over - Do NOT show me up"

"Hi there ladies. Me and my friend Chad couldn't help but notice such visions of loveliness. May we buy you a drink?"

"SOD OFF! We're married"

Don't show me up, she says! "Alice! don't be rude. Thank you, we'll have two halves of stout - Not EACH - Erm, are you Americans"

"Canadians ma'am. And It would be my pleasure to buy you ladies a drink"

HE GOES TO THE BAR

"Alice! What's up with ya? We're getting a free drink. So behave"

"I got nervous. I didn't know what to say. I've hardly talked to a man since Eddie got off - And don't tell 'em I'm a deserted wife. I'll think of summat if they ask"

"We're only having a drink. I don't think they'll want to know our life stories"

THE GENTLEMEN RETURN, WITH A TRAY OF DRINKS

"Well here we are. This is Chad, and I'm Billy. May we join you"

"Of course. Budge up Alice"

"Why've I got to budge up?"

"Cos I'm leaning against the wall and there's nowhere for me to go. BUDGE UP! -She's a bit deaf after all the bombings"

"I AM NOT! Anyway, ta for the drink"

"So what names do you ladies go by? I think I heard you being called Alice"

"You heard wrong. I'm Loretta, and this is Shirley. Would you just excuse us a minute. We need to powder our noses. Come on Fl -Shirley"

'LORETTA' AND 'SHIRLEY' GO TO THE TOILETS

"Alice! what on earth possessed you, to lie about our names?"

"Reputations Flo. OUR reputations. We don't know 'em from Adam. They could be the type who think that just cos a girl takes a drink, she's 'easy'"

"You don't need a drink! - I'm kidding - Well I think you're daft - And a cheeky cow for saying I'm called Shirley. Couldn't I have been Vivian or some other movie star? And as for calling yourself Loretta? Who round here would be called Loretta?"

"Well they don't know that, do they. They're not even from round here. They're from America"

"I thought they said they were Canadians"

"And where's Canada? It's in America you daft lump. Right, so I'm Loretta, you're Shirley. And we're typists in an office"

"Why typists?"

"Cos we're too posh to work in a factory - And we live in Cheadle Hulme"

"I hope they want to see us home. Or ask to see our shorthand skills. Come on before our beers go cold"

THE GIRLS RETURN. THEY HAVE A LIVELY TIME DISCUSSING THE WINNING OF THE WAR, AND AVOIDING ANY TALK OF TYPING SKILLS ...AFTER SEVERAL MORE DRINKS - AND A QUICKSTEP OR TWO. IT'S TIME TO LEAVE FOR HOME. BUT NOT BEFORE A FINAL VISIT TO THE 'POWDER ROOM'

"I tell you what Flo. That Chad's hands are everywhere"

"I didn't notice you trying to pull 'em off. Especially when you and him were dancing to 'IN THE MOOD' It was almost like, you WERE in the mood"

"Hark at you with the hypocrisy! You were practically in that Billy's ear hole when you were talking to him"

"It's loud out there. What should I have done. Brought a megaphone?"

"Excuses, excuses!"

"So what are we gonna do now, Alice? I think they want to walk us to the bus stop. And some idiot told them we live on the opposite side of Manchester"

"I wasn't born yesterday luv. I've got it covered. The last time you went for a dance with Billy. I told Chad that even though we lived in Cheadle Hulme, you're grandad lives in Newton Heath and we were on our way there, to stay the night cos he's got a bad cough And we only stopped by the pub to get him a bottle of tonic wine"

"You should work for the secret service. That's a brilliant cover story. I'm sure they believed every word" *Well they would if they were idiots!*

"You'll be thanking me, when your name's not 'mud' Are we ready?"

"Yeah"

THE FOURSOME TAKE A LONG SLOW WALK TO THE BUS STOP. VIA THE ODD ENTRY OR TWO. WHAT WENT ON. ONLY THE FOUR OF THEM KNOW. AND I DON'T WANT TO SURMISE COS FLO WAS MY NANA. AND IT'S 'GOING THROUGH ME' JUST THINKING ABOUT IT. BUT SAFE TO SAY IT WAS INNOCENT -ISH FUN.

AFTER 'PROMISES' TO MEET UP AGAIN. FLO AND ALICE - SORRY SHIRLEY AND LORETTA, GET ON THE BUS AND WAVE THEIR GOODBYES

"Are you really gonna meet that Billy again Flo?"

"Am I bloody 'eck! I only said that cos the bus driver had a face on him. He'd have driven off if we'd not got on. Are you gonna meet that Chad"

"Am I 'eck. I was doing the same as you"

"Oh. You DID seem keen though. And you did take your time when you went round the back of the shops"

"TO TALK!"

"Well why was your dress all skew wiff when you came out?"

"Swear you won't breathe a word"

"As God is my witness, Alice"

"I let him touch me bosoms. And we kissed"

"Nowt else?"

"What do you think I am?"

"Someone who goes down entries, with men she's just met - Put your face straight. I'm just kidding. We've just won a bloody war. You're entitled to a bit of fun"

"So what about you Flo. You disappeared for a bit. Did you let his hands wander"

"Oh no luv. My bits are just for Bob. I let him have a quick kiss though. And he was a 'tryer' bless him. He'll have a bruise or two when he wakes up tomorrow. I had to give him a poke when he got too fresh ... Right, here's our stop. We've got a bloody long walk an' all cos of you. Good job it's a nice evening"

"Int there loads of people about?"

"No blackouts anymore Alice. It's gonna be a different world now. The lads who have been lucky, will get to come home. And hopefully we'll be finished with the soddin' rationing. I'm gonna buy our Joyce a ton of lollipops...I hope Bob's in when I get back. I want to give him a cuddle"

"I wonder what I'd be doing now if Eddie hadn't left"

"Probably plotting his death. A leopard never changes his spots Alice. You're better off without him"

"You're probably right .. We're just round the corner from mine. Do you want to come in for a brew"

"No. It's been a long day. I'll walk you to your door, but I'm ready for me bed. Our Joyce comes home tomorrow, from her Aunty's. I want to get up early and bake her some buns"

"It has been a long day ... Do you think we'll ever see Chad and Billy again?"

"God forbid! It's alright for you I suppose, but I've got an husband at home. And with that in mind Alice. We will never talk about this thing or any thingy associated with it, ever again. Do I make myself clear?"

"As mud! - I'm kidding My lips are sealed luv. Here we are. Home sweet home. Goodnight Flo"

"Good night Alice"

13: A BIT MORE…

Second edition bonus chapter

BARRED!

"Flo? Guess where I've just come from?..And let me tell ya, I've never been so offended in my life"

"Well that rules out your house, unless you've managed to offend yourself. So which shop are we talking about?...It can't be the cake shop, cos you're already barred from there"

"I am NOT barred from the cake shop! I just choose not to go in when certain cheeky gits are serving"

"You ARE barred, Alice. I was with you and I most definitely heard her tell you not to come in the shop again"

"She said that, in temper, because i was showing up her shoddy goods"

"You were demanding your money back, cos the icing came off your iced bun. You're too quick to throw stuff away. It was only stuck to the paper bag"

"Well no way am I rooting through me bin once I've thrown

summat in it...And didn't I ask her for a box when she served me?...The tight cow. It wouldn't have happened if she'd given me a box"

"No-one's gonna give you a box for one iced bun. Me granddaughter get a trifle every week. They put it in a paper bag. She doesn't lose one jot of cream, cos she carries it like it's that exploding stuff in Westerns - Did you watch Bonanza the other night? Little Joe nearly got killed by it"

"I'm not bloody interested in daft telly programmes, Flo...Anyway it wasn't the cake shop, and I'm NOT barred"

"Well I'm VERY interested in Little Joe. He's dreamy...And I'll remember that next time you ask me to get you an Eccles cake...So go on then? Which shop or person has managed to get on your bad side today?"

"Him in the bloody Cobblers. There I was, stood waiting for me good courts and some tart walks in. Breezes past me like I wasn't there and chucks some cheap looking sandals on his counter, and goes "ooh luv I'm desperate for these doing today. I'm entering a fandango competition near the Town hall"

"A FANDAGO competition?!"

"Well summat like that. But the point I'm making is he said "I should be able to manage that for YOU luv. Come back at four o'clock. They'll be done and dusted for you"...Have you ever heard owt so cheeky?"

"Er...Who are you saying was cheeky? her or him?"

"HIM! Two weeks he's had my courts"

"Alice! You're being a tad unfair. It was only last night you remembered you'd left them in there"

"Yeah! That's his fault an' all. Cos when I took 'em in, he specifically said "I'm snowed under at the moment it'll be a few days...What if I'D had an emergency"

"You would have said, wouldn't you? And I'm sure he would have tried to help if he'd known"

"It's cos she was flashing her bosoms and I told him so"

"I bet that went down well"

"Well she tried piping up with some daftness but I soon put her in her place. She scarpered off, sandals in hand...Whatever she's fandangoing in tonight it won't be powder blue slip ons...And then I gave him 'what for'... 'I could spit and find a better cobbler than you' - I said"

"You got barred dint ya?"

"No I never! he only said "Don't come in here again" cos I said I wouldn't be going in there again..And then I stormed out"

"Did you get your good courts?"

"Put the kettle on"

"It's never off...Did you get your shoes?"

"In the kerfuffle, I forgot all about them...Will you pop in for me?"

"Why can't you go yourself? On your way home? It's only round the corner from your house"

"Cos I don't want to go in there again...I wouldn't be responsible for me actions. I'm still fuming"

"Not cos you got barred?"

"NO!"

"Right, I'll pop round in a bit... Will you do ME a favour?"

"Course I will"

"Whilst I'm brewing up, will you pop to the cake shop for a couple of custards?"

"Very bloody funny Florence!"

IT'S ALL GREEK TO ME

"Well that was a funny wedding wasn't it Flo?"

"I thought it was lovely Alice. Me feet are killing me. Shove the kettle on whilst I find me slippers"

"That'll be all that hokey-cokeying you did...To be honest. I thought it was a bit strange"

"I think YOU'RE strange. What do you mean by that? You're dead ungrateful you. You didn't think the buffet was strange did you? You was on bleedin' intimate terms with the buffet. You hardly left its side"

"I had a small plate! I was lucky I had a plate at all. Did you see 'em smashing 'em up?"

"That's their tradition. They're Greek. Its part of their religion to smash plates"

"Well they can't be Christians. It's not christian to break stuff"

"What about the walls of Jericho?"

"Some people will blaspheme, JUST to prove a point!...And Myrtle Grimshaw isn't Greek. I went to school with her. She's born and bred Harpurhey...And a tad common with it too"

"Well you'd know! And I'm didn't mean her, you daft mare. I meant her husband...Stavros"

"Well there's a funny to-do, an' all. I always thought he was called Steve"

"He is. A lot of people make their name more English. My parents did it with ours"

"Don't be telling me your real name's Rapunzel or summat foreign"

"I should get a medal for putting up with you. NOT me first name, me surname. Our original name was Kheim or summat like that. But you didn't pronounce the K. When my mum and dad came to England, they changed it to Kime"

"What do you mean? you didn't pronounce the K?"

"The K in Kheim!" (You idiot)

"How is there a K in Hime"

"Y'know what Alice? I haven't got time to waste on nonsense. Me parents had a different name. They came to Sheffield and changed it to Kime. End of story! Do you want a brew?"

"Course I do. Have you got any proper biscuits? Like a Bourbon or a Garibaldi. Them ones at the 'do' looked foreign to me"

"I've got rich tea or nowt. How you can be hungry after the amount you ate, is beyond me"

"It wasn't proper food though, was it? Did you see that stuff that was wrapped in leaves? No way was I eating a plant. It's not normal"

"Lettuce is a plant. In fact everything on the ham salad you have every Saturday, is a plant, except for the ham"

"Salad is a vegetable not a plant, Florence. If I want to eat leaves I'll suck on a privet"

I feel like throwing you in some! "It was a lovely wedding though. She scrubbed up well did Myrtle"

"That veil was a blessing. It covered half her face"

"Can you not be nice about anyone?"

"I'm not gonna lie just to make someone feel better"

"You didn't say anything to her did you?

"What do you think I am?"

"A cow on your best days. And an absolute cow on your worse"

"Well you're no Saint yourself, Florence. I saw you throwing daggers at Derek whojamaflip. What was all that about?"

"He borrowed our Bob's best waistcoat about six months ago. Cos he was in court. Not seen head nor hide of it since. Til he turned up wearing it at the wedding...I'll be knocking on his tomorrow...Hey! did you see who caught the bouquet?"

"Ida Jones. How it didn't burst in to flames when she caught it, is a bloody mystery to me. She's already killed two husbands"

"Alice! A German tank killed the first one. You can't blame her for that"

"Well what about number two? The only one out of her, and her kids from the first fella, to eat that vile stew she makes. And the only one to wake up dead the next day"

"Who told you that? You read too many murder stories you do. How on earth do you know what he ate before he died?"

"I got it from the horses mouth"

"What? Ida told you she'd poisoned her husband?"

"Not in so many words. But she looked a bit too gleeful when she was telling me how she gets comfort from the fact that her food was the last thing on earth he enjoyed...Enjoyed? Her butties, when we had the party for the Coronation, were given to the stray dogs...When was the last time you saw a stray dog round here?...I rest my case"

"You'd better rest your mouth before you get done for slander...Having said that, I've tasted her mince pies. You could be on to summat"

"They're worse than yours - WHAT?... You look like Betty Boop when you purse your lips like that"

"SOD OFF!"

PIE AND PALAVER

"FLO! grab your coat quick. There's a right barney going on on, six doors up - I'm surprised you didn't hear it with your front door wide open like that"

"I left it open for you. Cos as you can see, I'm up to me armpits in this pastry"

"Well leave it to settle - COME ON! we're missing all the good bits"

"TUT!

Flo and Alice depart for a casual stroll past the house six doors up

"Shove that kettle on Flo. I'm sure me tongue's shrivelled up a bit"

"You probably bit a bit off, trying to hold back when that Maisie called you a nosy cow"

"I'm just grateful you held me back luv...You could be visiting me in Bootle street as we speak"

"I wasn't holding you back Alice, I was shoving you on! We were meant to be ambling past not parking up outside her bloody house. You're too brazen Alice. We could have walked to Newton Heath and we'd have still heard the racket coming out of there"

"We wouldn't have seen the goings on in her hallway, though, would we? ...Mother and daughter, scrapping. You dint see things like that during the war...Can you imagine going three rounds with your Joyce along the length of your lobby, You'd both be hospital with broken legs...Int lino slippy? I nearly died laughing when they both slipped"

"My Joyce wouldn't dream! ...And that's why you should always wear clean underwear. That girdle was only held together by dirt...Remind me never to take a brew off her"

"Somehow I don't think we'd be offered...I mean, I might have been staring, but that gobful you gave her could bring tears to a lemon"

"Well! Never let it be said that I don't back me best mate up...Even if she is an idiot that brings it on herself"

"You'd have been crimping the edges of a pie if I hadn't come round. How exciting is that?"

"GOOD GOD! The pie! You don't care if my Bob starves to death, do ya? - Sort out the brews whilst I get it finished"

"What sort of pie is it?"

"Meat and potato...I've got a bit of pastry left over. Should I make you a little one, to take home"

"Let me see the filling"

"WHY?"

"I got one from the butcher's last week. They want reporting for false advertising. It wasn't meat and potato. It was potato and a hint of mince"

"Only lazy cows buy ready made pies. And mine is drowning in good quality stewing steak. Do you want the bloody pie or not? I can always make a little apple one if you don't"

"I don't fancy apple"

"Not for YOU, you cheeky sod, for my Bob"

"No, I'll have it. You do make a nice tater pie - Aw it's half day closing and I've not got any beetroot...Have you got any?"

"I can spare a slice or two"

"What are you having for afters?"

"Well now you've taken the last of me pastry, it'll have to be some tinned peaches and Carnation"

"Ooh I love a tin of peaches with Carnation milk"

"Have you got any?"

"No...And it's half day closing"

"Looks like you'll have to make do with what you've got in your cupboards, Mrs Hubbard"

"Eh! I'll have you know I've got a full pantry. It's only

coincidence that I haven't got the things you mentioned. I've still got a Trifle mix left over from me Hamper at Christmas"

"Have you got time for it to set? - No you bloody haven't...And who has Trifle on a week day?"

"The Queen!"

"Go and have tea with her then"

"I've got a tin of Mandarins. And a bottle of milk still unopened. I can have the cream off the top...It's not the same, but it'll do"

"All you need is a bowl and a plaintive look, and you'd be the spit of that kid in 'OLIVER'...I've got a spare tin you can borrow - And I want it back!"

"First thing tomorrow. I won't even have breakfast...I'll camp outside the shop...And with my knees an' all!"

"Well you can't leave 'em at home can ya? leave it til Friday when we do our big shop. I fancy trying that new Supermarket at the bottom of the lane"

"You've changed your tune!"

"I'm still offended at the fact I've got to pick me own shopping then pay for it and pack it meself...Remember old Jim who had the Grocer's? He'd be turning in his grave...Always had a chair for customers and his weights were spot on...And not a lot of people know this, cos he's always come across as a miserable sod. But when he heard folks were struggling, he ALWAYS weighed an ounce or two over...There was a time when me and Bob first wed and I insisted that I wasn't gonna live in a house with gas lighting, so we scrimped -"

"Was that it?...I just thought you'd both gone dead tight. Why didn't you tell me? I'd have helped"

"Bob would have gone mad if I'd breathed a word. He's a proud man. We could have got electric on the never-never but he wouldn't be beholden to anyone. So we saved, and we saved hard. If I'd let on to anyone he'd have left me... I'd be sat here today a childless single woman...A bit like you"

"I'm glad I DIDN'T help you now...I hope you suffered!"

"You've got no sense of humour. That was a cracker that was...Anyway, we did it in the end. But going back to Jim from the grocers. He must have cottoned on I was struggling a bit with grocery money cos for a few months, I got 13 eggs to the dozen and more than an extra rasher to me rhody bacon...He's in heaven is that man. On first name terms with God...I cried the first time I saw what he'd done. And Bob was right behind me. I had to pretend the onions were stronger than usual"

"I still would have helped. You are my best mate"

"I know you would. Anyway it's done now"

"So why do you want to go to the supermarket? We can still get everything we need off Moston Lane, and Conny Market"

"Cos that's where Maisie's daughter works"

"Ah!"

***

Time to go to the shops

"It's a proper trek is this Flo...Me knees are starting. I can feel it in me water"

"Lean on your trolley"

"Don't be daft. It'll tip over. Can I link ya?"

"Oh you know I don't like all that faffing about...Go on then - OY! stop leaning on me. You know I don't like being touched"

"That's probably why your Joyce is an only child - Bloody 'ell you can't stop dead like that, in the middle of the pavement! Why've we stopped? Are you going in the Ironmongers?"

"I'm thinking of buying an hammer. To hit idiots over the head with...You're not going a single step further with me if you continue that crudeness"

"What did I say? What did I say?"

"Casting aspersions on me and my Bob's private affairs"

"I was only having a laugh, to make the trip go quicker"

"We're only going to the top of the lane. Not the bloody Antarctic. And you know I don't like linking arms. We're not teenagers anymore. It looks daft!"

"We did it all the time when we were younger"

"No, YOU did it all the time. I've always hated it"

"Well you took your time letting me know...I don't know why we didn't jump on the bus"

"To go three stops?"

"If you've got a 'pass' use it, I say"

"We're here now anyway. Grab one of them trolleys"

"I can't pull one of them and push mine at the same time"

"Funny that. Cos in every other way, you're bloody contrary - I'LL PUSH IT! ...And if we see Maise's daughter DON'T be too bloody obvious"

"As if!"

"I have to say Alice. These displays look cheerful don't they? - The beans are tuppence cheaper here"

"If you're buying tins and you plan on using my trolley, you're pushing it back - Eh! Is that her by the cornflakes? Maise's daughter?"

"It is. Remember what I said"

"You can trust me...What's her name again?"

"Susan...And keep your gob quieter. We don't want her to think we've come here special" .

"Hiya Susan. I hardly recognised you stood up. Last time we saw you, you were being dragged the length of your mam's lobby...Innit Flo?"

I could kill her! "Are you alright Susan luv? Pay no mind to Alice.

We were just passing the other day and saw the kerfuffle with your mam"

"I don't have a mam!"

AWKWARD SILENCE

"I'm like that with some of my family, aren't I Flo? They're a bloody embarrassment. It's never come to fisticuffs though. So what happened luv?"

"ALICE!"

"WHAT?"

"Shut it! I'm sorry Susan luv. She's on new tablets...Whatever it was with you and your mam, I'm sure it'll pass. Me and my Joyce have had murders in the past"

"Has Joyce ever caught you snogging the Club-man whilst her dad's at work?"

FOR A FEW SECONDS, THE WORLD STOPS. WHILST TWO LADIES OF A CERTAIN AGE WEAR A GOBSMACKED LOOK ON THEIR FACES

"I can't say she has luv- Eh! these cornflakes are dead cheap. Chuck one in me trolley Alice and come on. We haven't got all day! See you around Susan luv. And never mind, worse things happen at sea"

***

"I don't believe you Flo. The biggest bit of gossip for ages and you say we've got to go"

"Well I need to get home quick"

"Why?"

"Me and Maisie have got the same Club-man and he comes today"

"Wanna get a taxi? I'll pay!"

OH GOD! DON'T LET HER SEE US

"COOOEEEY FIO"

"Oh God! Look who it is Alice...It's your fault this. I'd have had me key in the door by now if you hadn't dawdled to look in next door's window"

"Was it my fault there's no nets up? Did you see the wallpaper? I'd get an headache sat in her parlour. Who's shouting? I can't see that far in these glasses"

"Margaret"

"Margaret from the Chippy?"

"No. Margaret the Jehovah's Witness"

"Oh God!"

"Don't you start. I'm sure she'll mention him once or twenty times - Hiya Margaret. You've just caught us going out"

"Oh! I was trying to catch up with you for ages. I saw you from across the road when you was coming out of the paper shop...I thought you were just going IN"

"Int that what I said?"

"Margaret's right. You definitely said going OUT"

"Shurrup Alice! (You're dead later!) I'm on new tablets for me Angina. I've not stopped muddling me words up since...Well, come on in luv. You can chat to Alice, whilst I put me shopping

away - Have you got summat in your eye, Alice? You looked pained"

* * *

"Sit yourself down Margaret luv. I won't be too long getting sorted. Alice'll keep you company"

"I'm not stopping. I just wanted to drop off the new WatchTower. have you had time to read any of the other copies I've left you?"

"I've read bits. Erm...Let me just pop the kettle on and put this shopping away. Why don't you show it to Alice? She loves reading"

"Do you want a copy as well Alice? There's a lovely story in it, very pertinent to what's happening to the world today"

"Does it have recipes in it?"

"Well, it's funny you should say that cos isn't leading the life Jehovah wants us to live, based on a godly recipe?"

"Come again? -AND WHAT ARE YOU LAUGHING AT FLO? HAVE YOU GOT LAUREL AND HARDY IN THAT SCULLERY WITH YA?"

"I'M NOT LAUGHING. I BANGED ME FUNNY BONE...IT'S THAT NERVOUS LAUGH AND CRY THING...I'LL BE IN IN A MINUTE. I'M JUST POPPING OUT TO THE LOO. YOU TWO CARRY ON" *That'll teach you to dawdle...where's me fags?*

"Look at this picture on the front of the magazine, Alice. Where do you think that is?"

"Lovely flowers. Is it Piccadilly gardens?"

"It's HERE -

"Bogart hole clough?! - With LIONS?!"

"NO! Well, yes, but not just the Clough. Earth. This is how we could all live if we followed God's recipe for life. Why don't you come with me to the Kingdom Hall one day? I'm always trying to get Flo to go but she's so busy, what with the evening job and her husband being elderly"

Evening job?! "I know. She's a martyr!...The poor luv barely has time to watch the telly...I'd love to go Margaret. But I'm C of E, me. I feel like a Judas going in the Methodist church when they have a 'Jumble'...No offence meant luv, but I'm 'funny' when it comes to Gods. I'm just used to mine!"

"Oh, we've all got the same god. It's just knowing how to

worship him properly. let me just read you this passage from the bible -

"I can't read or listen to reading, at this time of day. I'm already late taking me tablets and, around this time, I go fuzzy for a bit...Maybe some other time. Either earlier or later but NOT at this time ... IS THAT BREW DONE FLO?"

"I'M COMING IN A MINUTE. I'M JUST WIPING DOWN ME TINS"

Cow! "Are you stopping for a brew Margaret? We'll have to rush it though. Her Bob'll be home soon and he hates anyone being here when he gets in. I think it's something to do with him being 'elderly'"

"I don't drink tea or coffee. Maybe I could pop round to yours one day and we'll finish off this discussion. I'll leave the magazine with you. When's a good time to knock on?"

You don't drink tea? No wonder you look haggard "Make it a Wednesday after six. I'm up to me eyes the rest of the week...I'll see you to the door"

"I'll see you then luv. Tell Flo I said bye. I'll leave her copy here on the sideboard"

***

"I heard every word"

"Did ya? Did you hear me choking when she mentioned your 'evening job'?"

"Well you've gotta say summat. I'm not one for being cruel. She means well...And you're one to talk. Telling her to come round on a Wednesday"

"SO!"

"You go to Bingo on a Wednesday"

"And you don't have a job!"

"Yeah, but you're being cruel. I don't have the heart to tell her I think it's rubbish. You're actually having her come out, for nowt"

"It won't be for nowt. That nosy cow next door is bound to pop her head out to see who it is. I bet she'll still have her on the doorstep when I get back"

AN ENEMY AT THE KITCHEN TABLE

"Aw Joyce. How long is it since we've been able to have a cuppa together without the kids? Love 'em to bits I do, but it's nice to have me daughter to meself"

"I couldn't believe it meself mam.Especially when he said he'd take all six of 'em out for the day. He'll be grey or bald when he gets back...Although I wouldn't be surprised if he's got some tart with him to watch 'em. Our Lesley won't say nowt but the little ones will so I'll find it all out when they get back"

"Aw Joyce, stop being mean, he's a lovely lad when he wants to be - Oh! That's the door. Why are they knocking? Did you lock it?"

"Mam, I keep telling you. Things are not the same as they used to be. You need to keep your door locked. There's some proper weirdos out there"

"It'll only be Alice"

"My point exactly!"

"Aw Joyce, promise me you won't start with her"

"As long as she doesn't start with me"

sigh "I'll get the door...Just 'watch it' madam. I'm still your mam!"

***

"Oh! hiya Joyce...Where are all the kids? Have you put 'em in an orphanage? -Only kidding"

"Hiya AUNTY Alice. No they're out with their dad. I was hoping to have a bit of time with me mam...Just us two"

"Int that lovely...Shove up then. You're sat in my usual place but don't worry about it. I can manage on this corner...Even though I seriously hurt me corns the last time I had to sit here"

"You're a martyr...I'm getting off soon anyway"

*Good!"*Eh it's funny you being here. Some new people have moved in my street and their kids - I say 'their' I've only seen her so far, but the kids are the same as yours"

"What? five girls and a boy?"

"No! Coloured. Do you know 'em?"

"WHY WOULD I -

-JOYCE ? Your brews going cold. Alice? its a bit daft to expect our Joyce to know a family just because the kids are coloured...Ignore her Joyce, she's on the change. It makes her daft"

"Have I offended someone? And I'm not on the change Flo. I'm too young. I just thought Joyce might know them, cos when I asked her where they'd moved from, she said Moss side, and your Joyce used to live there"

"For five minutes, Ten years ago! Mam? I'm going before I say something out of turn"

"Aw don't go on my account"

"She ISN'T! She was planning on getting the four o'clock bus anyway... I'll see you to the door luv... Say bye to Alice.Remember how you was raised"

"BYE!"

"Lovely seeing you" *Sod off you little cow*

***

"I don't know why I put up with YOU. I must need me head testing. You can't go round offending people. Especially MY daughter"

"What? - What did I say?"

"Just stop bloody presuming she knows every coloured person in Manchester. I don't go round pointing out idiots and asking YOU if you know them"

"Do you know what I've noticed Flo? Every time you've got someone else for company, you don't want to know me"

"Me daughter is NOT someone else. This is her home luv...And I let you in dint I?"

"I thought it was a funny to-do having the door locked in the first place. If I'm not welcome, you only have to say"

"I didn't lock it. I never lock it, as well you know. Our Joyce locked it cos she frets about me"

"What does she think I'm gonna do to you? Cos I bet she knew I was coming round"

"Oh! Shurrup thinking the world revolves around you. What do you want anyway?"

"Have you forgot?"

"Forgot what?"

"You've forgot!"

"WHAT?"

"We said we were gonna go through your Jewelry box cos I need a green brooch for me outing tomorrow"

"WE said WE were gonna go through MY jewelry box?"

"Yeah!...We were in the Paper shop yesterday and I mentioned I'm going to York Minster with that woman who get her feet done at my chiropodist's. Her daughter was supposed to go with her, but she's had a row with her husband and he won't let her go, so she asked me - The tickets all paid for, it's not costing me a penny - And I told you I wanted to wear me good green coat, but I didn't fancy dipping into me widows pension for a brooch that I'd only wear once"

"And where does my jewelry box come into it?"

"You said you had a green brooch"

"Did I?"

"Look! I'm not short of a bob or two. If you don't want to lend me the bloody brooch, I'll nip to Kendals in a bit and get one...What are you laughing at?"

"The thought of you 'nipping' anywhere. You need a weeks notice to get out of bed"

"Are you calling me lazy?"

"No, I'm calling you disorganised...And a snob. You'll need a brooch just to GO to Kendals"

"TUT! So can I lend one then?"

"Yeah - and it's 'Borrow'....They're not real emeralds, can you cope?"

"You can tell!...It's nice though, for what it is"

"Int it a bit daft wearing your green coat in July? You'll be boiling"

"It might rain"

"Wear a cardi and take an umbrella"

"We're going in the Cathedral. You can't just wear a cardi, it blasphemous"

"You don't see any statues of Mary wearing a coat"

"Well, that's Catholics for ya! I'm bloody wearing one... If Mary had lived over here she'd have caught her 'death' wearing them tea-towels and then we'd have had no Jesus"

"I don't think God would have let that happen"

"You're not wrong Flo. And I'm not even sure England was invented when Jesus was a lad"

"Were you born daft or is it just practice?"

"I don't like your tone"

"Sod off then"

"I will. I've got to put me rollers in anyway, and I'm not one of them common sorts that walks the streets in 'em...Ta for the brooch. I'll come round after we get back and tell you all about it"

"Don't come round too late. It's all good telly tomorrow night"

"Well, the sharra's due to drop us back off, around sixish. What time's 'too late'?"

"Anytime after three"

"You cheeky cow! I'm getting off...See you tomorrow. I'll get you a stick of rock"

"ROCK?!"

COMMON' MARKET

WELL THERE'S PLENTY OF 'WAFFLE' AND THAT'S BELGIAN

"All this Common Market business is doing me nut in. It's even in the TITBITS. I don't buy it for politics, I buy it for proper scandal. There are things about Dirk Bogarde, you wouldn't believe Alice...But if I wanted politics I'd buy one of them boring papers"

"He was never manly enough for me. Too pretty.And he wasn't a patch on Ronald Colman in 'A Tale Of Two Cities'...Why have they started remaking films they've already made? People today must be idiots. They couldn't have conned us into watching the same film twice Could they?"

"That's why I don't bother with the 'pictures' anymore. Seen 'em all, and I can see better films on the telly for free. If you don't count the telly license and the electric bill...plus the rental"

"So is there nowt worth reading in your magazine?"

"Well there's summat about Brigitte Bardot and her 'Les Melons' That's french, not got a clue what it means....I prefer Doris Day to her"

"Nowt in The Evening News? Has anyone we know been in court?...Or died?"

"That's even worse! Politics, from page one to the classifieds... Dead boring"

"Like the PINK?"

"Have you ever read the PINK, Alice? Cos I want to know where the politics page is in THAT"

"Have I eck! It's full of sport. I'd sooner watch paint dry"

"Eh, you did that once, remember? When you bought Dulux for the parlour...And sat there with your alarm clock ...You daft lemon!"

"Well, I wasn't gonna pay twice the price of distemper for summat that took ages to dry. They're conning us y'know, with all these fancy names for stuff. I'm sure Henry the eighth had a wall or two painted in his castle...Where was bleedin' Dulux then? Not even bloody invented...Have you noticed in the last ten years or so, how the list of things we need has grown?... I've got by all my life without a Kenwood Chef. And my rock cakes are second to none"

"You're not wrong Alice *Especially about them rock cakes. 'None' would be my first choice as well* I was in our Joyce's neighbour's flat the other day, and her living room floor was more dust than carpet. And she's got 'fitted'... Some people don't know they're born...So I thought to meself, I'd better give her a bit of a hint. She might be legally blind and not realise how dirty it is......Are we having a brew?"

"I wouldn't say no Flo. Me mouth's gone dry just listening to you...So, what did you say to her?"

"I said 'I'm not being funny luv, but your floor is filthy. Do y'know what she said back to me?"

"Summat like 'Get out of me house you cheeky cow'?"

"TUT! She wouldn't dream Alice. If it weren't for our Joyce, her kids would be coming home to an empty house. She's never in at home-time..No, she said, 'Me hoover's broke'... I wanted to slap her. Have you got a broom? I said. She looked at me like I was speaking a foreign language. I had to send our Joyce next door to get hers...Pass us the sugar?"

"She hasn't got a broom? No broom? Is this what we won two wars for? I'm almost glad we won't be around much longer.The world's going to pot...Have you bought different tea? Don't get me wrong - it's nice but different"

"It's Yorkshire tea, is that. I brought some back with me when I went to see me brothers last week"

"Well, to be honest, it's vile. Have you got any PG?"

"You cheeky cow!"

"I'm only kidding Flo. Sometimes I do it just to see your face"

"I can't really complain about YOUR brewing skills Alice, cos I can't remember the last time there was a blue moon"

"I was only joking luv! Sometimes, you can have a very cutting tongue, Florence"

"Well put your face straight, cos so was I. Do you want a Salmon paste butty?"

"Are you having one?"

"NO. I'm just gonna sit and watch you eat yours -OF COURSE I'M HAVING ONE!"

"Go on then - Is it best butter?"

"When has margarine ever crossed MY doorstep?"

"Just checking...It might have been Yorkshire butter"

"I only get that out when the Queen comes. You'll have to settle for 'Adams' ...There you go"

"Your knives could do with a sharpen. It's a bit of a doorstep is this"

"Luckily for you, you've got a big enough gob...I've got a couple of iced buns for 'afters' They're not due to go stale for a couple of days"

"I feel honoured!...So what were you saying before? about the Common Market ? I thought it was summat like a massive Conran street when I first heard it"

"That'd make a lot more sense to me. To be honest Alice, I'm not overly sure meself. Apparently, if me and you wanted to go somewhere like er, France or Germany, we could go, just like we go to Town"

"There's buses that go abroad?"

"No! We'd still have to get a boat or a plane. But we wouldn't need a passport"

"Well I'm sorry Flo, but if that's what the Common Market is all about, they should have asked us first. Who the eck wants to live abroad?"

"Well technically speaking, me grandkid's dad lives abroad"

"He does not! He lives here"

"Shurrup and eat your butty!"

"I wonder if they have salmon paste in France?"

"I doubt it... They eat frogs legs and snails...and a lot of onions with bread"

"Ooh! they're heathens...I bet them onions are not pickled either. I love a couple of pickled onions with me Tripe...They're not normal some of these foreigners - No offence to your Son-in-law"

"None taken... If my Bob was still here, he'd be turning in his grave at us getting all pally with people like the Germans. He'd sooner go to Newcastle for coal, than walk anywhere Hitler's been... Mind you he'd probably say he wasn't surprised. He insisted the royal family were Germans. He was a bit deluded my Bob. You don't talk like the Queen, I said to him if you're not a hundred percent English... Proper 'cut glass' is her accent. I have to put me crystal sherry glasses in the parlour when she's on telly doing her Christmas speech. And that's a bit inconvenient in itself. Christmas is the only time I use them... Her accent is the most englishey of any English accent I've ever heard. How can she NOT be English?"

"Do you think the queen says 'brew'? I don't mean in public! ...I mean behind our backs"

"How would I know that, Alice? I'm not one of her maids in waiting"

"I wonder what SHE thinks of this Common Market. Cos to me the Queen and 'Common' just don't go together"

"Ooh! I'm glad there's only me and you in here. It's vergin' on blasphemy saying the queen and common in one sentence. Wash out your mouth Alice. There's some carbolic on the windowsill"

"You daft sod!...Is there any more tea in that pot? I need summat to wash this iced bun down" *It's like sawdust!*

WINDOWS

"Aw innit sad Alice? Billy who does the windows has died"

"Which one?"

"What do you mean which one? How many Billy's who do the windows are there?"

"Well you wouldn't know cos you're still relatively new round here"

"Thirty odd years, is new? It's Moston not Brigadoon luv"

"Will you let me finish? Right! Before I was so rudely interrupted I was trying to say, that Billy who does the windows now, isn't really Billy"

"You mean he uses a stage name? Like Rock Hudson? who I'm betting, isn't called Rock in real life"

"What's his real name then?"

"I don't know, but what kind of mother calls her son Rock?"

"Eh! I wouldn't be too sure Flo. There's some strange women out there... Hitler had a mam"

"That's different. Adolf was probably a normal name in Germany til he got it. There's nowt normal about being called Rock"

"If you had a son and you could only name him Adolf or Rock. Which would you choose?"

"Neither. I'd called him Jesus, cos he'd be a bleedin' miracle at my age"

"I'm not standing near you when it's thunder and lightning, you blasphemer!"

"I'm part Jewish and part Christian luv. I'm laughing when I get to heaven. It can only be one or the other"

"God was only Jewish til he had Jesus"

"Alice? Why are we talking about religion?"

"You started it!"

"Well now I'm stopping it! What did you come round for anyway?"

"I was coming to see if you fancied a walk to the library. But me mouth's too dry to go anywhere now. Are you making a brew?"

"I'm sat here with half a rag rug on me lap. Do I look like I'm brewing up?...Do it yourself. You know where the kettle is...And then, you can finish off telling me about Billy. I've been told he's dead. but YOU Miss Marple, seem to know different"

"He probably is dead. He must be ninety if he's a day - I know why you're looking at me like that - You think I mean 'Billy' who does the windows now, but HIS real name is Gary"

"Am I dead? Is this what hell is? Your best mate waffling on like a mad woman for all eternity"

"I wouldn't know Flo. I'm going to heaven luv. I've never missed an Harvest festival...Anyway, let me just finish off these brews. I'm not like SOME people. I don't just waft the tea at the water ... Right, here we are, a proper brew...Now pin your lugholes back cos if I have to tell you more than once, it becomes gossip. And I don't do gossip"

"Shush! Hang on a minute Alice"

"What? What is it? Did you hear summat funny?"

"No. But I was expecting lightning"

"Come again?!"

"When you said you didn't gossip"

"TUT! Do you want to know about Billy or not?"

"Go one then. I'm all ears"

"The person you call 'Billy the window cleaner' isn't really Billy. The real Billy was cleaning windows before your Bob was even a twinkle in his dad's eye...And that's going back some"

"Shurrup about my husband's age. He's still here in't he? Where's yours?"

"Gawd! Don't you get easily offended? I was only trying to explain how old he was. I didn't mean nowt personal"

"I'm sure you didn't! So does this story have an ending, or are you planning on movin' in?"

"What? And leave my inside loo? I think not (Put THAT in your pipe and smoke it) Anyway back to Billy... When the proper Billy -the one whose probably just died -sold his round. Well to be honest, no one really noticed...They're only windows. It's not like being a baker and you don't sell on the secret recipe. And everyone starts saying 'These cakes don't taste the same since whatsit left' You don't need special training to wipe a 'shammy' round a pane of glass, do you?...So everyone carried on saying 'Billy who does the windows' Even though it was actually Gary"

"Is that it?"

"How much more do you want?"

"Well the way you were going on, I was expecting Billy to be Crippen the second or summat like that"

"There's no pleasing some people...Do you fancy that walk to the Library?"

"No thanks. I think I've had enough 'stories' for the day"

***

THE END...FOR NOW

ABOUT THE AUTHOR

Born in 1960 to an English mother and Barbadian father, the author spent her early childhood growing up in the Manchester suburbs of Moston and Collyhurst.

After living for 3 years in Barbados as a teenager, she returned to her hometown where she has lived ever since.

Her first book, A NORTHERN LIFE was published in 2013.

She currently resides in Bolton, Greater Manchester, where in between writing, she works as a carer for her best friend.

She is a proud Mum and Nana, and is constantly on Facebook showing off about them.

16300958R00211

Printed in Poland
by Amazon Fulfillment
Poland Sp. z o.o., Wrocław